REAL ESTATE AT A CROSSROADS

The Insider's Guide for Agents, Brokers, and Execs

By Gregory Charlop

CONTENTS

Interviews with the Experts

Introduction	1
Chapter 1: Agents and Future Agents	19
Chapter 2: Brokers and Executives	98
Chapter 3: Elite Agents	174
Chapter 4: Virtual Assistants and Chatbots	213
Chapter 5: Emerging Technology	244
Chapter 6: Philanthropy and Real Estate	281
Chapter 7: The Path Forward	308
Endnotes	323

All rights reserved. No part of this book may be reproduced or used in any form or by any means—graphic, electronic, or mechanical, including photocopying or information storage and retrieval systems—without written permission from the author.

The scanning, uploading, and distribution of this book or any part thereof via the Internet or any other means without the permission of the author is illegal and punishable by law.

Published by Gregory Charlop Walnut Creek, California.

Copyright 2019 by Gregory Charlop

Interviews with the Experts (in order of appearance)

Tom Ferry, Top real estate coach, speaker, and CEO of Tom Ferry International
Dave Phillips, VP of Industry Relations with Realtor.com
Ken Potashner, Angel Investor, Chairman and CEO of Home Bay Technologies
Nick Bailey, Former President and CEO of Century 21®
Adam Gothelf, Co-founder and CEO of Disclosures.io
Anthony Vitale, President of Talk2Tony, a residential real estate consulting service
Nav Athwal, Angel Investor, Proptech enthusiast, and Co-Founder/CEO of District
Matt Murphy, Venture capitalist, real estate expert, and partner with Montage Ventures
Darren Johnson, Marketing expert, Co-founder and CEO of AgentZip
Suzy Truax, Board of Directors, eXp World Holdings
Kim Hughes, CEO of virtual assistant firm Kim Hughes & Company
Tamir Poleg, Founder of Real
Daniel Ramsey, CEO and Co-Founder of virtual assistant firm MyOutDesk
Michael Lam, Chatbot expert and CEO of Kaydoh
Bridget Frey, CTO of Redfin
Ragnar Lifthrasir, Founder of the International Blockchain Real Estate Association
David Ament, Philanthropist, international speaker, business advisor, and investor
J.R. McKee, Philanthropist and Founder of Home In Silicon Valley.com

INTRODUCTION

The real estate business will never be the same. Here's why

Caution: The old world of real estate is over.

You remember the whoosh of air when you pushed the door open to your first home showing. The new-house smell, the feel of cold granite and soft carpet, the squeals of excitement as the kids ran around their future bedroom, and the giddy smiles when the young family looked around with awe and disbelief at their new home.

That is why you're here.

You're here for empty nesters looking for a home that will preserve their independence. You're here for the young college graduate buying his first home. You're here for the adventurer looking for a new future out West, on a farm, or down the coast. And, you're here for the retiree searching for a home near her new baby grandson.

You change lives.

But now, real estate is changing around you. Modern technology, radical transparency, empowered consumers, iBuyers, and internet brokerage companies are transforming the business of real estate into something new and nearly unrecognizable. It doesn't feel the same.

Gregory Charlop

The real estate biz is changing.

Those happy families and sold homes may become a distant memory unless you keep up with the new rules of real estate. You need to adapt. Unless you understand the influence of technology, you'll struggle for business, be blindsided by brokerages, and miss out on what you love most: welcoming families to a new home.

That's why I wrote this book. I want to prepare you for the modern world of real estate. I'll show you how social media, augmented reality, Zillow, internet brokerages, flash briefings, Bitcoin, the ubiquitous MLS, Facebook, artificial intelligence, robots, chatbots, and modern technology are transforming your job.

If you're a real estate agent, aspiring agent, broker, notary, lender, appraiser, real estate firm executive, or CEO, you need to know what's coming. I'll show you. I'll give you the tools you need to thrive in our new era of technology. I'll help you best your competitors and avoid costly mistakes.

This book will pull back the curtain on the future of the real estate industry. Once you understand the transformative impact of technology on your real estate practice, you'll make the right career decisions.

Your team of experts

To help you, I've brought together an army of the best minds in real estate. This team of power players will show you what's going on in the real estate industry and what you need to know.

For the first time, one book contains the candid advice of America's top real estate authorities, including leading influencer Tom Ferry, CEOs, and top executives from Realtor.com, Redfin, Century 21, Real, and eXp. Several of the world's top real estate technologists share their expert views about where tech is heading.

Since you need to know how to use these tools, I interviewed the CEOs and founders of companies specializing in real estate virtual assistants, lead generation, chatbots, and Bitcoin. We also explore the world of philanthropy and chat with leading social entrepreneurs. We'll show you how to help your community and your bank account!

The country's top real estate experts are all here to help you and share their wisdom from the front lines of the real estate revolution. Take advantage of these great minds; learn their secrets.

Some of you will read this and decide that it's time to switch careers or take an early exit from real estate. After all, the new world of real estate won't be for everyone. I'll tell you right now, the job market will get tougher. Indeed, one of the biggest impacts of technology is that we'll need fewer agents. You have to decide if you're up to the challenge. Once you read this book, you'll be able to make an informed career choice.

I hope most of you will stay in real estate and use the tools and tricks outlined here to crush the market and make your financial dreams come true. If you embrace technology and use it to your advantage, your business will succeed beyond your wildest expectations. While we won't need as many agents, it's likely that the top agents will dominate the market. You want to be a top agent. This book will show you how.

Even if you don't use modern tech, your competitors will. Real estate firms, marketing tools, and client acquisition will change, whether you like it or not. The relationship between salespeople and their brokerages will transform in the next couple of years. Whether you embrace new technology or not, you should educate yourself so you're prepared. While I believe that it's possible that a low-tech agent could still survive in certain limited markets, it will be an uphill battle. The team assembled here will help you.

Armed with their insights, you'll be prepared for life in the real estate industry. We'll help you answer burning questions such as:

- Will we still need real estate agents, or will technology replace them?
- It is worth becoming a real estate agent, or should you choose a different career?
- How can your brokerage remain competitive in the face of new, internet-based rivals?
- What technology should you use to supercharge your real estate career?
- How should you use technology to advertise properties and locate quality leads?
- Will virtual and augmented reality take over real estate?
- How should you keep up with the latest technology?
- What is Bitcoin and how will Bitcoin and blockchain impact real estate?
- What should you do if you want to start your own real estate technology business?
- How can you differentiate yourself from the other real estate agents/brokers/brokerage companies?
- What is a social business? Should you include philanthropy as part of your business model?

This book is your one-stop guide, regardless of whether you are an agent, broker, or executive. It will give you a rich understanding of technology and the future of the real estate industry. Use the tools and skills in this book, and your career will flourish. Strap yourself in and prepare for a ride into the future of the real estate biz. You now have the best team as your tour guide!

Changes are coming

Recall the days before the internet. Most homebuyers and sellers were clueless about the marketplace. They had little idea about home prices, neighborhood demographics, or how to transact a home. They didn't know what properties were for sale or how much they could expect for their own home. In short, the general public was nearly helpless.

Back in the not too distant past, most people didn't have an easy way to find a real estate agent. Nothing was transparent. They couldn't just hop online and see the top local salespeople.

Instead, someone looking to buy or sell a home would flip open the Yellow Pages (remember that?) and look for a real estate *firm* they recognized. Brokerage firms back then invested a lot in brand recognition because that's what drove prospects to call them in the first place. The agency would then act as the matchmaker and connect the potential client with a salesperson and take a hefty cut of the commission along the way.

The agent would then have to do all the heavy lifting: review books and binders with MLS data, create comps by hand, and photocopy listings to show to prospects. Since buyers were stuck with small black and white pictures, they didn't have a good feel for a property before walking in the door. Home tours were difficult, frustrating, and inefficient. Agents worked hard for each client.

The client, in turn, was dependent on the associate's research and recommendations. Other than switching agents, the transacting public had nowhere else to turn. There was no Redfin or Realtor.com to research listings. Zillow and Trulia weren't around with their detailed neighborhood insights. The general public was in the dark.

At the same time, real estate salespeople were nearly dependent on their brokerage firms.

Why? At that time, there was no way for the general public to determine the best agents in their community. The public didn't know which associates made the best sales, and review sites were non-existent. There was no easy way for the public to track down good agents. Moreover, advertising was expensive and inefficient in the pre-internet days. Other than hosting open houses, sales associates were limited to branding bus benches, passing out pens and notepads, and papering neighborhoods with flyers and signs. Needless to say, none of these tools worked well.

As a result, unless one of your clients sent you a referral or you met someone at an open house, you, as a real estate agent, were nearly dependent on your brokerage for prospects. You needed your firm to put food on the table. You needed their advertising and prestigious brand name to bring in business.

In short, the large real estate agencies pulled the strings, the associates controlled the knowledge, and the transacting public was at their mercy.

How times have changed.

Thanks to transparency, the entire paradigm of a helpless and ignorant general public depending on "trusted" real estate brokerages to locate salespeople is out the window. Moreover, agents are now able to reach prospects directly due to social media and reduced advertising costs.

The system used to function well for the brokerages. The large, powerful real estate companies served as a trusted point of contact for the general public who lacked easy access to information. The brokerage firms and their franchisees controlled the tools of the trade including MLS access, photocopiers, conference rooms, FAX machines, etc.

The brokerage firms were the only entities that had the resources to create meaningful advertisements. They could afford full-page ads in newspapers and magazines. Most associates could only afford pens, notepads, and the occasional shopping cart display. The salespeople needed the firms' advertising, infrastructure, and access to prospects.

The brokerages served an important role as a central hub of supplies, information, and prospect/agent connection.

Not anymore.

When was the last time a home seller flipped open their Yellow Pages and called a real estate firm looking for a salesperson?? That era is over.

The truth is, our current system of transacting real estate no longer makes sense. The internet increased transparency, and easy access to advertising blew up the old system.

The marketplace can be cruel to outdated and inefficient systems. Just ask Blockbuster.

Let's do a thought experiment. Imagine that you are creating the real estate system today from scratch. You're starting from a clean slate. What would the system look like?

The process, of course, would begin with the clients. Imagine that Maria is looking for a home. She just landed a great new job in Colorado. She's moving her husband, two tots, and family dog out West.

What would Maria do?

First, she'd hop online. Maria and her husband Joe would do their own research on websites that list all Denver homes for sale. Perhaps she'd even ask her Alexa. They'd narrow their search based on their needs. They'd review neighborhood information including schools, crime rates, commute times, local weather, access to parks, and walkability. They might even drive the neighborhoods themselves to see how they feel about the different communities.

Once they've done their homework, they'd need a little bit of help to navigate the system. After all, this is their first home purchase. Maria and Joe wouldn't quite know how to review inspection reports, arrange mortgages, file government-mandated documents, or negotiate prices. And, Joe wants to ask someone how difficult it is to replace popcorn ceilings. Maria needs some advice about whether it's realistic to move into a 1,400 sq. ft condo with two young kids and a Dalmatian.

Although they've done their research, Maria and Joe need a human consultant. They need someone with kindness and experience who will walk them through the process. They need a real estate agent.

Again, Maria will jump online. She and Joe will look at the review sites and check out who had the biggest sales in their neighborhoods. They'll probably read some bios and look for someone experienced in relocating families. Then, they'll pick an agent.

Let's pause for a moment. While this flow seems natural to us today, it stands in stark contrast to the process from a decade ago. Today, homebuyers and sellers are empowered. Agents have a defined, consultative role.

And the real estate brokerage firms?

Welcome to the new reality of real estate transactions. Homebuyers like Joe and Maria can do almost all the research themselves. They don't need you or anyone else to run comps or evaluate neighborhoods. They still need the insight of a human real estate agent, but that role will be more circumscribed. And, without significant innovation, the role of real estate brokerage firms may shrink beyond recognition.

The impact of these changes cannot be overstated.

Let me summarize. We have too many real estate associates. Agents are paid too much for some transactions. Underperforming and part-time agents will struggle. Real estate brokerages will need to reinvent themselves to survive. And, top agents will own the market.

The internet changed the rules of the game. Technological supremacy will determine who survives and who is sent packing.

We'll help you master the dramatic forces reshaping the residential real estate industry. Once you recognize the storm on the horizon, you can position yourself to be a winner in the new real estate economy. You'll learn how the current legacy system is poised to be swamped and how you can safely stay afloat amidst the changes.

Don't face your career and your business with your eyes closed. In *Real Estate at a Crossroads,* we will give you the real deal. We tell you the good, the bad, and the ugly. Know what's coming and prepare yourself!

Who should read this book?

Future real estate agents

"Why do these changes to the real estate industry matter to me?"

If you are considering a career in real estate, you need to know what you're in for. This book is your glimpse into the future. The current model of real estate employment is about to experience a major disruption. Most young potential real estate agents imagine that they will study, obtain their real estate license, and find a brokerage. The brokerage will tutor them and help them generate leads. The broker would provide them with clients, an office, and administrative support.

Although new real estate agents understand that they eat what they kill, many still view the world of real estate as being somewhat protected. After all, you have an experienced broker who is looking out for you.

Prospective associates assume the broker will train them, oversee their work, provide beautiful offices with computers, review their contracts, help them find health insurance, and generally keep them out of trouble.

Moreover, potential real estate agents are drawn to the profession because it appears to allow for part-time work and work flexibility. You could work as much or as little as you want, the thinking goes, and still do well. If you only want to work

20 hours a week, no problem! If you want to work on certain days and be home with your family for the rest of the time, no sweat!

With such a prevailing view of the real estate industry, it is no wonder that so many people aspire to become real estate salespeople. After all, who would not want a job that is largely protected by a nurturing mentor, has unlimited income potential, and allows so much flexibility that you could work as much or as little as you want? It's perfect!

Unfortunately, it is also no longer true.

Sadly, many people risk being lured into the world of real estate sales under false pretenses. These folks will be in for a rude awakening as the new dawn of the real estate industry melts their plans.

If you are considering starting a career as a salesperson, you must read this book carefully and share it with your friends and family to discuss. The business of real estate is not what it seems. I don't want you to make the mistake of entering a profession with one expectation only to have the industry leave you behind, broken and disappointed.

It is no small matter to establish a new career. Young real estate agents must study for and pass multiple exams, obtain licenses and insurance, and work hard to obtain initial clients. This work requires effort and potentially expensive advertising and communication tools. You do not want to jump into real estate if you do not know what you're in for!

I asked some of the leaders in the field for their advice to anyone considering a career in real estate, and their answers might surprise you. Read on and find out what they recommend.

Am I saying that nobody should go into real estate? Absolutely not! Once you read this book, you will have a greater understanding of the future and a better sense of whether your skills and drive match the new marketplace. If you have what it takes, you may make more money in real estate than you ever imagined. But, if you have the wrong expectations, you will almost certainly be doomed to failure. So put that real estate exam training book down and read this first. Don't waste your time until you know for sure whether real estate is right for you.

Current real estate agents

Times are changing, and you need to be prepared. You will soon find that the standard operating procedures you've developed over the years will no longer work. Technology and marketplace changes are upending the traditional ways of doing business.

On the plus side, real estate brokerage companies will lose their grip on you and your commission check. You can expect to keep a larger and larger cut of your sales.

Technology is swamping traditional techniques for lead generation, advertising, and running your business. If you master the new rules of tech, you'll hit the jackpot. If you fail to keep up with the technological times, your business will suffer.

As a real estate agent, you face the increasingly dire threat of technology replacing some or all of your services. I'll show you how to keep yourself relevant in the face of a constant computerized onslaught.

If you're a top agent, the picture is completely different. Market forces are in your favor. It is likely that you'll vacuum up an ever-larger share of home sales. You may become more successful than ever before. In the chapter on top agents, you'll learn the skills needed to exploit the new marketplace and how to prepare for the upstart agents gunning for your lofty perch.

Real estate brokers

What if you are an experienced real estate agent who is considering transitioning to a broker? This book will give you a glimpse into your future.

The life of a real estate broker used to be fantastic! After all, you've paid your dues and now you are the person at the top who's calling the shots. Your associates are doing most of the work and, as long as you provide mentoring and great facilities, you can largely kick back and benefit from their labor.

Real estate brokers enjoyed great commissions from their associates' work. In a very real sense, the associates were dependent on you. Yes, they could always switch to another broker, but people generally try to avoid that. The brokers as a collective wielded great power. But this will change as the structure of real estate brokerages evolve.

The fate of real estate brokers is tied to the brokerage system. In this book, we will explore how the system came into being and why the system in its present form is doomed to oblivion. Disruptive change is on the way and, as a real estate broker or the owner of a real estate company, you need to be prepared.

Don't let the winds of change in the real estate world drive you into obsolescence.

If you are a broker, the time to act is now. If you are not prepared for what is coming, you will be at a distinct disadvantage against the startups. I will show you the danger on the horizon and how you can navigate the waters to safety.

Executives and CEOs

Real Estate at a Crossroads may be the first and only book dedicated to the structure and future of real estate companies. We explore how technology, Millennials, and radical transparency are transforming the old real estate business model. In some ways, real estate CEOs need this book more than anyone, as your entire livelihood will be upended by innovation unless you are prepared.

We feature an entire chapter dedicated to executives. We'll look at the dangers you face and how you can respond. Learn how to harness technology as an engine of growth, whether you should hire a Chief Technology Officer (CTO) and centralize innovation, what types of associates and markets you should target, and how to make your organization more philanthropic (and successful!). You are at a pivotal moment in history. The decisions you make now will determine whether your organizations thrive or collapse. This book is your team of experts dedicated to help you win the future.

Mortgage brokers, underwriters, and other professionals

If you're involved in a real estate-related field such as mortgage broker, underwriter, escrow officer, or transaction coordinator, we have important information for you. Technology such as blockchain, Bitcoin, and automation tools may slash the need for escrow officers in the future. Artificial intelligence (AI) is undermining underwriters. Automation is taking aim at mortgage brokers and transaction coordinators. Millennials won't tolerate the old, slow way of originating mortgages. The future of these careers is technology. Don't take the conventional route. Find a technological way to do things better and you will be richly rewarded. We'll discuss how technology and Millennials are changing these fields throughout the book.

Important Disclaimer

This book is not about how to invest in real estate. We make no predictions about housing prices or whether it's better to buy condos or vacant land. We make no claim about the long-term value of real estate vs. the stock market. If you're looking for investment advice, there are plenty of other great books on the topic. Rather, this book is strictly about the real estate industry and what you need to do to become a successful real estate pro.

About the Author

I don't fit the mold of a typical real estate writer. As a result, I can offer you a perspective that you won't find anywhere else.

I am the founder and host of the premier real estate flash briefing on Amazon Alexa devices, The Real Estate Flash (www.TheRealEstateFlash.com). Every day, I share the most important news and I interview top industry insiders. We take a deep dive into industry trends, emerging technology, and threats on the horizon. Real estate pros across the country stay current by listening to my broadcasts every morning. Click on this link to join the Real Estate Flash community on Facebook. If you have an Alexa, be sure to sign up for my free flash briefings. Just say, "Alexa, enable The Real Estate Flash!"

Real estate has immense power to improve lives. I am the founder and CEO of Dignified Housing, Inc. We are dedicated to helping seniors and the disabled find affordable and safe homes that will reunite them with their families. Our goal is to end senior isolation and help the aged find meaning and purpose. We work with top real estate agents and manufacturers who are equally passionate about aiding the elderly. Visit DignifiedHousing.org or look for us on Facebook to learn more or join the team. We'd love to hear from you!

As an expert in real estate technology and senior housing, I'm a regular contributing writer for the websites Inman News and Real Town. I write about innovations, industry trends, accessory dwelling units, and the latest news. I feature interviews with leaders throughout real estate. Here's a link to my Inman writer's page and another for my Real Town page.

Gregory Charlop

I founded the Real Estate Tech Expo, a series of conferences held in California. We bring top real estate technologists and CEOs together with the front-line agents and brokers. Our speakers and attendees are united in the goal of using technology and innovation to help the less fortunate.

As the founder of the Real Estate Flash and Real Estate Tech Expo, and writer for the top real estate websites, I know most of the leaders in real estate and technology. I know what's hot and what's not, what people are using, and what's just over the horizon. With my deep industry connections, I know where the marketplace is headed. With this book, I'm now able to share with you my special access with these thought leaders. Consider this book your insider's pass to the greatest executives in real estate.

The Real Estate Tech Expo, Real Estate Flash, and Dignified Housing have philanthropy woven into their DNA. My goal is to mobilize real estate pros to help the community. Real estate agents and executives have just the right insight and specialized knowledge to benefit their neighborhoods and society. There is a chapter on philanthropy at the end of this book and I encourage all of you to roll up your sleeves and join a local charity or start your own!

My first startup, Visionary Remodels LLC, used data analytics and augmented reality to help real estate agents prepare homes for sale. I understand the pain points involved in selling homes, and I know technology can make the process easier. Cutting edge at the time, we aimed to use artificial intelligence to automate the process of remodeling homes to optimize them for the market. While the company has been shelved so I could focus on consulting and senior housing, it was a great crash-course deep inside the world of real estate tech.

I traveled down an unusual road to real estate technology. In fact, I didn't start out in the real estate field at all! I'm a pediatric anesthesiologist by training and I care for children during complex and dangerous surgeries. As a result, I constantly read and review the latest research. A child's life depends on it.

As a trained physician and data expert, I understand what the numbers tell us and I critically interpret trends. Now, I bring this data-driven perspective to the world of real estate. I offer you powerful analytical tools and an outsider's perspective of the complex world of real estate.

As the CEO of a tech-based real estate company, journalist, and the founder of the Real Estate Tech Expo and the Real Estate Flash, I've met the key players in the field including senior executives from major real estate companies, marketing firms, finance, and remodeling. As part of the startup tech community, I regularly speak with leaders from the new breed of companies that are reshaping the field.

I know the inside scoop.

It is with this background, with views from both the inside and outside, that I'm able to bring you this book. Since I'm not part of any silo, I can integrate the whole field of residential real estate. I've been involved in every side, from entrepreneur, to investor, to executive. And as a physician, I know how to critically look at facts and reach difficult conclusions.

Now I'm sharing what I've learned so you can prepare for what's coming. This book will pull back the curtain and give you a front-row seat to the future of the real estate industry. Whether you're an agent, broker, technologist, potential real estate agent, or brokerage CEO, you'll benefit from my outsider's view and insider's connections.

I am available for consulting or speaking at your next event. Reach out to me on LinkedIn so I can help your real estate business thrive.

Now, let's get started!

CHAPTER 1: AGENTS AND FUTURE AGENTS

Do you have what it takes to succeed in the new world of real estate?

Your life as an associate is about to change. Perhaps you're already feeling it. The job that you have known over the years already seems different. The world is evolving, and you have to adapt.

This chapter is a guide for what the future may hold for you, and how you can prepare. It is a must read if you make your living helping folks buy and sell homes.

You've always known that your success in real estate depends on how well you sell, and there have never been any income guarantees. The more you sell, the more you make, and a dry spell could lead to tough times. There has always been turbulence.

Now, that income variability will explode. The successful associates will be even more successful, and the unsuccessful ones will have a harder time recovering. Success will beget success like never before, while failure will be more damning. The safety net, such as it was, will vanish.

Thanks to modern technology, you have more freedom than ever before to find new clients. You really are the captain of your own ship. But you'll find yourself without the protective bubble of real estate brokerage firms as you chart your path.

In this chapter, we will talk about what leads to success and failure for real estate agents. Under the new rules of the real estate marketplace, success may primarily be driven by your willingness to embrace technology and specialization and your work ethic. We will explore in detail what you need to succeed as a salesperson.

We'll begin this chapter by exploring how you will find clients. Increasingly, customers will be finding you, and you need to be ready. How can you reach these people? How will they find you? Hint: performance matters more than ever.

As we discuss elsewhere in the book, real estate brokerages are experiencing a radical transformation. Many of the institutions you grew up with may soon disappear, while technology-based upstarts will quickly replace their market share. There's a good chance you'll either work for a new brokerage firm or change your business strategy in the face of technology upstarts like Opendoor and Home Bay. (We describe Opendoor and Home Bay later in the book.)

We will look at how the rise and fall of other real estate brokerage companies will directly impact you as an associate. It will be a constant struggle to add value, as more and more companies look to reduce transaction costs for real estate sales. You will need to prove your worth!

A lot of folks enter real estate with the goal of working part-time with a flexible schedule. Will that still be possible in the new marketplace? Short answer: it won't be easy. However, we'll consider some options for those looking to work part-time.

Finally, we'll conclude the chapter by focusing on folks considering starting a career in real estate. This is not your father's real estate industry. Apprenticeships will be tough to find and competition will be fiercer than ever. We will look at whether a career in real estate is right for you. If you want to become a real estate associate, you must read this chapter, so you know what's to come.

In the new world of real estate, winners take all.

Back in the day, folks looking to buy or sell a home would call the major real estate firms in search of an agent. If you happened to be on floor duty that day, you would take the call and likely land a new client. The callers didn't know you from Adam, but they heard of your company and trusted you by association.

Real estate brokerages spent vast sums of money advertising their brands in order to build that trust, and the sales agents benefited from the association.

The buying and selling public had no idea how good you were or how hard you worked. They didn't know if your former clients loved or hated you. And they had no way of judging your performance.

The sales and satisfaction data either didn't exist or wasn't accessible to the lay public.

There was no transparent, online system for evaluating real estate agents. From the public's perspective, as long as you had your license and a decent brokerage affiliation, you were just as good as the next person. You could work part-time, be fresh out of training, or have smelly feet. It didn't matter. As long as your broker decided to send incoming business your way, you had an opportunity.

Of course, you still needed to perform.

The quicker you moved houses, the greater your income. And, like any salesperson, you would lose clients if you didn't close deals. Your broker would tire of you if clients started complaining.

But the point is that almost all associates, regardless of their level of training or part-time status, would still have ample opportunities thrown their way by their brokers.

Not anymore.

The Yellow Pages have gone the way of the Dodo bird, and floor time ain't what it used to be. There's a whole new way that customers find representation, and results matter.

The internet changed everything.

The public is watching you. They know how well you compare to every other agent in their area. They know how many homes you've sold and whether you negotiated prices above or below market for their neighborhood. They know the top agents in their town because they can see the results online.

They also know whether your former clients like you. You're being reviewed by everyone and those reviews are posted everywhere. They know how many stars and points and smiley faces you've earned on each of the sites.

In short, your customers know all about you before you meet.

What are the consequences of this explosion of publicly-available information?

The most obvious change is that home sellers now search for particular associates rather than real estate firms. The clients want to be represented by winners, and now they know who the winners are.

How do potential clients find the premiere agents? The technology and companies may change, but the three main channels of inbound agent discovery are MLS portals, review sites, and agent connection sites.

Currently, popular MLS portals are Trulia, Redfin (also a brokerage), Zillow, and Realtor.com. For finding high-performing salespeople, they all work the same way. Home sellers search their town and review all of the most killer sales. They see who transacted the deals, and presto, they know the most successful agents in their community.

Success will beget success. Associates with the top sales in any given area will vacuum up most of the future listings in that neighborhood.

As powerful as marketing or brand affiliation can be, I doubt that either of those can carry more weight than a proven track record of success. And since the effectiveness of each salesperson is quantifiable and readily available, no puff piece or glossy brochure will convince a customer that you're better than you are. The proof is in the pudding, and it is out there for the world to see.

A second way inbound clients will discover you is via review sites like Yelp and Trulia. While long popular for restaurants and coffee shops, Yelp is playing an increased role in rating professionals. You can expect that more and more of your clients will hop online and rate their experience with you on one or more rating sites. And your potential clients will read those reviews.

Nobody wants to work with a jerk, and if you develop a bad online reputation, it may be tough to recover. There are enough agents out there that homebuyers can afford to select someone who matches their personality.

Homelight and similar sites represent a third way for home sellers to find agents. These sites function like virtual matchmakers. Customers enter their location and the site suggests agents based on their proprietary algorithm. In essence, the website serves as an intermediary between the client and the associate - no brokerage involved!

There are two consistent themes to these online services. You will be judged by your performance, and your agency doesn't matter. Technology lifted the veil, and your successes and failures are there for the world to see. No more hiding behind clever marketing or large brokerages.

This transparency will create a further consolidation of sales among the top agents.

The 80/20 Rule

Real Estate at a Crossroads

You're probably familiar with the 80/20 rule, also known as the Pareto Principle.[1] The idea is that 20 percent of the effort creates 80 percent of the results, or 20 percent of the salespeople generate 80 percent of the sales. In most instances, an elite group of top performers are responsible for most of the results. The rest of the sales are distributed along the long tail represented by the rest of the agents.

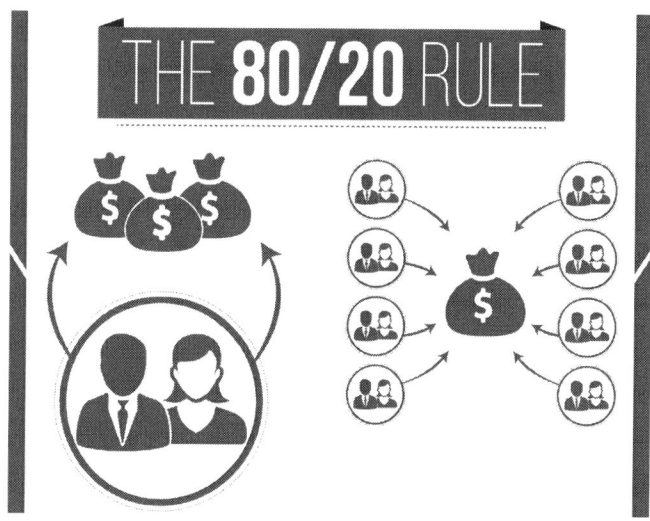

As more and more home sellers gravitate towards the top agents (since they now know who those top agents are), the 80/20 rule will likely intensify to 90/10 or even 95/5 in most markets. The top agents will attract more clients which will further solidify their status as top agents thereby attracting even more clients. It will become a virtuous cycle with the top associates vacuuming up the sales while everyone else is left fighting for the scraps.

This is great news if you're a top performer. Each sale will improve your score on the matchmaking sites, generate more positive reviews on Yelp, and increase your appearances in

25

MLS searches via Zillow and Realtor.com. As a result, you'll enjoy more inbound success and secure more clients. When you close those deals, you'll gain more positive reviews, matchmaking connections on Homelight, more hits on the MLS, and the cycle will continue.

Life will be good!

Unfortunately, the news is not good for everyone else. If you aren't a star, the internet's unprecedented transparency will work to your disadvantage.

Your upset former customers, lack of experience, or bad deals will alarm your prospective clients. Clever marketing materials and prestigious brokerage companies won't protect you from the harsh light of a troubled history. When customers select between your beautiful website or the associate who sold the house down the street for a killer price, you already know who they'll hire.

Real Estate at a Crossroads

As a result, you cannot count on a prestigious brokerage firm to fill your pipeline. All you have to rely on is yourself. Your skills, history, work ethic, and market positioning are all that matter now.

Your clients are changing

You might ask, why should we expect such a sudden change in the marketplace? After all, rating sites and Zillow have been around for several years now, and there are still lots of real estate agents out there making a living.

There are two major reasons to predict a massive shift in real estate sales. The folks buying and selling houses are younger, and the use of the internet for home purchases has exploded recently.

Despite being derided as adult campers in their parents' basements, Millennials are out there buying homes. In fact, Millennials comprise a third of all home buyers—the largest segment of the market—and 36 percent of Millennials now own homes.[2] To have a successful real estate career, it's likely that you'll need to appeal to this demographic.

These younger home buyers were raised online. They take the web for granted. It is a natural part of their life.

They don't go out to stores to shop, they turn to Amazon.com. Real estate is no different. While it's true that even Millennials rarely complete an entire home purchase online, they use the internet for as much of the process as possible. They are initiating their search, browsing, researching, and comparing online.

Here are the numbers: 44 percent of all homebuyers initiated their homebuying process with an online property search. Most do this even before contacting an agent, speaking with friends, or driving by homes. And 99 percent of Millennials

27

and even 89 percent of older Baby Boomers search for homes online.

Even more incredible, almost half of Millennial homebuyers placed an offer on a home sight-unseen.[3] With each passing month, more and more people will depend on the internet to research homes - and to research you!

You must be ready for these new clients. If you aren't on the forefront of the online marketplace, you will be left to a shrinking pool of prospective homebuyers that haven't yet embraced the new ways of doing business.

And if you are not well-positioned to take advantage of the internet, you will either need to change strategy or change careers. Sadly, a time will come when most new agents will drown and even experienced but average pros will disappear as the elite soak up all the prime deals.

What can you do? For those of you considering a career in real estate, we'll cover how to launch your career later in this chapter. For now, let's take a look at how mid-career pros can survive in today's changing landscape.

Target specific buyers

Will clever advertising help you compete? In other words, can you compensate for a history of lackluster deals with a slick advertising campaign? The short answer is: maybe.

Modern advertising techniques are beyond the scope of this book. This technology is improving and changing every day.

Having said that, targeted campaigns aimed at specific buyer segments will likely be effective. For example, Facebook, Instagram, and Google campaigns designed to promote your expertise in particular neighborhoods or niche market segments can work. You can potentially promote yourself as an expert in a particular community or neighborhood by blanketing the internet with targeted ads.

With clever use of keywords and audience targeting techniques, Facebook and Google can help you zero in on your specific audience. For example, you could arrange for your ads to show up anytime someone mentions your community in a Facebook or Instagram post. Repeat exposure will make your name familiar to would-be clients.

If you couple the advertisements with offers for free services like a market analysis, you might be able to position yourself to win business with the force of your personality.

Unfortunately, advertising is an expensive approach. It's estimated that the average agent spends about $400/month on ads.[4] While the internet has driven down the cost of targeted ads compared to the old days of print media, it still remains remarkably expensive if that's your only way of acquiring customers.

You will have a hard time running a successful business if you're totally dependent on advertising to drive business. You need inbound traffic.

Outbound vs Inbound marketing

Outbound marketing is what most of us traditionally think of as marketing. It includes TV and radio commercials, email blasts, mailings and other printed materials, billboards, and our favorite: cold calls. Outbound marketing is when we scream at our audience, interrupt them, and attempt to gain their attention.

When that commercial intrudes on your favorite show or that pop-up sneaker ad appears while you're reading the news, that's outbound marketing. And every time you make a cold call during dinner or send a potential customer a postcard, you're attempting to interrupt them and capture their attention.

Although we've historically spent lots of time and money on outbound marketing, it has a low yield. A 2017 HubSpot report (State of Inbound 2017) revealed that only 16 percent of marketers felt that outbound marketing generated the highest quality leads for their teams.

The problem is that people just don't like to be interrupted. There are a lot of advertisers competing for attention, and they are all shouting at the public. Frankly, people just try to tune out the noise. And most of your advertising, unfortunately, is noise.

Inbound marketing focuses on attracting clients through content. Common examples of inbound marketing are blogs, social media posts, and search engine optimization. I would argue that MLS portals and review sites are also a form of inbound marketing since folks use those technologies to find you. Your reputation is another form of inbound marketing as homeowners seek out successful agents. These forms of advertising don't aim to interrupt folks. Rather, they seek to attract consumers by offering them something free and searchable.

Success through technology

Don't rely on the old ways of reaching clients. Branded notepads, little ads in the corner of magazines, and cold calls just aren't going to cut it anymore. Nobody cares about those things except in particular niche markets. Prospects are online and on their mobile phones (although not for talking). And, they don't care about your business card.

Technology will turbocharge your business in three different ways. First, you can use the web to find and connect with clients through inbound marketing. Next, you'll use modern real estate focused customer relationship management (CRM) programs to groom potential homeowners. Finally, you'll need to harness the latest apps to close deals quickly and successfully.

"I think agents need to utilize technology for organization and automation," said Darren Johnson, co-founder of Agent Zip. "They need a website with a feed of homes that will give them analytics on what homes and features their prospects are searching through. The MLS is no longer a physical book; you need your own website that is very intelligent. Pair it with a good CRM and you have a solid foundation. I get mind blown when I hear agents say they don't have a website," Johnson added. "I think every single agent needs to utilize retargeting. If you go on Nike's website and you start looking at shoes, you're going to start seeing those shoes follow you on other sites. Through Google display ads, through Facebook—that's all retargeting. I notice many agents don't retarget their visitors. I think it's one of the most underused tools out there and it has the highest rates of conversions." Click here to read the full interview with Johnson.

Let's review some technological gems with the usual caveat that by the time you read this book, some of these companies may have changed, folded, merged, etc. You can always keep up with the latest by visiting my LinkedIn page and signing up for my free daily Alexa

show, The Real Estate Flash.

You can get the show by saying "Alexa, enable The Real Estate Flash!" Then, each morning, ask Alexa to play your flash briefings. I'll be there sharing the latest industry news, current trends, coolest technology, and top interviews. It's the easiest way to stay up to date with the evolving world of real estate technology.

Search, social, and local

You need to be where your clients spend their time. Now you can be in their cars, bedrooms, offices, vacations, and everywhere they go thanks to the magic of Facebook, Google, You-

Tube, and Instagram.

Search and social media. That's where you want to be.

While the best strategies to optimize these channels are well beyond the scope of this book and change daily, here are a few basics.

First and foremost, you want to be present on at least some of these channels. It probably isn't necessary to be engaged with all of them (that would be overwhelming). Pick your favorite two or three and get involved.

My recommendation: optimize your inbound marketing efforts with these platforms and experiment with some outbound techniques.

Snag inbound traffic with Google using a technique called search engine optimization (SEO). Use SEO correctly and Google will point potential clients your way rather than to your competition. Don't assume that clients will find you on native search unless you put some effort into SEO. Do some reading or consult with an expert to find the best techniques for SEO and put Google to work for you.

MASTER SEO AND APPEAR AT THE TOP OF SEARCH RESULTS

"Humm, let me search for a top real estate agent"

Joyce Smith

SEO

You can also experiment with some outbound advertising on Google. Did you ever notice Google search results in bold on the top or side of your screen? Those are sponsored results. Google has sophisticated tools to help you create your own paid search results. You don't have to spend a lot of money to test whether this tool will work for you. For example, spend $20 per day for a week and see whether that drives you any new homebuyers. It's fun and easy to try! You can do the same with Google's smaller and less expensive competitor, Bing (www.Bing.com).

An interesting emerging platform to engage with the local community is Nextdoor.com. It allows you to create a free business page.[5] If you're an active user, you can become the face of the neighborhood. You can use Nextdoor's tools to showcase your listings and generate interest among the locals. The platform appeals to real estate agents because all of

33

the users have verified addresses (they live nearby) and nearly three quarters are homeowners.

Experiment with social media

Social media is the new king of the internet. Facebook, LinkedIn, Instagram, Twitter, and perhaps Pinterest and Snapchat are the new faces of client engagement online. Your neighbors are on Facebook. Your potential clients are already looking at houses on Instagram and Pinterest. And, homebuyers are perusing your competition's LinkedIn profile as you're reading this.

Willie Sutton was asked why he robbed banks, and he famously replied: "Because that's where the money is." The internet and social media are where your customers are. Most homebuyers turned to the Internet first when looking for a home, and nearly three-quarters of all Americans use social media.[6]

Surprisingly, many real estate agents today aren't as sophisticated as the bank robbers of old. Not enough agents are using social media. Almost a third of agents don't use social media at all. Half of real estate agents admit that keeping up with technology is one of their firm's biggest challenges in the coming years.[7]

You can do better. Join one or two social media sites and set up an account.

How should you use social media? Engage with your community by providing useful content and experiment with outbound advertising. We will discuss content shortly, but first let's address social media advertising.

Google, Facebook and other social media giants empower you with sophisticated advertising targeting. Take a few minutes and review the Facebook Ads Manager. You'll be amazed by how specifically you can target your desired audience. In many ways, Facebook knows more about its users than their friends do. Use that power to your advantage!

Just like with Google advertising, I suggest that you create a few Facebook advertising campaigns. Test some different messages and audiences and see how it goes. For as little as $10-20 per day, you can experiment with laser-precision ads. Check them out, it's worth a try. In a recent survey, 81 percent of social media users believe that social helped bring in clients.[8]

When you're experimenting with social media advertising (or any advertising, for that matter), remember that you are actually testing two different things: the message and the ad itself. The message is the primary point you're trying to convey in the ads. Are you the neighborhood expert? Do you have the best sales in the area? Do you have access to a lot of off-MLS deals? Do you have an interest in certain buyer categories like the elderly or international buyers? Without testing these various messages on ads, you won't know which are most attractive to your target audiences.

The second thing you're testing with the ads is the format, appearance, targeting, and placement of the ads themselves. Are they better on Facebook or Instagram? Are your prospective clients young professionals or retirees? Does your ad look better in red or blue? Is your call to action (CTA) clear?

For example, imagine you place an ad on Facebook for a week targeting young homeowners. You emphasize your connection to the international community and your ability to locate and deliver international buyers. To your disappointment, very few people click on your ads. What went wrong?

It's possible that your target audience is wrong. Maybe young homeowners in your area don't want to sell. Perhaps your message is wrong. It could be that these people do want to sell, but they don't care about whether you can find international buyers. Or, it could be that you found just the right target audience and you have a terrific message, but your ad is so ugly or subtle that nobody bothers to click on it. Agh!

You won't know what works unless you experiment. Once you find the right combination of message, audience, and advertisement, you will feel like Facebook is printing you money!

Think this is too much work? I'm telling you, optimizing your social media advertising is much more fun (and takes less time) than those cold calls you've been making. You'll see.

Please note, although this chapter focuses on Facebook as the quintessential social media platform, all of the same arguments and reasoning apply to the other social media sites including Instagram, Snapchat, Pinterest, etc. You should direct your time and energy to channels that you and your target audience use most.

Entice with content

The crown jewel of inbound marketing is content—generally free material that you publish online that's useful for your target audience. The goal is for your target clients to discover your content via organic (Google or Facebook) search. The prospect reads and appreciates your content and then discovers you. Examples of content vehicles are blog posts, video blogs (vlogs), and curated content such as reposting interesting articles. Your content can either be on your website, social media accounts like Facebook or LinkedIn, or on standalone blog sites. If you enjoy video, consider creating a YouTube channel for your material. YouTube has the added bonus of showing up on Google search results.

Does content marketing create a better connection than someone clicking on your outbound ads? You bet! For one thing, content doesn't cost you anything to post. It's hard to beat free! More importantly, you create a relationship with your ideal prospect. If they read and enjoy your content, you generated some good-will. They're more likely to trust you and view you as an expert. They may feel indebted to you and ultimately decide to hire you.

Imagine Jane, an ideal potential client in your primary neighborhood. Jane is considering selling her home, but she isn't sure. So, she jumps on Facebook in search of information about the ideal time to go on the market. Up pops your article. She reads it and likes what you have to say.

Who do you think Jane is going to call to discuss selling? You!

Do the math. You just scored a new client in exchange for an hour of writing. Not a bad deal. Even better, your post might be read by dozens, hundreds, or thousands of people. How many Janes are out there searching for your post? Share your neighborhood knowledge, and the prospects will come.

As a real estate agent, you're loaded with local expertise. I bet you know a lot more than you think you do, and you should use that knowledge to your advantage.

Perhaps you have some insight into local real estate trends. Or maybe you have some info about the new shopping center or fancy restaurant opening in the neighborhood. You should write about it! That's useful information and your local prospects want to know. Someone buying or selling their nearby home will appreciate the news you shared about the development. They just might turn to you to be their agent.

Your material should have good information; it also needs to be well-written and engaging. There are lots of books (and blogs!) about how to write the best content. Check those out to help with your style and improve your SEO.

Two suggestions to improve your posts. First, don't do any hard selling. If your piece reads like an advertisement, folks will treat it as such and tune it out. Remember, your goal is to impress your prospects by generously sharing knowledge, not to make a hard sell on your services. Secondly, the only way you'll get better at writing is to write frequently. Practice all you can, and you'll see your writing improve before your eyes. Reading about writing helps too. My favorite book is *Stein on Writing* by Sol Stein.

Audio is another emerging communication platform. I've engaged with a lot of great people on my Alexa show, The Real Estate Flash. You can make your own flash briefings with the help of companies like SoundUp Now. They're the company I use to publish my flash briefing and I highly recommend them.

I asked Sean Mckenna, the co-founder of SoundUp Now about the importance of voice technology like Alexa. "As a Realtor, the use of audio and voice cannot be overestimated. Home search and valuation with the simple ask of a question to a voice assistant device isn't the future - it's the 'now'."[9]

From connections to clients

Now that you've connected with prospects using a mix of inbound and outbound advertising, SEO, social media, blogs and videos, your next task is to nurture these folks. You need to convert them from connections to clients.

In an ideal world, prospects will read your post, be swept away by your insight, call you and hire you on the spot. That does happen, but not often. Usually, the first step is to capture the prospect's contact information: email address, phone number, or social media account names will do.

Congratulations! Now you have one of the most valuable resources for any business: a list. Your list is full of folks who live in your target area and like what you have to say. They may already view you as an expert. And they are players in the real estate market. These are the people you want, and they already know you.

Technology cuts both ways

The good news is that modern technology makes client cultivation easy. Tools like customer relationship management (CRM) software, enhanced email services like MailChimp, manual and automated social media engagement, webinars, and Facebook Live are fantastic ways to manage and interact with your list and generate business. The bad news is that these modern tools of engagement aren't optional. Your tech-savvy competition is already using these techniques. You have no choice but to keep up. Otherwise, the technology meteor shower will rain down on your town and leave you like the dinosaurs.

One last thing about content. Don't regurgitate! I strongly advise you against signing up for some Facebook content factory that makes generic, bland posts. People will be bored by it and pass right over your posts. Your Facebook or LinkedIn ranking will fall, and soon nobody will see your stuff at all. So, if you post something, make sure that it shows your personality. Make it original or add meaningful commentary or opinions to someone else's information. Don't plagiarize or repost generic junk!

Be sociable

Social media is meant to be, well, social. Yes, you can use Facebook and Instagram as one-way conduits of information for your interesting posts, pictures, and information. But to really harness the power of these networks, you need to actively engage with your prospects.

There are a number of different ways to increase your social media engagement. The first and best is for you to post frequently. Your followers will lose interest if you rarely post. You can accomplish this by either posting directly to the social media channels of your choice or by using products that post to multiple social media outlets at once like Buffer or HootSuite.

To rule social media and wow your followers, you must go beyond just posting to your account - you must engage with theirs. Like their posts, scan for any comments that mention you, and comment on blogs or forums that are popular with your community. When folks see that you're active, they will engage more with you. And the more active you are, the more visibility you'll enjoy.

To boost your social media presence, consider hiring a virtual assistant. A virtual assistant (VA) is someone who typically lives in another country and can help you by engaging with others on your behalf. They're surprisingly affordable and some are very good. Most large companies have a social media person who does this stuff for them—and thanks to VAs, you can have one too! If you do hire a VA, I suggest you use a real estate VA service or a reputable site like Upwork to hire them. Make sure they come equipped with great reviews and experience. We discuss VAs in greater detail in a later chapter.

Rather talk than write?

Check out Facebook Live. Facebook Live allows you to create and stream videos right from your phone's Facebook app. Your video will spring to life and your friends will be notified that you're broadcasting.

Live makes creating simple videos easy (and even publicizes them for you). Your job is to make your videos fun and engaging. While you can use Live to promote your listings, I think it's real power is in introducing yourself by sharing useful information. Show your audience that you're the neighborhood expert.

Leading real estate coach Tom Ferry's advice about videos: be authentic. "The best videos are always real, "Hey guys, I'm just walking to this open house. Oh my god, look at this bathroom! What do you think?" It's you being you." Click here to read the full Ferry Interview.

For example, imagine you're walking near a new housing development near downtown and you want to share your insights about the place. You simply fire-up Facebook Live and engage with your followers in real time. Your friends will be notified about your broadcast and can immediately click over and watch you. It's also interactive, allowing your followers to type and ask you questions while you're presenting. And Facebook will save and post the video for you so folks can view it long after you're done with your broadcast. Don't forget, you can also transfer the finished videos to a YouTube channel, website, or LinkedIn page. Just Google how to download Facebook Live videos, and you're off to the races.

Picture this. Li and May are relocating to your town from another state. They're researching condo communities online and discover your video review of a wonderful new development. They love what you have to say, laugh at your jokes, and are inspired by the footage of the swimming pool and playground—perfect for their young daughter. Who do you think they'll contact to buy that beautiful new condo? You!

One last thing. As of this writing, Facebook favors showing videos created using Facebook Live over other platforms like YouTube. Therefore, your friends are more likely to see your Facebook Live video than other videos you upload. So, if you like making videos, give Facebook Live a chance.

Custom domains

Imagine you're real estate agent Jack Garcia in the fictional town of Fall Oaks. You have some serious drive. You want to own this town! You want folks to think of you when they think of Fall Oaks. Most importantly, you want them to go to

Gregory Charlop

you first when they want to buy or sell in Fall Oaks.

How best to do it? You need a website and email address that is yours and yours alone. Own a website such as www.falloaks.com and the email address: JackGarcia@FallOaks.com.[10] (Warning: they aren't real.)

When people search for Fall Oaks online, they'll find your website. Whenever you email someone from your custom email address, they'll know what you're all about. Each email you send will build your brand.

Real estate guru Saul Klein said, "Your domain is more than the "address" of your website. Owning your own domain also puts you in control of your most important asset, your client communication. By combining your domain with your email solution stack, you make every piece of email you send a marketing piece."[11]

Another reason to own your identity online: If you end up leaving your brokerage, you want to take your name with you. You don't want to rebuild your internet presence from scratch if you take a new job. You must own it!

I recommend picking a website that ends with .com or the newer .realestate, which is now available from the National Association of Realtors (NAR). You can easily search for available domains from GoDaddy or My Real Town. Once you reserve your domain, make sure you get a matching email, like in the JackGarcia@FallOaks.com example above.

How do you pick your domain? If you have a business name already, you might want to choose that as your website name. Here are a few other options to consider:

- Geography - Pick the name of the city where you focus most of your efforts, as in the Fall Oaks example.

- Neighborhood - If you specialize in a particular part of town or large housing development, pick it.

- <u>Your name</u> - For example, use JackGarcia.RealEstate. Depending on how common your name is, you might need to be a bit creative, since it's a little tougher to find available sites with someone's name. Fortunately, the .realestate domain is more available.

It remains to be seen whether the .realestate or other novel domains such as .io or .info ever take off. Since it is impossible to tell, and domains are cheap, I suggest buying as many relevant domains now and holding them. You can always use them later, sell them, or let go of the useless ones.

Beyond Facebook - How technology can help you close

It's hard to sell a house if it doesn't look good, but sellers often don't know how to fix their place up before selling. They're often unwilling to spend money, or they don't see anything wrong with their green shag carpet. These design decisions are tough!

My first startup, Visionary Remodels, made it easy to prepare a beautiful home for sale. My housing research data combined with computer algorithms and AI, took the guesswork out of selecting colors, materials, and finishes. These tools even took the pain out of finding available contractors and tradespeople by finding them for clients!

I eventually closed down Visionary Remodels because I wanted to focus my efforts on helping seniors find affordable housing with my newer company, Dignified Housing. But there are many other good companies that use augmented reality and other tools to help real estate agents showcase a beautiful home and close deals.

Visual aids

Once you've prepared your home for sale, there are some great products to promote it. Your buyers are visual people. Make your listing crackle online. Show the place off! Some of my favorite tools are Virtual Tour Cafe and RoOomy.

Buyers expect video. Virtual Tour Cafe and similar sites make it easy to create fun and effective video tours accompanied by music and social media integration using simple images of the home. Don't settle for flat pictures!

RoOomy creates interactive 3-D models of your home and will even virtually stage it! Check out the site, you'll be impressed. Your home will look its best even if you use a regular camera. Remember, Millennials represent the largest segment of homebuyers, and they love this stuff. Make ads that will appeal to this crowd.

Porchd uses the wisdom of the crowd to make your listings look great. You can upload your potential listing pictures to their site and receive anonymous feedback from other users. More on Porchd in the chapter on brokerages.

Matterport is the gold-standard in online walk-through home tours. You'll probably need a pro to use their camera, but the beauty of their final product is undeniable. If you're listing a high-end home or you're targeting foreign buyers who might purchase the property sight unseen, you need Matterport. Even better, CoreVR converts your Matterport images into shareable virtual reality. Go to their website and check out how great this looks!

Two younger companies in the augmented reality space with cool tech are restb.ai and Magicplan. Restb.ai uses computer vision to tag and classify your property photos. You have to watch the videos on the company's website! Magicplan creates detailed floor plans and virtual tours using computer vision.

Facebook Live is another useful video tool. In addition to

using vlogs to promote your personal brand by sharing useful neighborhood content, you can also use Facebook Live and YouTube videos to narrate a tour of your client's home. Try it! Turn on the camera and create a 2 to 3-minute walkthrough of the house. Point out the highlights and share what you love about the property. This is your chance to sell the benefits of the home without interruption - use it. Once you've made the video, post it to Facebook, YouTube, and your home's website and make sure you've optimized it for search.

Here's how going the extra mile with video can help you. Imagine Juan and Gerald, ages 30 and 32, are considering moving to your area. Like most Millennials, they're active Facebook, Snapchat, and Instagram users. They stumble on your page after reading your post about how young people are relocating to your town. They're intrigued and feel like you "get them." With permission, you add them to your real estate CRM and send them periodic updates about interesting events in the area. They enjoy your Instagram posts of new restaurants and bars in town. Now, they're excited.

Then you release a narrated video tour of a new lifestyle condo loaded with amenities like a first-class gym and racquetball courts. They can't resist! They call you up with their pre-approval letter in hand.

Once you have some interest in your property, it's time to send out disclosures. Many agents consider this one of the most painful parts of a transaction - but it doesn't have to be. Disclosures.io streamlines the entire process of preparing and sharing disclosures. It even tracks and measures the disclosures, so you know who's really interested in your property. Very cool.

Adam Gothelf started out as a real estate agent. That's how he discovered that managing disclosure documents was harder than it should be. He founded Disclosures.io to remedy the situation.

"We build software that helps real estate agents manage property disclosures," Gothelf says. "We provide one online location for agents to manage important information like documents, marketing materials and offers for their properties. We have all the crucial property info, whether for listings or buy sides, in one location."

"Imagine you share a property package with 10 different buyer parties who came to an open house. If you're just sending out a pdf or a DropBox link, you have some idea who's looking at the disclosures, but you don't have a sharp sense of how many of the 10 agents are really interested. With our product, you can see that two parties are very interested and they're highly likely to write an offer. Our product gives you that insight. To read everything Gothelf had to say, click on this link.

With technology, it can be this easy!

Real estate is becoming more competitive by the day, and you can bet your competition is using these tools as a weapon against you. It's a fight, and you want to be armed. Use social media and SEO to boost your online presence and locate prospects with a mixture of inbound and outbound marketing. Nurture your leads using a real estate CRM and social media engagement. Build your brand with useful content and videos. And close sales with photo optimization, video, 3-D tours, and automated disclosures.

Success through specialization

Your potential clients already know the top performers. They read the reviews on Yelp and checked out the top sales on Zillow and realtor.com. They know who closed all the best deals —and it isn't you.

The simple fact is you won't be able to compete directly with the top agents. Period. To beat them, you need to change the rules to the game.

Leveraging technology is critical, but you'll need to do more. You need smart specialization. There are a lot of books out there that address different types of specialization including *A Guide to Making it in Real Estate* by James R. Carter. Here, we'll focus on how you can segment the market so you can get your foot in the door without directly targeting the top performers.

The four types of smart specialization are location, property type, client, and technology. Pick one or more of these areas. Carve out your own niche and dominate it.

Location refers to hyper-targeting very specific communities. Aim for a narrow area, not a whole city. Become the boss of one or two neighborhoods or complexes. Your weapons are content and targeted marketing.

Imagine that you've chosen the Heather Farms neighborhood of Walnut Creek, California (in the San Francisco Bay Area). You know that people move to the area either because they're young families with kids looking for schools or retirees looking for quiet and proximity to nature while still in an urban area.

Now, you position yourself online as the local expert with content and targeted advertising. Write Facebook posts about the remodeled neighborhood pool. Blog about some of the new restaurants. Share Instagram pics of recent festivals in the park. And create videos about homes for sale and exciting neighborhood developments. Finally, produce some inexpensive Facebook and Google ads targeting folks looking at that community.

Before you know it, your posts, blogs, videos, and ads will pop up anytime someone searches Heather Farms. You'll become familiar to the prospects and soon you'll be a trusted resource. They will turn to you for advice when they're ready to take the plunge and move! And, best of all, they'll be so comfortable with you that they won't even care about your lack of Yelp reviews or successful sales!

Differentiation based on **property type** segments the market into the usual suspects: single-family homes (SFH), condos, townhouses, land, etc. Unfortunately, this type of segmentation only works if you either pick a very specific segment (i.e. land or manufactured homes) or if you couple property differentiation with neighborhood specialization.

For example, you can easily make a name for yourself if you are the go-to person for undeveloped land sales in your city. Spend some time researching land sales so you know your stuff. Then, share that knowledge with valuable content! Write about permits, utilities, and acceptable use. Use Facebook Live and show off that beautiful plot with the stream and city views. You'll be the only one doing this and the buyers and sellers will be banging down your door!

Alternatively, you can position yourself as the condo expert in, say, Boulder, Colo. There aren't that many condos there. Learn them all and you can own the market. When a buyer seeks the condo lifestyle and wants to live by the mountains, take their business!

Client type. Smart segments include retirees, young Millennials, same-sex couples, families with kids looking for top schools, urbanites, investors, and international clients. Learn about the needs and search habits of these buyers, and you will become their go-to resource.

Retirees/elderly

Retirees are unfairly stereotyped as internet-ignorant. According to Pew Research in 2017, two-thirds of seniors use the internet and the proportion of seniors using smartphones has doubled in the last 4 years![12] While social media use by seniors still lags (only one-third use it), there are plenty of ways to recruit senior clients. Currently, your easiest opportunities might be partnerships with events and locations with senior patrons and non-social media internet channels like search engine marketing (sponsored search results on Google or Bing). While slightly more challenging to reach, seniors are great potential clients because many can afford to move. And it's a great feeling to help these folks find the perfect place to live.

Never lose sight of why you went into real estate in the first place. If you're like many agents, you entered the field because of a genuine desire to help people during one of the most important transitions of their lives. What could be better than helping senior citizens move closer to their beloved grandchildren? Or finding a place the elderly could live independently despite physical handicaps?

If you're interested in working with seniors, it's worth familiarizing yourself with different housing types so you help them find the right home for their needs.[13] The most common are retirement communities, co-living spaces, aging in place, assisted living, and accessory dwelling units (ADUs). My company, Dignified Housing, Inc., is dedicated to helping seniors find the right affordable home. I'd love it if you'd check out the site and join our team. We want to celebrate and promote real estate agents who share the same passion for advising seniors that we do. We are expanding rapidly across the country and we're always in need of new partners!

Millennials

On the opposite end of the spectrum are young Millennials. Now the single largest demographic block of homebuyers, Millennials were raised with the internet, and social media is an integral part of their lives. If it's not posted on Facebook or Instagram, it didn't happen.

And that is good news for you because you know how to reach them! Engage with them on social media, create voice content, post cool pics on Instagram, and vlog about activities in the neighborhood that will appeal to this demographic. And, by all means, promote your listing's high-tech features and powerful broadband. Your competition may be overlooking this demographic. But you know better.

Other client segments

Same-sex couples, families with kids, urbanites, and investors all have particular needs and interests. If you have an interest in any of these demographic segments, learn about what would be useful to them and share it online! They're all great communities and they tend to have friends with similar interests. If you can win them over, they'll be a fountain of referrals!

Do you have a connection to another country? If so, use it to your advantage! Whether you speak a foreign language or have a close cultural tie, you should parlay those strengths into sales. NAR reported that foreign buyers spent $153 billion on U.S. residential real estate in one year between April 2016 and March 2017.[14] One out of every 20 existing home sales were to foreign buyers. It's time for you to claim a piece of that action!

If you're fluent, create web and social media content in foreign languages. Promote local restaurants and markets that would appeal to international clients. Advertise your listings on websites popular with foreign buyers. And make yourself available for international consultations via Skype. Create online tours with Matterport and virtual reality. With your special access to these markets, you have an advantage over your competitors! Use it, and win business.

Win business with technology

Picture the usual initial sales call you might make to a potential client. You go over to their home and take a quick tour. Then, after some small talk, you sit down at the kitchen table and open up your binder. You unload boring glossy brochures and pamphlets all over the table. You show several ads you made for prior sales, a few graphs about the benefits of using an agent, and perhaps some positive quotes by clients you've helped in the past. Yawn!

While the binder certainly has some value, you don't need to limit yourself to it anymore. Relying on a binder full of glossy flyers is a relic and it's what your dated competitors are still doing. They don't know any better, but you do!

Now, imagine a different scenario. You meet your new prospect Ming at her home. While she shows you around, you snap a few pictures using a virtual tour app. After the walk-through, you sit her down and flip on your tablet. You dazzle her with your sophisticated social media campaigns. She loves your video blogs of the neighborhood. Finally, you close the deal with interactive tours from Virtual Tour Cafe or RoOomy that turn her home into a virtual showcase.

You'll knock her socks off and win her business.

Technology does more than locate and nurture prospects. Use technological tools to differentiate yourself and prove that you're worthy of your client's business. In fact, once you've established yourself as a technological innovator, clients will beat down your door to see how you can use your tech savvy to help them!

Remember, Millennials live on the internet and are used to seeing ads on Snapchat and virtual reality movie promos. When, they see agents with binders and pamphlets they are not impressed. They don't want a dinosaur selling their home.

Embrace technology and win over this demographic. They are waiting for someone who understands them. You can be that someone!

The value of hard work

Technology alone won't make you successful, you still need a strong work ethic. Fortunately, hard work can be the great equalizer, allowing new agents to compete against the top dogs.

When discussing the value of work, Tom Ferry said, "The National Association of Realtors puts out these wonderful statistics. They say that 78 percent of consumers go with the first agent they meet. So, for a brand-new agent, it's very simple: You need to do more meeting and greeting and connecting and prospecting and marketing than Gregory, the experienced rock star in your town who has done it for decades and still does it. But everybody's marketing. The Borrell report tells us that somewhere in the range of $15-16 billion a year is spent on advertising. If an agent just gets out in the marketplace and meets and greets, does more open houses, knocks on front doors, makes phones calls, goes after all the myriad of available lead sources, a new agent's going to win.

Unfortunately, the math tells us that the vast majority of them won't do those things and, therefore, will fail. Some say it's as high as 87 percent, but that doesn't shock me because 90 percent of all small companies fail. So, why would 90 percent of startups fail, and real estate agents succeed at a higher level? It's a dog-eat-dog world. But a new agent who has the discipline to talk to as many people as possible, who knows what to say, has the ability to communicate, connect, engage, ask questions and bring value to the customer will win." Click here to read the full Tom Ferry interview.

Success through a cause

Save the neighborhood parks. Build houses with Habitat for Humanity. Hold fundraisers to support the local animal shelter. Organize volunteers to help feed, train, or provide food for the homeless. Read to disadvantaged kids at the local library or school. Donate compassion at the senior center. Support your community!

The goal is specialization. What better way to make a name for yourself, help the neighborhood, and boost your business than by committing to a good cause? Find one that motivates you. We're each driven by different passions. If reading to kids doesn't appeal to you, volunteer at the art museum. The opportunities are endless! Find something that resonates with you.

You'll be known as the person who saved the local playground. People will admire your dedication. Then, when they're looking for a real estate salesperson, they'll think of you.

The beauty of specialization through good deeds is that you don't need any real estate experience. You don't need a portfolio of sold homes or lots of Yelp reviews. You can go out and do it today, even before you put up your website.

Just remember: support your charitable cause because you want to, not solely for self-promotion. People will see through that and it will remove all the good will from your good works. Just do the right thing, and business will follow. We have a whole chapter dedicated to social responsibility later in this book.

Join a local real estate organization

While going out and meeting clients (either online or in person) is the best way to generate new business, you shouldn't neglect your real estate colleagues. They can be a rich source of advice, mentorship, and leads. Dave Phillips, VP of industry relations at Realtor.com and former CEO of the Pennsylvania

Association of Realtors® offered this advice:

"I've seen plenty of really super talented Millennials who come into the business thinking they're not worthy yet. I've heard many Realtors® who have been there for a while say, "We need to get this new person involved," and they push them forward. They help them go forward early in their career. But sometimes the new Realtors® are reluctant to take the step. They think, "I'm not quite ready," or "I need more experience," or whatever. I don't believe that's the case anymore. I think what you need is innovative thought, and when you get someone new to the business or, someone very young who hasn't lived through the last eight real estate cycles, you get some fresh thought—some fresh juice in the organization."

"What we've always found is that the people who are engaged in that sort of leadership and participation—at whatever level of the realtor organization—are the ones who'll still be in the industry years from now. Anybody who's involved in that sort of volunteerism gets more out of it than they put into it. They become more knowledgeable and have new doors open up that they wouldn't have known about without being involved." Here's a link to the full interview with Phillips.

Is part-time still possible?

We all want flexible hours and control of our schedule. In fact, that's the most commonly cited reason folks went into real estate.[15] Two-thirds of agents surveyed by NAR in 2017 cited flexible hours as their primary motivation to become a real estate salesperson.

As an associate, you can arrange your schedule to take the kids to school, root for them at soccer games, or even treat yourself to a mid-day manicure or workout. You enjoy the luxury of time that many of your 9 to 5 peers can only envy.

Beyond simply wanting control of hours, many folks are drawn to real estate with the dream of working part-time. Perhaps you plan to work only 20 hours per week by limiting your new clients. Alternatively, you might try to job-share and split a full-time real estate job with a friend. In that scenario, you would both work together for all of your clients. You're still working part-time, but (theoretically) your clients are still enjoying full-service.

Unfortunately, the new world of real estate will make it more difficult to work part-time. The primary reason is that prospects will see who's making the sales. They can hop on Zillow, Redfin, or Realtor.com and find all the top agents in their neighborhood. And, most likely, those top sellers work full-time.

Now that the MLS is transparent and easily accessible to everyone, I suspect that most prospects will gravitate towards the busiest agents. Social media provides social proof for the biggest sellers.

Here's an example: I follow Jordan Mott, a real estate agent in the Silicon Valley area, on Facebook. You should too. The guy is amazing! It seems almost every day he has a new listing. It isn't uncommon for him to have simultaneous homes he's preparing for market. Even when he's on vacation, he's landing new deals. And, most remarkably, his properties perform. Jordan is always working, and he crushes the market.

Now, I've never met Jordan. But, if I had a home to sell in Silicon Valley, there's a pretty good chance I'd be calling him up. I see how well he does on Facebook. He's a winner with a great track record, and that's who I want on my team.

As a part-time agent, it would be tough to keep up with top producers like Jordan. A part-time person would never have the sales volume or social media successes to compete against a powerhouse like him. That's not to say it's impossible, but you'll find it increasingly difficult to remain competitive against successful agents - especially when their success is visible for the world to see.

If you do decide to give part-time a go, here's what you'll need to focus on to succeed. Much of this advice also works for new or underperforming agents.

- **Lead Generation**: While lead generation is important for everyone, folks working part-time will especially struggle here. You'll have fewer reviews on Yelp and won't have as many successes on Zillow. You'll lack the social proof of an impressive track record. As a result, you'll need to work hard to acquire leads. Consider creating valuable content, purchasing leads from sites like AgentZip, or paying for advertising.

- **Maximize the QUALITY of your reviews**: Since you work fewer hours, you'll have fewer deals. As a result, you're likely to have fewer online reviews. Therefore, you must make sure that each deal results in a great review. Once you sell a home, ask your client to post a glowing review on key sites like Homelight, Zillow, and Yelp. Don't be bashful! It's possible that your sterling reviews might carry you over the finish line.

- **Differentiation:** A track record of success is probably the best differentiator. As a part-time agent, you'll have fewer closed homes. Instead, look for alternate ways to differentiate yourself. Find a niche such as a limited geographic area, housing type, or buyer profile. Alternatively, differentiate yourself with your commitment to social causes! We expand on this strategy later in the book.

- **Outsource**: You have fewer hours per day to work. Therefore, you must make each hour count! Use virtual assistants (MyOutDesk, Kim Hughes), Chatbots (Kaydoh, HelloAlex), and natural language systems like Google Duplex when available. Have the computers do the work for you. Let your assistants screen prospects, make appointments, and handle routine tasks so you have time to focus on the core responsibilities that only you can do.

New rivals and the future of commissions

You've always had to prove your worth, but now you have new rivals: the machines. There are so many new ways to sell a home, you will need to prove that not only are you better than the agent down the block, but that your human touch is superior to an inexpensive computer algorithm. Companies like Home Bay and Opendoor will transact a house with little human involvement and much lower cost. Auctions are soaring in popularity and require little agent participation. New models are surely on the way. All of these may cost less than half the price of a traditional real estate agent. You need to show the client that you're worth it.

With all the new competition, the typical 5-6 percent commission is sure to drop. You have new electronic rivals that cost about 1 percent, and they will impact your pay. On the other hand, real estate firms have less power over you than they used to. You have new options like eXp and Purplebricks. While your overall commission will drop, you'll pocket more of it and your brokerage will take less.

Angel investor, proptech enthusiast, and real estate expert Nav Athwal had this to say about agent commissions: "I think charging 6 percent commission, regardless of what type of market you're in, is going to erode away slowly. In markets like San Francisco, where you're very supply constrained, and the transaction sizes tend to be larger, 6 percent is very expensive. Those homes typically start at $1M and are going for $1,000+ a square foot. I think taking 6 percent of that transaction doesn't really make sense, and the value the agent brings doesn't justify it. Whereas, that same type of transaction in a market like Phoenix or Dallas does make sense, because the size of the deal is smaller, and the supply/demand balance works much differently than in primary markets like SF or New York." Here's a link to the full Nav Athwal interview.

Starting out in real estate - Is it a good idea?

If you're considering starting a career in real estate, congratulations! Real estate is one of the most exciting and interesting fields out there. As much as I love real estate, I'll share some cold, hard truths with you, so you know what you're in for. I'll give you an honest and complete picture of what's coming so you can decide if real estate is right for you.

In some ways, it's easier to become an associate than ever before. You can sign up for an online class, and for a couple hundred bucks and several weeks' time, you can sit for your exam. You'll need to study, but the whole process doesn't take too long or cost too much. And, you can do almost everything from the comfort of your home or the local coffee shop.

That's where the easy part ends.

Once you score your license, you'll want to be an apprentice. These days, securing a good apprenticeship is tougher than ever. Here's the problem: most of the boring, repetitive, or annoying tasks that the experienced mentors would assign to an apprentice are now either automated or outsourced. Chatbots, real estate automation tools, and virtual assistants are doing those jobs. Therefore, an experienced agent has less incentive to take you under her wing. She just doesn't need you as much.

Full-service real estate companies are also more reluctant to train you. As a new associate, you cost a lot to develop. If you drop out or never succeed, companies have wasted their time and money. If you do succeed, they fear that you'll switch over to a virtual brokerage like eXp and take all your valuable training with you! Brokerage firms are in a bind, and new trainees like you are the ones who suffer.

As a salesperson, you'll be locked into a constant struggle to add value. Every day and with every client, you'll need to prove your worth against fierce human and machine competition. Computerized real estate systems improve each day as their artificial intelligence learns and grows. If you're just starting out on what could be a 20+ year career, you'll face a lot of new technology. We can only imagine how powerful computer systems will be in 5-10 years, and some of them will be your adversaries. You will need to prove that your uniquely human qualities justify your high cost.

We already have too many real estate agents. Most associates quit the field after 5 years, and technology will continue to drive down the number of required agents for two reasons.

First, some agents will simply be replaced by tech companies like Opendoor. Those agents will simply vanish. Second, each of the remaining agents will be more efficient because of technology. They'll show properties with virtual reality, and enhanced AI will make shopping for homes easier. A typical salesperson might only need to show a buyer 2-3 physical homes rather than 10-12 today. As a result, the amount of time per transaction will decrease - reducing the number of agent hours needed in each city.

Extra competition and streamlined sales processes will drive down commissions. Don't expect to pull down 5-6 percent from your transactions. It ain't gonna happen.

Competition against your human rivals will be even more fierce. The transparent and ubiquitous MLS means that every home seller can hop online and review all the sold homes in their neighborhood. They'll see for themselves who had the killer sales and read who has the best reviews. As a newbie, you'll have to convince these sellers to go with you instead of their town's top agents. Not an easy task!

From the moment you start out, you'll be battling it out against the top dogs. That's a tough match to win. That's why I suggest you find a niche or specialization - so you don't have to confront the elite agents head-on. Your best play is to find, develop, and own a specific market segment. With the power of technology, market segmentation is easier than ever.

Another option is to start working for a company like Redfin or another internet-based brokerage. They are sometimes willing to hire new associates. They'll train you, and you may ultimately choose to spend your whole career with them. When you're with a firm like Redfin, the clients come to you through the company, so you don't need to worry about your limited track record. You'll still get business!

I asked top investor and real estate expert Ken Potashner (click here to read the entire interview) what advice he'd offer to someone considering starting out in real estate. He said, "I would steer people away from getting a real estate license if they're going to work with a traditional entity. If you get a real estate license, go with a company that's heavily leveraging technology to facilitate transactions."

Not everyone is concerned about the future of real estate agents. Nick Bailey, former President and CEO of Century 21® said in an interview, "Real estate agents who continue to provide value to the home buying and selling client will always be necessary. While there is a lot of information online today, the agent possesses the knowledge of the market, the 'ins and outs' of the transaction, and they have the negotiating skills to get the client from start to finish; something the Internet simply cannot do. The irony is that the digital revolution has helped scale the importance of human knowledge and shared experiences, and consumers across generations are 'pushing forward' the value of working with a person. In fact, according to a CENTURY 21-commissioned study by Wakefield

Research, Millennials—despite being incredibly tech-savvy—overwhelming (92 percent) believe it is important for a real estate sales professional to get to know them personally before choosing to work with them. An agent who is equipped with the tools and technologies that help them facilitate human-to-human connection, augment their abilities and serve to enhance the human involvement consumers demand and deserve from their real estate company will be a step ahead of the market, the industry and the competition."

You might want to consider joining or creating a startup. Tech startups are hot right now! If you love real estate and technology, the startup life might be for you. You can even work in real estate for a year or two to develop an understanding of the market and then jump over to tech. Adam Gothelf took that path. He was a real estate agent who transitioned to technology and co-founded Disclosures.io. Here's a link to the Gothelf interview.

While it may be tougher than ever to be a traditional real estate agent, there are more opportunities for a creative entrepreneur than ever before. Go out there and experiment. Innovate, and you may be surprised by the result.

Gregory Charlop

Interview with Tom Ferry, Top real estate coach, speaker, and CEO of Tom Ferry International

Gregory Charlop: Tom, you have a very impressive background. Tell us a bit about yourself and how you developed your interest in real estate?

Tom Ferry: I've been involved in the industry since I was 18. Most people were raised on milk and cookies. I was raised on real estate—real estate sales, real estate sales training, and real estate management. My father was a real estate agent. My grandfather, who helped raise me, was a real estate agent back in the 50s. So, it's really been the only industry I've ever known. I've been absolutely passionate about it and in love with it for three decades.

I've built two $50 million-plus coaching and training companies in the space. I've done that because I am very mindful of what matters to real estate professionals, what matters to consumers, and bridging the gap between the two. In 2008, I started telling real estate professionals, "You need to start a YouTube channel and start producing content and educating consumers on the dos and don'ts and the things to avoid in buying and selling."

In 2007, 08, 09, I did everything in my power to get as many agents as I could to build their profiles, and then turn around and participate in platforms like Facebook and Twitter, and eventually, Instagram and others, all because I understood that's where the consumer was going. And rule number one in sales and marketing is: be where your customers are.

As a business coach, I've done a little over 30,000 hours of private coaching sessions. I've been named the number one real estate coach for the last five or six years in a row. Today, we have 162 business coaches managing thousands of clients all over the world and helping them basically run their businesses more effectively.

Gregory Charlop: You're also an author.

Tom Ferry: Yes. Three books. One New York Times bestseller. The last book we published was purely for the real estate industry, called *Mindset, Model and Marketing.* Because I do so much free content on YouTube, where we've got millions of views and videos with hundreds of thousands of views, that when I published a book, I thought: "Put it on Amazon. Make it digital. Sell it for 99 cents. I don't care." And we sold a gazillion copies. Books are great.

Gregory Charlop: Let's talk about leads and customer engagement.

Tom Ferry: We're now in the on-demand environment. Imagine if you went to Netflix tomorrow and you could only watch the show you wanted 50 percent of the time. You would absolutely get rid of that service in two seconds. Well, the studies show that if an agent gets 100 leads from lead services, on average, they're only touching 35-40 percent of those people, leaving 60 percent of them with a really bad experience. So, in the on-demand environment, what's happening is smart companies and smart agents are building tech that allows every consumer to get what they want in the timeframe that they want it. Smart agents are partnering with those companies. Solutions like Zillow, Agent Legend, or Agentology are doing a tremendous service for both the agent and the consumer by eliminating a horrific phenomenon in real estate called lead follow up.

As a buyer, I want information in real time. In a perfect world, I don't want to talk to anybody, and the internet has done that for us. Agents are talking about how their tech causes their sellers to sell faster, to sell for more money, and, ultimately, create a better-quality experience.

Look at Dotloop.com. Imagine you're a consumer buying a

home every seven to ten years. You meet with an agent. You look at a bunch of houses. You identify the one that you want. You write up an electronic offer. It gets submitted, and from there you have absolutely no optics on what's happening until your agent calls you and notifies you. With the technology in Dotloop, I am given access as the buyer, as the seller, as the selling agent and the buyer's agent, as the loan officer, the title rep. Everyone involved and associated with the transaction can see in real time what's happening. It's another beautiful degree of separation that has enabled a lot of agents to serve their clients at a higher level through transparency.

Gregory Charlop: As you know, the top agents tend to land a disproportionate share of the real estate business. I think the 80/20 rule definitely applies in real estate, well maybe more like 95/5. What can a newer or less experienced real estate agent do to compete with these top dogs? Can they compete through specialization or better use of technology?

Tom Ferry: Here's the good news. Are you ready? The National Association of Realtors puts out these wonderful statistics. They say that 78 percent of consumers go with the first agent they meet. So, for a brand-new agent, it's very simple: You need to do more meeting and greeting and connecting and prospecting and marketing than Gregory, the experienced rock star in your town who has done it for decades and still does it. But everybody's marketing. The Borrell report tells us that somewhere in the range of $15-16 billion a year is spent on advertising. If an agent just gets out in the marketplace and meets and greets, does more open houses, knocks on front doors, makes phones calls, goes after all the myriad of available lead sources, a new agent's going to win.

Unfortunately, the math tells us that the vast majority of them won't do those things and, therefore, will fail. Some say it's as high as 87 percent, but that doesn't shock me because 90 percent of all small companies fail. So, why would 90 percent of startups fail, and real estate agents succeed at a higher level? It's a dog-eat-dog world. But a new agent who has the discipline to talk to as many people as possible, who knows what to say, has the ability to communicate, connect, engage, ask questions and bring value to the customer will win.

Gregory Charlop: So, if the new agent can get in front of the seller before the experienced agent does, they have a good shot at winning the business?

Tom Ferry: Yes. I usually modify that NAR quote and say, it's not that 78 percent of consumers go with the first agent they meet. I say, 78 percent of the consumers basically settle for the first agent they meet. Agents have to do a better job of bringing value and nurturing the people that they already know, people in their database. And if you're new and don't have the technical know-how, I tell them to align with another agent. Get a mentor. Take on a temporary partner. Join a team. On the flip side, they must have multiple lead sources that they can go after, because, again, it's not that 78 percent of consumers are going with the first agent they meet. They're settling for the first agent they meet. Agents just need to talk to more people.

Gregory Charlop: This is a controversial question, but it's on the minds of many people that I speak to. With all the new real estate technology and the rise of Internet-based real estate companies, many real estate agents are really worried about what the future holds for them. Do you think that we'll still need real estate agents, in the next five years, or do you think technology will replace them?

Tom Ferry: Century 21 was the first real estate franchise. And the second one? It was a discount broker that was basically looking to get rid of real estate professionals.

The reason I bring that up is this: the only people who are nervous about this are agents who should leave the industry anyway. Good agents will never be replaced by technology. Good agents always have that fiduciary responsibility to walk you through the process, make sure you make the right decision and feel good about the decision, and that you have someone to talk to through the range of emotions that take place inside a real estate transaction.

This is a human business that is tech-enabled, not a tech business that will replace humans. There are a ton of examples of technology completely displacing humans, and I can show you an equal number where the human absolutely matters. I bought a very expensive Tesla in seven minutes online with a salesperson. "What about this? How about this? Does this matter? Do I need this?" I used that salesperson to guide and direct the experience. I could've done it online, right? I still want that salesperson experience. When you're talking about a house, the vast majority of people, still want that human element to help them make a good decision.

So, do I think real estate agents will be here in five years? I would bet everything I own times a thousand that they will be. Then I would go out 10 years, 20 years, 100 years, and I'd say the same exact thing.

Now, what might change is model and compensation. There is plenty of room for new models and changes in how agents are compensated, but somebody's still going to be there guiding and directing. Did WebMD get rid of doctors?

Gregory Charlop: No, not at all. Thankfully!

Tom Ferry: Right. Doctor Google usually is a scary place to go.

Gregory Charlop: That's a great analogy. You heard it here first! Tom Ferry says that if you're doing a good job, your job is secure in real estate.

Tom Ferry: 100 percent.

Gregory Charlop: What are your thoughts about the future of virtual or augmented reality in real estate? Do you think those will become industry standards, or will they remain kind of niche players? And how can real estate agents take advantage of these tools?

Tom Ferry: The great news about real estate agents is they are independent contractors. They're entrepreneurs. For the most part, they're people oriented. They're experience oriented. Real estate, generally, is really adaptable to new technology.

There will always be the early adopters that go hard. But once you begin to see traction, once you begin to see it is the cultural norm, real estate's usually ahead of that curve.

So, I feel super bullish about VR. I'm looking forward to Siri or Alexa having every possible real estate question downloaded and ready to go. I remember when agents would pay $5,000 to have a video produced. They now do it for free on their iPhone. Agents will pay early and often until it gets disintermediated and becomes free and accessible to all.

Gregory Charlop: You mentioned Alexa and so have a couple of other people I've interviewed. What technological tools do you think real estate agents really should be using that they're underutilizing today? Are they leaving technological tools on the table that they should be using?

Tom Ferry: The answer is always yes. Number one is any kind of CRM. Studies show that the vast majority of agents don't have one, and they have no way to really manage their relationships and their contacts. I'm a huge fan of Contactually. We even partnered with them to provide every one of our coaching members The Tom Ferry CRM Powered by Contactually within a business portal we created called The HUB. Another great tech tool in The HUB is on-demand video role plays. This allows people in our ecosystem to go online, connect with another agent and practice their scripts together live on video.

And I still think agents are totally under-utilizing Facebook Live, Instagram Live, Instagram Stories, and, ultimately, YouTube for creating content and distributing it to as many people as they can in their marketplace. If you asked me for the one thing they're under-utilizing, it's their phone. They still think of it as a texting, calling, and emailing device, when it's really a device that is connected to 2.1 billion people on the planet—depending on which platform you're on.

Gregory Charlop: I'm with you. I think things like Facebook Live are great, and I'm honestly surprised that it's not being used more by real estate agents.

Tom Ferry: It will be. The challenge, though, is that the vast majority of agents are hung up on: how do I make this look as good as my normal marketing that gets airbrushed and perfected? But then I remind them that at the end of the day, customers choose you because you're likable, you speak their language. They feel good about you. You've got smiling eyes.

Google shared with me a bunch of data about how agents are selected. A high number, around 49 percent, select the agent based on trust. How do you create trust? You let your hair down. You become vulnerable. And on top of that, your brand, your reviews and all the other things that would go along with that. So, most agents are just afraid. That's okay. I remind them all the time: your friends know what you look like, get over it.

Gregory Charlop: I heard international speaker and author Gary Vaynerchuk talking about this exact topic: that people aren't using Facebook Live because they want their hair to be perfect or their makeup to be perfect. They worry so much about making it professional quality, that they don't do it at all. And they're missing out on just what you described.

Tom Ferry: 100 percent. The best videos are always real, "Hey guys, I'm just walking to this open house. Oh my god, look at this bathroom! What do you think?" It's you being you. They're all trying to impress someone rather than just realizing I'm just having a conversation with my friends. Just ask yourself, "How do I talk to my friends?" I don't go, "Hey there Gregory! How are you? I'm Tom Ferry, professional." I'm like, "Hey man, what's going on?" Right? You go live being yourself. You do that, and you're gonna win.

Gregory Charlop: I completely agree. One last question: If executives of a major traditional real estate company asked for your advice about how they could remain current and relevant in today's high-tech world with these newer technologically oriented firms, what advice would you give them?

Tom Ferry: First, I would say, "Congratulations, you have a massive advantage." Because they've got a huge brand, lots of identity. People know who they are.

I would create a culture first where executives and leaders are doing what they want their agents to do. So, I would look at every CEO and say, "You want agents to go, 'Hashtag Century 21' and do a video. So where is your three times a week video?" I would put it right on the executives. Sharing what's going on in your business as the CEO, the executive of the company. You do that, and it will trickle down throughout your entire organization.

That's my first advice: Do what you're asking them to do. Get out of the ivory tower or off the golf course and say, "How do we get 100,000 of our agents to use these hashtags to drive more traffic to our website?" Start doing the work would be my first thing.

Second, I would say, "You are never too old. I don't care if you're 30 or 80. Get on your phone. Hit Google, and type in,

'How do I do a Facebook Live?'"

Third, I would advise executives to start creating a company culture around the tools that they want the agents to use. So never do a conference call as long as Zoom, Twilio, or a Facebook Live private group is available. Just utilize all the tools, and let the agents see you doing it!

Bob Goldberg, the CEO of NAR, is doing an excellent job with a company called Relola. Relola is a geotargeting app that allows the executive members of NAR, as they're traveling around the country talking to their agents, to post their activities on the Relola map, making it transparent that my representatives today are in Kansas, tomorrow they're in Wyoming, and the next day they're in Michigan. So, using these tools from an executive level on down is better than, "Hey, let's hire a trainer to teach our agents how to do this stuff."

Interview with Dave Phillips, VP of Industry Relations with Realtor.com

Gregory Charlop: Thank you Dave for joining us today. You have a very remarkable resume, including holding many important leadership and executive positions in the world of real estate. Can you tell us a bit about your background?

Dave Phillips: I actually got into the real estate business as a meeting planner, running the real estate conventions in Virginia. I just loved the industry, loved the people, loved real estate in general. I went on to be an association executive for a local association in Charlottesville, Virginia, for 12 years, and then, onto the Pennsylvania Association of Realtors to head up that entire state association for about six or seven years. So, I've been around a while, participated in a lot of NAR volunteer activities and different things along the way. It's been a great run for about 27 years and I feel like I'm just getting started.

Gregory Charlop: In addition to that, you do a lot of other activities, right? You give speeches and leadership courses—that type of thing.

Dave Phillips: I've always believed in giving back. I love to do training, particularly on leadership and strategic planning. I've done a lot of strategic planning for organizations both in and out of the real estate business. In my current job as vice president of industry relations at Realtor.com, I get to work with a lot of the largest MLSs in the country. All this helps me keep up with what's going on in the real estate world from the MLS and association viewpoint. I travel around to a lot of different meetings, conventions and give presentations on behalf of Realtor.com and explain all the great things we're doing.

I've been fortunate to be able to share my industry knowledge as well as my association management knowledge in lots of different platforms all over the country.

Gregory Charlop: Very impressive! A lot of our readers are interested in developing their own leadership skills. Can you share some advice about becoming a better leader?

Dave Phillips: Sure. My wife, Dr. Jan Phillips and I have just published a book called *Time to Lead*. She's a great leader, as well. So, we collaborated on this book because we believe that in today's society everyone is so busy and have many different things pulling for our attention and our priorities, that we lack time to lead.

The book focuses on three different gifts—as we call them—and if you take advantage of these gifts, you will actually find you have more time to lead. Focusing on the three gifts gives you the ability to focus on positive things rather than always putting out fires or dealing with the latest employee crisis. We need to know how to prioritize what we do as leaders, as well as real estate agents or individuals, to make sure we're getting done what's truly important and build the foundation that allows you to be less stressed with time restraints and more focused on the results that you want.

Gregory Charlop: Can you share with us what the three gifts are for leadership?

Dave Phillips: The first one is the gift of learning. We believe strongly that if your leadership and the culture of your organization supports learning for your employees—such as taking training classes, attending conferences, or reading books—you will find new solutions to every challenge. If you constantly encourage your organization to learn more and to experience more, new doors will be opened that wouldn't have been discovered without expanding your horizons. Even if it's not direct learning for that particular job, just the process of learning and the mentality and culture of learning is a gift to any organization. It allows you to expand your base and reach your successes in ways you would've never thought of without that learning.

The second gift is the gift of caring. We believe that both the leader and the organization need to care not only its employees, but for its customers, as well as the community they serve. If the organization cares about employees as humans and cares about providing them with some sort of a life-work balance, employees will care about the company. By caring, we mean: understand what's going on in their lives outside of work. Because in today's crazy busy world, we can't expect employees to go to work nine to five and not have to co-mingle work and life. This is especially true with millennials but is really true of all generations of workers.

Life is a complete merry-go-round of everything that is going on in our lives, both work and personal stuff. So, whether it's having to take your parent/child to the doctor or attend a neighborhood meeting or whatever, it's pulling on our time. If we don't acknowledge that and embrace it as part of the work-life balance, we can't really care about our employees. If we do not allow employees to be successful humans as well as productive employees, we will miss out on the loyalty and dedication that those employees could have to our organization.

The final gift is the gift of planning, which we too often ignore. We don't have time to plan for the future, but we've found that when you have a plan, it actually frees up time because you can focus on the plan rather than on wondering what you're supposed to be doing. If you don't have a written plan, then you just wander in many directions. That takes more time than it does to actually plan.

Gregory Charlop: You've been involved in leadership at many levels. What are some ways that real estate agents, brokers or executives could become more involved in leadership? And do you recommend it?

Dave Phillips: Absolutely, I recommend it. There are a multitude of ways to be involved in real estate leadership, both as a broker leading your firm as well as a volunteer at a Realtor® organization. This could be anything from serving on a committee or being president of your local association or chairman of your MLS or some sort of state director. There are many ways to give back to the real estate industry.

What we've always found is that the people who are engaged in that sort of leadership and participation—at whatever level of the realtor organization—are the ones who'll still be in the industry years from now. Anybody who's involved in that sort of volunteerism gets more out of it than they put into it. They become more knowledgeable and have new doors open up that they wouldn't have known about without being involved.

It's actually related to the gift of learning. When you're out there operating in a leadership environment as a volunteer or even as an industry leader, you are learning about the industry. The knowledge that you gain from taking the time to invest in your industry is what really opens new doors for you that you never would've thought were there.

Gregory Charlop: Who would you recommend becoming involved with leadership? You mentioned volunteering in organizations or joining boards. Would it be someone who's been in real estate a long time? Is already established? Or someone who's just starting out? Or both?

Dave Phillips: I'd say both. I think we're way beyond the, "Hey, you have to pay your dues," type of situation where someone who's only been in the business a few years is not encouraged to serve. Whether you're young or not young, you can lead. Even if they've only been in the business a few years or a few months, they can still have leadership skills and knowledge that is very valuable. One thing that the real estate industry always had is a lot of second career people. So, if you come from the mortgage banking industry and now you're in real estate, you might be a really good addition to a leadership role that involves dealing with financial issues.

We're seeing more and more millennials stepping up to the plate instead of feeling they have to pay their dues first. They're sharp, young, charismatic people who can be great leaders.

Gregory Charlop: It sounds like new people in the industry shouldn't be afraid to start getting involved with these organizations almost from day one.

Dave Phillips: I think, actually, they hold themselves back. I've seen plenty of really super talented millennials who come into the business thinking they're not worthy yet. I've heard many Realtors® who have been there for a while say, "We need to get this new person involved," and they push them forward. They help them go forward early in their career. But sometimes the new Realtors® are reluctant to take the step. They think, "I'm not quite ready," or "I need more experience," or whatever. I don't believe that's the case anymore. I think what you need is innovative thought, and when you get someone new to the business or, someone very young who hasn't lived through the last eight real estate cycles, you get some fresh thought—some fresh juice in the organization. That can really be good.

It's still comes down to fundamental leadership. Whether you're charismatic and brilliant or whether you're young or old, it still comes down to understanding your role as the leader. That's why I like to help people learn how to lead, because I think anyone can be a leader if they understand how to lead.

Gregory Charlop: As you know, a lot of young people or people just starting out in real estate won't end up surviving in the real estate industry for very long. It's a tough business. Do you think that by getting engaged in these organizations early, they may improve their chances of success?

Dave Phillips: I definitely do. Certain people like to volunteer for everything, but you have to keep it in perspective. The ones that are successful typically find a balance of business and volunteering in their early career. Most find a mentor and attend as many training sessions as possible. They look for people who they can share their ideas with and learn from. It is critical to find someone to work with right out of the gate, a team or a broker that can help you understand the fundamentals of real estate.

Gregory Charlop: Switching gears a little bit, you've been involved with the real estate industry for a while now, and I imagine that you've observed some pretty dramatic changes. How has the industry changed over the years?

Dave Phillips: Two things. One, the business model of real estate has changed very little. There's been some peripheral stuff around the edges, but largely we're still a commission-based, independent contractor business. It's been like that my entire real estate career. That said, I think this industry has demonstrated that we're very adaptable to change—maybe slow to change, maybe reluctant to change, but we also actually change.

Here are a few examples of how we have adjusted to change. When the internet first appeared, nobody understood it. The internet started getting popular, and industries like travel agencies were put out of business because they did not adapt to the new environment. Disintermediation was the word that everybody used back then. We were worried about being disintermediated. The real estate industry actually rose up and embraced the internet, which is pretty shocking. So, in the mid-nineties we were putting listings on the internet, and Realtor.com came about. We were putting listings on the internet when a lot of people weren't even on email yet.

You could say we didn't embrace the internet quickly enough, but we did embrace it before it was too late. I remember a headline in a national magazine that said, "Internet zero. Realtors one," meaning that the real estate industry had actually won the battle and avoided disintermediation.

It was a good example of us saying, "Okay, we have to adapt." And we have adapted in other ways too. We have continued to embrace technologies as they've come out, and we've continued to embrace new ways of doing business. Back in that same period -the nineties – is when buyer agency came out. There really weren't a lot of people who understood buyer agency back in the nineties. And it wasn't until then that the entire industry had to change and become more transparent and more service-oriented toward the customer. Before that, it was just really doing deals and marketing properties. So, that was another fundamental change that the organization adopted instead of waiting for regulators or the legal system or an outside innovator to force change on the industry.

Gregory Charlop: The example you mentioned pertains to my next topic. I think that granting access to the MLS to the general public—say in their living room or on their phones—has had a profound effect on the real estate industry model. I think that that's been a major transformational change. How do you feel that giving public access to the MLS at home is altering the industry?

Dave Phillips: Well, I think it has altered it. When we first did it, we started seeing some really good statistics that flew in the face of the fears that were out there. The fear was, "When we do this, they won't need us as real estate agents. They won't need us to help them buy or sell homes." We really underestimated the value of a real estate agent and what we bring to the table, but that was the fear. And the reality was that the industry became more efficient; the process of looking for a home became more efficient for both the consumer and the real estate agent.

When you look at the statistics, they used to have to show a buyer dozens of houses before they found the one they liked. All they had was a crappy little picture in a black and white MLS book to look at before they went in and actually saw the house. So you often had to look at a bunch of houses before you could find the one that you actually liked.

Then, when the internet came along, you could see some color pictures, and that's only increased over time. We used to have just a few pictures with a listing. Now we have a hundred pictures on some listings. But even in the early days of the internet, you could see the house online and decide whether you liked it or not. You could search under certain parameters and rule out all the ones that you didn't want to see or that didn't meet your criteria. So, it saved both the consumer and the real estate agent a lot of time. And that's what, I guess, wasn't even thought of. It was more about losing control of the data. But I think that the statistics really show what happened there. It had a very positive effect on the productivity of real estate agents because they spent less time with clients.

I think the best example out there—I just used this when I sold my home in Pennsylvania—are the new 3D virtual tours. They are quite amazing. I asked my real estate agent to do a 3D tour of my home. A company called Matterport is leading the way, and there are others as well. This was great to experience because my house sold in 12 days. It only had four people look at it. Two of them made an offer, and two expressed continued interest but just weren't ready to make an offer.

What that told me was that these people had already been

in my house. They'd already seen everything they needed to know, and the people who didn't come see my house had already seen everything they needed to know and decided it was not for them. Only four people came in, which isn't a huge amount of traffic in 12 days, but they were all extremely qualified or interested buyers. To get two offers out of four people seeing it says to me that I used that 3D tour as a pre-qualifier. No one wasted my time as the seller by wanting to come look at my house to decide whether they liked it. By the time they came to see it, they already knew they liked it and the chance of them making an offer was much greater.

Gregory Charlop: I'm glad you mentioned the 3D tours, because I agree with you. I think that consumers, at a minimum, are using the internet as a way of pre-researching the market before speaking to an agent or going to visit homes because nobody wants to waste time. I think technology like 3D tours gives consumers a great opportunity to preview houses in a more immersive experience. Do you have any thoughts about virtual or augmented reality in real estate? Do you see those having a role anytime soon?

Dave Phillips: Absolutely. In fact, we've got some pretty cool features on our Realtor.com mobile app now that use AI and AR. We just introduced a feature on our mobile app called Street Peek. It allows you to walk down the street and hold your phone up to a house to get market information, such as how many bedrooms and baths and the price. A little bubble pops up above the house on your phone, and you can see data being augmented to your reality.

You hit the nail on the head when you said it's all about saving people time. All these innovations that we're coming up with —augmented reality, virtual reality and artificial intelligence —are all converging and helping the consumer and helping the Realtor save time. Consumers can now research a neighborhood as they drive through it. They don't have to go back and do several different searches to see what the houses are worth.

I think its key, and we have to embrace it more and more. We've created a lot of big data in real estate, we now need to use that big data to augment the reality that consumers are seeing and that real estate agents are providing.

Gregory Charlop: What technologies should real estate agents be using now, that are available now, but they simply aren't using enough?

Dave Phillips: I'm betting on the 3D tours. I think that's key. I like to talk about a technology tipping point that I believe we're reaching in the industry. One example is digital photography, which was invented in 1975, but in the late nineties Kodak still had a huge business printing pictures. But a few years later, in 2001, they went bankrupt. So, that's a tipping point. Suddenly everybody had digital photography capability right on their phone. And it created that tipping point, putting Kodak out of the picture printing business.

I think there are three technologies right now that are ready to hit that tipping point and disrupt the industry. Agents need to start paying attention to them now and look for ways to embrace and understand these technologies. They are artificial intelligence, augmented reality, and virtual reality. The third one is probably a little bit further behind the other two in terms of the tipping point but will probably be prevalent in more like five years instead of three years.

The 3D tours are amazing but having to strap on one of those headsets to transport yourself to a different reality, is still a little clunky and a little costly. AI and AR are starting to pop into every application. So, when we reach the tipping point, it will come fast and hard, leaving behind those who weren't paying attention.

Gregory Charlop: I have just two more questions for you. One of them switches gears and focuses more on real estate firms and brokers as opposed to real estate agents. We discussed how having the MLS in people's living rooms has made the process more transparent. I think one of the consequences of that is it has eliminated the larger brokerages and firms as gatekeepers for information, both in terms of helping a customer find an agent and helping a customer learn about homes. Also, it's made the agents a bit freer. How do you think that public access to the MLS and greater transparency are impacting the brokerages and these larger real estate firms?

Dave Phillips: I think, in large part, we're on the mature end of that change. It's been happening for decades, but some in the industry still think we control the data. We've had real estate listings on the internet for over 20 years. And Realtor.com is over 20 years old. So, it is not a new phenomenon. A large part of this transformation has already occurred and is now just being tweaked and refined. I've seen the transformation happen, and there are still a few who want to hold the information, when the reality is: that ship sailed a long time ago.

Each listing today is typically on hundreds of different websites, if you include all the IDX websites. Listings are on all the brokers' websites in addition to the big portals like Realtor.com. Your listing is on many different sites, so to think that you can do anything to restrain that is silly.

I do think that there are some minor issues that are still working their way through. We've seen a real reluctance over the years to display sold data to the public. But the consumer is firmly in charge today, and they want more data. They want 100 pictures, 3D tours, neighborhood information, market information and historical data. To hide anything, any data, from the consumer just makes them lose trust in the industry.

The fear is, of course, that instead of having to come to the real estate agent to get that information, consumers can now get it on the internet. That is so 1980's thinking. Anything that wastes the consumer's time, or the agent's time, is a deal killer today.

Gregory Charlop: Last question, kind of a fun one. What is your favorite feature of Realtor.com? Or the best feature that not a lot of people know about?

Dave Phillips: I'm going to say Sign Snap, which is an artificial intelligence feature we have on our mobile app. It allows you to go through the neighborhood, take a picture of the sign in the front yard, and instantly the listing information on that particular property pops right up on your phone. You don't need to get out of the car and go up to the little box and grab a flyer. You simply snap a picture. I think that's super cool. It's becoming popular on our mobile app now, but it's still probably relatively unknown to folks.

Interview with Ken Potashner, angel investor & CEO of Home Bay Technologies

Gregory Charlop: Thanks for joining us. You are the executive chairman of Home Bay Technologies. You have a remarkable background, and you didn't come from real estate. Can you please tell us your story?

Ken Potashner: I'm a Silicon Valley tech executive. I've been involved with building several companies that have gone public and created a north of a billion-dollar market cap. My initial executive roles were in the disk drive sector. I then became the CEO and chairman of the company that brought the first MP3 player, the Rio, to market. I've also taken a San Diego company and transitioned it from a defense focus to a commercial focus. So, I absolutely consider myself a tech guy, not a real estate guy. We've taken a technology platform focus, in terms of how we disintermediate the transactions that real estate agents do. We do it in the context that we believe the value proposition is solid. For someone to get 6 percent of your house for facilitating a transaction, we think, is outrageous. We point to the very large technology mindset and ask: how do we disintermediate everything that a traditional agent does, automate it, add efficiencies, and offer a platform solution to transact in real estate?

Gregory Charlop: Does that mean that Home Bay sells properties without the use of real estate agents? How does that work?

Ken Potashner: We use agents in a support capacity. If, at any point, one of our customers needs to talk to a person, we have people available. Very highly qualified people available to get on the phone with them. Very rarely is there a face to face interaction required. And we find that our customers aren't looking for that. They're very comfortable talking ... texting, making calls—but predominantly using the platform.

Think of it in the context of a Turbo Tax type experience. You're being guided through a step-by-step process, a lot of data is being given to you. You're totally aligned. In real estate, a traditional agent, may be trying to get a transaction done, where, in our case, we're supporting your thinking, your valuation for your home. Things of that nature.

Traditionally, it would apply 50, 55 hours of human time to a transaction. We're spending about an hour and a half of human time. And we're not compromising at all the customer experience. As a matter of fact, the ratings we've gotten back from customers are dramatically higher than you would get with a conventional agent. We set off to design something that has a stronger customer experience, better results, measured in terms of the ultimate price you get for your house, as well as the time your house is on market. And an extreme increase in the responsiveness. And we're doing all this at a dramatically reduced cost.

Gregory Charlop: When a customer does ask someone on your team for help, are they speaking to a real estate agent, or broker? Or are they speaking to a receptionist? Who's actually answering their calls or texts?

Ken Potashner: Agents. We've hired a fleet of agents who have done, I think the minimum is 500 transactions over their lifetime. Traditionally, an agent spends a great deal of time trying to recruit new business, identify leads. Our entire lead generation is done online. Facebook, Google, Bing. So, we've got agents who are doing nothing but supporting customers. Therefore, we're able to get a tremendous amount of bandwidth on the key issues, and we have agents who are supporting 20, 30 clients at a time.

Gregory Charlop: It sounds like you do all the work of finding the customers, using your platform and your advertising. And all the agent has to do is facilitate the transaction remotely.

Ken Potashner: That's correct. It's done with a tremendous amount of data learning analytics with a bit of AI thrown in. We're operating at the ZIP code level, understanding what's normal and not normal on a given transaction. And the platform's identifying an offer you got. The buyer has asked for these things that are not traditionally offered. You may want to consider this proposed counter. So, it's a blend of the system with the human intervention.

Gregory Charlop: Well, it sounds like a remarkable product. It'll save a lot of people money.

Ken Potashner: Yeah. On average, we're saving $16,000 per client. Our average price point has been about $600,000, and that price point's moving up as we begin marketing in a more aggressive fashion.

Gregory Charlop: Very impressive. You obviously have a keen eye for how technology can disrupt industry. That's what you've done during your career—not only in real estate but in other fields. What did you see in the real estate industry that made you think that it was ripe for a change?

Ken Potashner: I guess the starting point was the value proposition being offered by traditional agents today. Again, the 6 percent of your house. We realized that there's a tremendous margin with that type of a proposition, and we knew that, through technology, we can offer a much more compelling experience as well as a much more aggressive price point. So that convinced us that the value proposition was there. Then it became, can we define and execute on a platform that delivers those dynamics? So, whenever you see a disconnect between the value being provided and the cost being charged for that, it's a green flag, right? Here's something ripe for disruption.

Gregory Charlop: In other words, it seems like the real estate industry was overcharging for the amount of service it was providing.

Ken Potashner: Absolutely correct.

Gregory Charlop: The current system for buying and selling residential real estate is essentially based on large, traditional real estate companies, broker supervisors, agents, and high commissions. And this has been around a long time. When this system first started, information was pretty scarce, and companies, frankly, held all the cards. How do you think that increased information transparency and access to the MLS in everyone's home or on their cell phone will change this long-standing model? In other words, do you think that the current system of large firms, brokers, and agents will even continue to exist? Or will they need to change radically?

Ken Potashner: You hit it right on the head. There's tremendous transparency now in terms of data flow. Zillow provides a great deal of data. People go in now with a preconception of what their house is worth. They're able to see comparables in a way that they weren't able to years ago. We're in a data information-rich environment. In the distant past, you would have had to rely on your broker and trust your broker to steer you through valuation. Therefore, given the existence of the information, the brokerage needs to define differently what value add they're providing to the equation. They need to either look for different ways to add more value or change their value proposition from a cost perspective to align with how much data is flowing freely to the consumer.

I think you'll see everything on the spectrum. I think you'll see some guys dig a moat and build a wall higher, trying to entrench themselves in how they do it today. And I think you'll see other guys move pretty aggressively to take advantage of technology. Those who ultimately disrupt themselves are going to be viable downstream. But those who simply connect the way they've done it in the past won't be here in the future.

Gregory Charlop: In a similar vein, if the board of directors of a leading real estate company asked you for specific suggestions about how to deal with technology and with the changes in the industry, what would you say?

Ken Potashner: My advice would clearly be, you want to be the ones that disrupt yourself. You don't want to be in a reactive state when dealing with technology disruptors that are going to put you in a catch-up mode—a mode by which you're encumbered by the agents that you have in place. You need to always have internal efforts that span the breadth of technology progress, information progress. You can't sit there hoping that somebody doesn't come along and deploy the new technology in such a way that can compromise you.

In some cases, there are multiple channels. At the very high end of your market, you may want to continue the way you've done it. But with more and more people having their sleeves rolled up in their transactions, or looking for discount services and such, if you want to participate in that part of the segment, you'd better have that technology within your portfolio.

Gregory Charlop: If you met a young person, maybe someone just out of college or out of school, who's considering a career in real estate, what advice would you give that person?

Ken Potashner: Clearly, I would steer people away from getting a real estate license if they're going to work with a traditional entity. If you get a real estate license, go with a company that's heavily leveraging technology to facilitate transactions, like we're doing.

Gregory Charlop: Why? Because you just don't think there would be enough work for them in the future?

Ken Potashner: Think of the efficiency that we get. Our agent can support 30 times the transaction volume of a traditional agent in a traditional company. Maybe 50 times, even. So the inverse of that suggests I can replace 50 agents with one of mine, using my technology. There should be a pretty significant excess, or available workforce already of agents out there that will need to be redeployed. So, I would not be recommending that somebody begin training to add to what will be an overinflated workforce for that kind of work.

Gregory Charlop: You're an expert in both business and now in real estate, with quite a track record. You went from technology and business to real estate. If you met someone who wanted to do the opposite—a broker or an agent who wanted to go into business, either as an investor or as an entrepreneur starting their own real estate-related company—what advice would you give that person? In other words, how could they go about finding a career in business?

Ken Potashner: Let me correct your earlier statement. I don't consider myself having gone from business and tech to real estate. I still consider myself 100 percent a tech guy—a business guy who, by the way, now is operating in real estate surrounded by folks who know real estate. So, I'm probably the weak link on the team in terms of really understanding real estate. In the same way, I doubt that the leadership team on Uber were really guys who were fluent in the taxi industry. So, they built a software platform and pointed it at the challenge: how do I get people from point A to point B, give them a great experience, and save them a lot of money. In the same way, this is a tech company, not a real estate company. If you looked at the resumes of my team, I'd say 90 percent of them are tech guys, and then we've surrounded ourselves with the agents I discussed.

To your question, though, I think what's really key is core skills—business or tech—that can be flexible enough that they can be pointed at any industry. I don't think that whole degree of specialization is necessary. I think that actually would be limiting. The secret would be acquiring core skills that can move back and forth across different sectors.

Gregory Charlop

Interview with Nick Bailey, **former president & CEO of Century 21 Real Estate**

Greg Charlop: Nick, you have a very impressive background. Can you tell us a bit about your journey and how you became interested in real estate?

Nick Bailey: My interest in real estate dates back 21 years when I first started to list and sell as an agent, coincidentally with CENTURY 21® and shortly thereafter as an unaffiliated broker-owner. In the process, I realized the value of franchise and affiliation. Giving people an entrepreneurial opportunity to own their own business, provide for their family and be proud of what they've done for a living has been at my core over the last 21 years in the real estate industry.

Greg Charlop: Virtual and augmented reality are attracting a lot of attention in real estate. What are your thoughts about the importance of virtual and augmented reality? Do you see it as something that is ready for prime time now, or do you think it will be a while before customers expect that as part of their homebuying experience?

Nick Bailey: There are any number of technologies, new and old, that help market properties for clients to sell their homes. Consumers will ultimately decide when, or if, VR or AI are ready for prime time. As president and CEO of Century 21 Real Estate, I see technology and innovation from two buckets: One is serving consumers—buyers and sellers—and the other is serving real estate professionals. We must figure out, from a technology perspective, how to satisfy both of these constituents. My job is to help C21® agents be productive, close more deals and simplify the transaction for their clients. Right now, mobile is where everyone is. Our organization is always fine-tuning our comprehensive C21® mobile-first platform to help connect buyers and sellers with our real estate professionals and help them take their buyers and sellers from search to close. If we can make that process easier for our affiliated agents, which in turn makes it easier and transparent for consumers, that to me is a winning formula. This is where VR or AI can make a difference, and we are discussing ways in which these applications can make that happen in the real world.

Greg Charlop: What are your thoughts about Bitcoin and real estate? Will Bitcoin play a major role in the market, or do you think that will remain more of a niche interest?

Nick Bailey: Cryptocurrencies are certainly gaining a lot of attention, but right now there are many risk factors that could impact the success and security of a transaction, for example, the volatility of Bitcoin and the current timing associated with the various steps in the real estate transaction. That said, new processes always come with 'pros and cons' and we'll definitely be watching to see if cryptocurrencies become a viable solution for more buyers and sellers.

Greg Charlop: Years ago, consumers were almost entirely dependent on their real estate salesperson for information. Now the MLS is essentially public, and consumers can find practically any kind of data online themselves. How does the easy availability of data impact the role of the real estate agent? Will real estate agents become unnecessary?

Nick Bailey: Real estate agents who continue to provide value to the home buying and selling client will always be necessary. While there is a lot of information online today, the agent possesses the knowledge of the market, the 'ins and outs' of the transaction, and they have the negotiating skills to get the client from start to finish—something the Internet simply cannot do.

The irony is that the digital revolution has helped scale the importance of human knowledge and shared experiences, and consumers across generations are 'pushing forward' the value of working with a person. In fact, according to a CENTURY 21-commissioned study by Wakefield Research, Millennials —despite being incredibly tech-savvy—overwhelmingly (92 percent) believe it is important for a real estate sales professional to get to know them personally before choosing to work with them. An agent who is equipped with the tools and technologies that help them facilitate human-to-human connection, augment their abilities and serve to enhance the human involvement consumers demand and deserve from their real estate company will be a step ahead of the market, the industry and the competition.

Interview with Adam Gothelf, co-founder & CEO of Disclosures.io

Gregory Charlop: Tell me a bit about you. You obviously have a deep background in real estate, but how did you decide to start Disclosures IO?

Adam Gothelf: During my time in real estate I felt a lack of technology to support my clients and my own workflow. A key part of the transaction is managing disclosure documents: sharing, reviewing and interpreting them with your clients. So we decided to start there.

Gregory Charlop: So, before this, you were working directly as a real estate agent. And then you discovered a problem. And you decided to start a company to solve it?

Adam Gothelf: Correct.

Gregory Charlop: That's very inspirational. Did you have a background before, in either starting companies or creating technology?

Adam Gothelf: Not really much tech background. I had a few different companies that I started after college before I got into real estate. I just have the entrepreneurial bug, I guess.

Gregory Charlop: That's exciting that you would make a big leap like that. For our readers who aren't familiar with Disclosures.IO, can you tell us a bit about the company? What is it exactly that you do?

Adam Gothelf: We build software that helps real estate agents manage property disclosures. We provide one online location for agents to manage important info like documents, marketing materials and offers for their properties. We have all the crucial property info, whether for listings or buy sides, in one location.

Gregory Charlop: So, you help listing agents prepare disclosures and distribute them? How does a real estate agent use the product?

Adam Gothelf: Yeah. We help agents compile the disclosures, reports, basically whatever they want to share about the property. We make sharing really easy and insightful. We are also integrated with DocuSign, so signing is very easy.

Gregory Charlop: You have an ability to track when the disclosures are reviewed or sent out?

Adam Gothelf: That's correct. For example, imagine you share a property package to 10 different buyer parties that came to an open house. If you're just sending out a pdf or a DropBox link, you have some idea who's looking at the disclosures, but you don't have a sharp sense of how many of the 10 agents are really interested. With our product, you can see that two parties are very interested and they're highly likely to write an offer. Our product gives you that insight.

It's also useful on the buyer's side. Often, when your buyers request to see the disclosures, you send them and it's "crickets". They have lost interest in the property and you don't hear from them. With our product, you get an insight into whether or not they are actually reading the disclosure documents.

Gregory Charlop: That sounds like a great tool. Most agents probably create a pdf. And then ultimately they use DocuSign. So, if you're comparing, say Disclosures IO to that traditional method, it sounds like you're getting a lot more information about who's looking at the disclosures and how popular it is. Plus, they're easier to prepare and keep organized.

Adam Gothelf: Correct.

Gregory Charlop: And does the agent on the receiving end need to be a Disclosures IO customer in order to review and use disclosure packets?

Adam Gothelf: No. There's no friction on the buyer's side. They don't have to sign up or create an account.

Gregory Charlop: I'm a big fan of data. It seems like Disclosure IO offers a great way to measure and track engagement. How would agents use that information to their advantage?

Adam Gothelf: Let's say you have fairly light interest on a listing. Maybe you only share three disclosure packages to interested buyer parties. With our product, you can see who's looking at what. You see who's actively reviewing the descriptors, which is the key next step in the process of writing an offer. If you just email a pdf, you don't know if the agents are engaging with the disclosures.

You're having a hard time deciding whether to set an offer date. With our products, you can see that, "Wait a minute. I only have one party who's actively reviewing the disclosures." The other two have not looked at it at all! In that case, you may not want to set an offer date. You may want to just let that one buyer surface. You can continue marketing the property or do some more open houses.

If you have a lot of interest, go set an offer date. That's how the agents could use that data.

Gregory Charlop: In other words, it might be better sending out 3 packets and having those parties heavily reviewing them, rather than sending 10 offer packets that nobody is looking at. And knowing that information could help the seller's agents tailor their strategy.

Adam Gothelf: Correct.

Gregory Charlop: That's a clever idea. Who typically purchases this product? Is it usually an individual agent, broker, or brokerage firm?

Adam Gothelf: We try to build for individual agents. There's a lot of bureaucracy in real estate. The agents are on the ground doing the hard work interacting with clients. They have a unique workflow and by building products for them, we think we can really provide a service that's highly valuable to them.

Gregory Charlop: So, most of your purchasers are individual agents, who want to improve their productivity?

Adam Gothelf: We have many brokerage-wide accounts, but the product is really more focused on the agent as opposed to the brokerage needs.

Gregory Charlop: Excellent. Now, Disclosure IO really seems like a great product. Adam, I'm curious: how were you able to transfer from selling real estate to Silicon Valley entrepreneur? Did you hire someone who knew how to program? How did you even go about that?

Adam Gothelf: All of the above. It's been a long road for me. The companies that I started before getting into real estate were not really tech companies. This has been a long road.

About 5 years ago I had an idea for a real estate app. So, I raised a little bit of money, and I outsourced the development. I don't know how to code, but I know real estate. I spent all this money on building an app that targeted a pain point that wasn't really sharp. It was just sort of fuzzy pain. And it fell flat because nobody really wanted to use the product, the app broke, and I had no money left. The entire time I was trying to find co-founders, and it was really hard to get people to turn on to real estate tech. I went to all these meetups, events, etc. It really sucked.

Around that time, I linked up with an old friend, Brian, who's mom happened to be a real estate agent. We started kicking around some ideas for a new real estate product. Brian was working as a product manager, leading a team of engineers at a company called Opower. So, Brian had great experience working with engineers. He and I came up with a product idea that was very different than disclosures. We went on the hunt together for an engineer.

We met with a bunch of people, but this time the conversations were a bit different. We met our third co-founder Paul, who at the time, was working on Transaction Rooms at DocuSign. We put out a beta version to about 10 or 15 agents in San Francisco, and we crafted the product a little bit more and had really strong positive signals from those early users. We all went full time after that. The key was finding a really sharp pain point and building the right team.

Gregory Charlop: That's a great story. And excellent advice. Now, we probably have a number of people reading this book—either real estate agents, or brokers, or perhaps even executives—who also have an entrepreneurial interest. What advice would you give to a real estate agent or broker if they came up to you and said, "Hey, I'm thinking about starting a company or developing a product, as well." What advice would you give that person? What next steps should they take?

Adam Gothelf: I'd say a couple of things. One, test it without building any product. I really wish that I had understood this and knew this when I was first starting because you don't really need to build anything. You can catch a lot of problems with tools that are available to you today, such as a Google form and email.

Two, talk to your potential customers. Just go and ask them, " Is this a pain point for you? How sharp is it?" And dig into that. The two key things for that is, is it something people want? And number two is, what is the minimum viable thing or experience they need?

CHAPTER 2: BROKERS AND EXECUTIVES

How to survive and thrive in the marketplace of the future

Top real estate companies and brokers are great at nurturing talent. You know how it works. You hire young associates right out of training and pair them up with your more seasoned salespeople. The newbies learn the ropes from the experienced folks in exchange for running open houses and shuffling papers. Throw in some classes from the brokers and a nice library of resources and, after a while, you have a great farm team! Everybody wins.

It was a great deal for you. The inexperienced associates didn't really cost you anything. They provided cheap labor for stuff nobody wanted to do, like filing and phone calls. The experienced agents didn't mind giving up a fraction of their commission for the team. And you built a great bullpen as your senior agents retired or left.

Sure, a lot of the newbie associates would fail, leave, or quit, but that was no problem. They were practically free, and new ones are banging down your door every day to replace them.

This apprenticeship model, as I call it, sustained large real estate firms throughout the generations. In fact, this system of cultivating talent was a huge benefit to the large firms. After all, the largest brokerages would have a vast pool of experienced salespeople and huge libraries. The top shops had the most inbound calls during floor time. And there was an endless supply of new grads ready to work for next to nothing.

It was a dream! The system perpetuated itself.

Senior associates jumped ship or retired? No big deal! They could easily be replaced. You could either promote the top of your bullpen or hire another experienced associate drawn to your firm's prestigious reputation. Turnover among the trainees? Not to worry! New folks were lining up around the block for a chance to work under your tutelage.

All the while, you'd collect a nice cut of the commission from all the action! Buying or selling, senior associate or junior apprentice, complex transaction or routine business. It didn't matter. Either way, you'd get paid. And, paid quite handsomely!

The whole system depended on your brokerage. The junior people required access to your senior salespeople to learn the ropes and for a cut of their deals. The senior people liked your constant supply of newly minted associate worker bees. Everyone loved your grand conference rooms, prestigious addresses, and fancy photocopiers. The whole team benefited from your firm's advertising, which was far too complex and expensive for individual associates to arrange on their own. And, of course, everyone was legally required to work under the supervision of a designated broker.

You held all the cards.

All you had to do was keep up the office, monitor compliance, and maintain the corporate advertising. Throw in a little teaching here and there, and you were done. If you kept up your part of the bargain, you were nearly assured of a steady flow of willing associates and a flood of effortless commissions. You were the Don.

Now, the rules have changed. The successful senior associates aren't playing ball.

The marketplace is more transparent now. The general public has access to MLS portals like Zillow, realtor.com, and Redfin. As a result, homebuyers and sellers know the top agents. The public knows who made the killer deal on the house down the street. They know who's racked up sale after sale in their neighborhood. And, thanks to review sites like Yelp and

Trulia, folks know the most popular associates in town. The ratings are out there for the world to see.

Everyone wants a real estate salesperson who's successful and well-liked. Thanks to the internet, potential clients can hunt those unicorns down on their own.

The general public cares that their agent has a proven track record of success and happy clients. They do NOT care about that salesperson's brokerage or real estate firm. I repeat. They care about the salesperson, not the company.

Moreover, most of the public doesn't care about your magnificent offices. Tamir Poleg, the founder of internet-based brokerage Real, said in an interview, "If you ask brokers about their expenses, about 50 percent of the expenses go to either rent or maintaining the physical space. It doesn't make sense to spend so much money on physical locations because customers do not need it anymore. Nobody wants to drive to visit your fancy or not-so-fancy office."

Your senior associates know all this.

Top agents are more empowered than ever, and that has huge consequences for your brokerage. The Agents and Future Agents & the Elite Agents chapters supply more information about this critical concept.

Winner takes all

When you do a web search, you Google it. Looking to buy a book or sunscreen online? You visit amazon.com. Seeking an original edition of the first Star Wars videotape? Time for Ebay. Remember Myspace or Friendster? Neither do I. Facebook toppled them. The winner takes all.

A small fraction of salespeople generate most of the sales (the 80/20 rule), a small number of countries produce most of the world's GDP, a tiny fraction of software bugs saddle us with most of the errors. We see this over and over again.

Winner takes all, and the 80/20 rule will increasingly dominate real estate. In fact, you can already see it now....

Look around your sales floor. Your new agents earn less than $10K a year from real estate.[16] In fact, most of them will exit the business without renewing their license. Your top agents, on the other hand, are cleaning up. They close deals and vacuum up referrals. They are your Thoroughbreds.

Radical transparency consolidates sales at the top, and everyone else will be left in the dust.

Consider this scenario. It's the year 2000 and someone wants to sell their home. They need to pick a salesperson. Other than through referrals, how did they choose?

You already know.

They went with the first person they found. Perhaps that was the associate who answered the phone at your real estate agency when they called. Or, it was the guy holding the open house down the street. Maybe it was nice lady they bumped into in the cereal aisle at the grocery store! The point is, folks chose their agent largely by chance, not by merit!

Fast-forward to today. Folks do everything online, from buying shoes to selecting their real estate agent.[17] Within minutes, the public will figure out the best agents in their neighborhood. It's not a secret. Clever advertising, floor time, and extra visits to the cereal aisle won't change that. Data is transparent, and the best agents are out there for all the world to see. After referrals, internet search is the leading way people find real estate agents. That trend will only increase.

Once the public finds out who the top agents are, they won't go anywhere else! Why would they?

We will see a robust virtuous cycle where the top associates have the most impressive MLS track records and the best reviews. More folks will flock to those elite salespeople which will generate an even more impressive track record and a flood of positive reviews and the cycle will repeat. Success begets success.

Real estate sales will be dominated by the few, and you want them on your team.

Focus on top talent

The old farm team model is broken, and you won't be able to fix it. Don't count on the top performers sticking around long enough for you to groom the next generation of high-achievers. It ain't gonna happen.

Unless you create a compelling reason for the top folks to stay, they're going to jump to another firm. If that happens, you will lose.

As the talented few come to dominate real estate sales, your firm's model will have to shift to keep up. The old model of a constant cadre of superstars coupled with nurturing a farm team won't cut it anymore.

To put it bluntly, you need the top agents. Without them, you'll be in for tough times. Therefore, you will need to reorganize your system to do whatever you can to attract the top salespeople even at the expense of losing your farm team infrastructure. The top agents are paying your bills; the underperforming folks are taking up desk space.

Sure, some of your new agents might one day turn into superstars. Perhaps one day an agent who's been mired in the third quartile of sales may bump up to the second. But that will take time, money, and luck.

You might ask, "Why can't we have both, top agents and a farm team?" The trouble is, the infrastructure needed to attract and retain top agents is almost 180 degrees opposite what you need to nourish and cultivate novices and underperformers.

Why is that?

To nurture your farm team, you need some sort of hiring or talent manager who can review all the applicants and determine whether they have the potential for success despite lack of a track record. That's a unique skill! You also need a broker to provide legal coverage. Then you need to support these folks with advertising, mentorship, and significant technological resources—as well as more senior people who will always be available to provide them with work and tips. You might even want to make a big, beautiful office and conference room to provide these trainees with a veneer of success. In short, you will need to spend a lot of money to make these new agents successful!

How do you pay for all the training, conference rooms, advertising, and technological support? High fees and a large cut of the commission. You give these folks a rich, nurturing environment, but you need to charge them for it. You're a business, after all.

What do the top performers need?

Well, they'll still need the broker for legal coverage. Some of them may want some assistance with technology such as a web page or CRM. And that's about it.

They don't need all that much help. And, to be candid, they may not want it! They have their own way of doing things that works for them and they probably don't want you to impose your system on them. What they're doing is working, and you should get out of their way.

They work hard and deserve to be rewarded. What they truly want is a flexible, inexpensive system that lets them keep their commission.

YOUR TOP AGENTS GENERATE MOST OF YOUR REVENUE

Herein lies the problem. The newer folks need to be pampered and monitored. They need lots of advice and lots of stuff. And, they're willing to pay for it since they know they won't generate sales without all the help. Conversely, the top performers want an inexpensive, agile system that doesn't interfere with their routines or their paychecks.

The needs of the savvy elite agents and the underperforming beginners are so diametrically opposed, it seems nearly impossible to house them both under the same roof and deal justly with either camp. Skimp too much on services and supervision, and the newbies will falter. Build up a full-service shop with systems, support, and fancy conference rooms and you'll scare away the best producers.

What's a brokerage to do? That's easy: focus on the top performers. They bring in the business and pay the bills. Do whatever you can to keep those folks with your brokerage. Just a couple master associates will generate more revenue than legions of more mediocre salespeople. The 80/20 principle rules the day.

You know what you must do to attract and retain the cream of the crop. Let them keep most of their commission and be available to help with some technological challenges. For example, you could help create a website or a drip Mail Chimp campaign; offer them tools like TLCengine, Porchd, Voiceter Pro, The Real Estate Flash, and a virtual assistant. But, for the most part, you should just stay out of their way. Don't impose your systems or personnel on them. Let them chart their path.

I know what you're going to say. You reserve your highest charges for the newbies and bill the top performers a smaller cut of their commission. You charge a lower rate or cap your fees after a certain level of sales for your top people. Perhaps you even have secret deals with your elite performers. That's all great.

But, is that really enough to compete with the discount and internet brokerages that are springing up everywhere? I think not.

The trouble is, you have high fixed costs: rent, building maintenance, utilities, branded advertising, your receptionist, that fancy photocopier, and franchise fees. What do your online competitors have? A website and a couple of computer programmers? The contrast couldn't be starker. You have bills to pay that they don't.

How do you cover your costs?

Let's be honest. You aren't making that much from your novices and lower quartile agents. Sure, you charge them a higher rate. But, a large percentage of zero is still zero. You need your racehorses. And you have big bills to pay for the whole infrastructure you've set up to train the apprentices. You can only reduce your charges to the top folks by so much if you want to keep the lights on.

With all of your expenses, you'll be hard-pressed to keep your charges in line with the lean, mean, online brokerage machines.

You're also in a bind in terms of flexibility. You've created a magnificent system of CRMs, websites, integrated pathways, etc. These are a great help to the novice, but they might tie the hands of the pro. Do you really want to impose bureaucratic hurdles on your rock stars?

To make this business model work, you need to keep your costs low and your systems simple. The plush conference rooms, expensive photocopiers, and prestigious corner addresses won't help you. They just drive up your expenses. At the same time, you need to avoid excessive rules, and needless one size fits all solutions to problems which will snuff out the creativity and individual prerogative of your elite performers.

In short, you need to focus like a laser on your winners. To do this, you may need to fundamentally restructure your business model to make your company appeal to the cream of the crop.

◆ ◆ ◆

A Quick Aside: Tragedy of the Commons (Tragedy of the Novice Agents)

Humor me for a brief diversion.

You may ask: "if I just focus on recruiting top talent and neglect novice agents, what happens if every other broker does the same thing?" If every company only wants the best-established players, who will cultivate and train the next generation of associates?

Fair question.

The trouble is that the trainees aren't economically productive now, but the future of real estate depends on them. Right now, the newbies cost money to train, require an expensive infrastructure to nurture, and rigid systems to keep them on the right path. They need mentors and leads. And they aren't generating revenue.

Yes, most will fail or go on to mediocre careers, but not all. The fresh-faced kid of today who doesn't know the difference between an APR and the LTV may very well be the top agent next year. But, if everybody snuffs out their training and mentorship programs today, she'll never have the opportunity to become a successful salesperson.

It's a tragedy. Better yet, it's a Tragedy of the Commons.

The Tragedy of the Commons (TOC) is a classic demonstration of game theory. First described in 1833, the TOC explained why we as a society tend to ruin collectively-owned resources.

Consider this example. Imagine that you are one of many cattle ranchers adjacent to a large community pasture. The pasture is a public good - nobody owns it, and it benefits everybody. The field is perfect for grazing cattle, and anyone can use it. The pasture is loaded with lots of tender grass for food and streams for refreshment; it's a cow paradise.

But, you're in business to make money. Since the more cows you raise, the more money you make, you have an incentive to keep buying and breeding cows to put on the pasture. The trouble is that all of your competitors have the same incentive.

As a result, you and all your competitors keep loading the pasture up with more and more cows and eventually the pristine place is swamped with hungry bovines and ruined. The public good is destroyed by overuse and neglect.

It was in the rancher's collective long-term interest to maintain the pasture and not overgraze it. After all, if they each used the pasture at manageable levels, the pasture would be around for all of them forever. But, it was in their individual best interest to jam the pasture up with as many of their own cows as possible to maximize their short-term profits.

Moreover, if one rancher decided to be a team player and limit her use of the pasture, how does she know that the other ranchers will follow suit? In a valiant effort to protect the future, she may restrict her use of the public good, only to have her greedy competitors force even more cows on the pasture. After all, the more cows they have, the more money they make. As a result, unless ALL the ranchers cooperate to save the pasture, the place will still get destroyed and the good folks will just lose out sooner.

How does this relate to newbie real estate associates? Cultivating new real estate associates is like tending to the public pasture. Creating and maintaining a large pool of talented real estate salespeople is in every agency's long-term best interest. However, focusing on the newbies offers no short-term benefit at all. Worse, if you spend time and money training new folks and your competitors don't, you might be squandering your precious resources only to have your top apprentices leave and set up shop with an online brokerage which didn't spend a dime training anyone!

◆ ◆ ◆

Some low-cost options

The Tragedy of the Commons is a tough problem to solve. If

you do decide to take on new agents, one way to help them might be through *specialization*. You won't turn novices into pros overnight, but you might be able to train them to master a specific niche within a reasonable time. Throughout this book (particularly in Chapter 1 about real estate agents), I offer some suggestions about how to specialize.

Two other options to pay it forward and help the community of new real estate associates are pro bono help within your firm and apprenticeship matchmaking between novice applicants and your top agents.

Pro bono help within your firm might take the form of regular lectures, meet and greets, office hours, and access to your library of educational materials. The idea here is to offer a helping hand to folks just starting out *without* structuring your business around them. In other words, you can pursue a low-cost strategy needed to attract the top agents and just add some useful teaching (for free) that might benefit novice associates. You'll feel good knowing that you're supporting the next generation of associates, and you'll generate some great PR. The newbies will appreciate you, and your brokerage will be a destination for those agents once they come of age.

Matchmaking works by connecting interested new agents to willing experienced mentors. It is a true apprenticeship. You don't structure your systems around the newbies—you keep costs low and routines flexible. Instead, you create an optional sign-up form that helps interested novice volunteers sign up to ride along with your top dogs. This way, you're enabling motivated freshmen agents to find willing mentors without structuring your entire business around this process. It's inexpensive, easy, and will give you some great PR.

Not every brokerage will be able to lock down the top agents. After all, there are only a few top agents around, and competition to sign them will be fierce. If you're unable to recruit exclusively top agents, fear not! Here are two other strategies to help you win the marketplace of the future.

Alternate strategy #1—The Long Tail

The first strategy is to focus on the long tail. Amazon.com and Netflix used this strategy to win the market and crush their brick and mortar competitors. Here's how it works. Imagine it's the 90s and you want to rent a video. If you wanted a top movie or new release, you were in luck. The shelves of Blockbuster stores were busting with chart-topping new movies. But, if you wanted to see a rare, old, niche, foreign, or campy movie, your odds were not too good. After all, Blockbuster only had so much shelf space, and most of that was consumed by the new releases. They had very few older or obscure titles. Those older, rare, non-mainstream movies are known as the long tail.

It's true that the top 20 movies were the best sellers, but there was considerable demand collectively for movies in the long tail. That was the opening for Netflix. Netflix cornered the market on the long tail. Did you want to see that surfing movie from the 60s? That campy sci-fi flick from the 50s? A documentary on the history of Thailand? You had to go to Netflix. Netflix captured the video rental market by owning the long tail.

Amazon followed the same strategy with books and music. Since they were online and offered nearly every book and album, they captured the long tail and ultimately snuffed out iconic brands like Borders, Tower Records, and Virgin Megastores.

You can do the same with real estate. Sure, single-family homes, condos, and townhouses represent the bulk of real estate. But, you can focus on the long tail.

Own the niche! Corner the market on vacant lots, four-plexes, short sales, cloudy title sales, distressed sales, international buyers, senior living, mixed-use, or vacation property. Encourage your associates to specialize. Find folks who like bankruptcy sales and RV parks and get them on your team. Train them! They'll stay with you because your brokerage specializes in just the stuff they like.

Control the long tail. You may not sell the most 3/2 single-family homes, but you might capture everything else.

Alternate strategy #2—The Boutique Full-Service Brokerage

Make your brokerage a destination.

Throughout this book, I make the claim that the massive physical assets of traditional brokerages are liabilities. The corner offices, impressive conference rooms, and beautiful office furniture are expensive to maintain and drag down profits. You need to take a large cut of your associate's commissions just to pay rent. How can you compete against an internet agency like eXp or Purplebricks with their low overhead?

Here's one way you can.

Tony Vitale, president of residential real estate consulting service Talk2Tony, advocates a concept he calls real estate 3.0. The idea is to turn your physical liabilities into an asset. Convert your office into a place agents want to work and clients want to frequent. Transform your brokerage into a destination!

Offer your clients more than just a real estate transaction. Help them remodel their homes by turning your office into a showroom. Hold free classes on remodeling, mortgages, and short sales. Go from a real estate transaction office to full-service hub for real estate needs. Make your brokerage a place clients want to visit even after they buy their home. Here's Tony's roadmap:

"As you know, every home we sell affects roughly 40 local businesses—cleaners, landscapers, painters, carpet stores, kitchen renovation centers, handymen, swimming pool installers, deck people even doctors, dentists and attorneys. You get the picture.

We real estate agents have the first contact with new residents coming into a community, and our connection is valuable. As the industry enlarged, it left behind that valuable relationship. Real estate agents once provided the community a conduit between the new homeowners and local business owners —the "Welcome Wagon" of the Real Estate 1.0 era.

We once again have an opportunity to monetize all those valuable warm and fuzzy connections in a new and potentially highly profitable way. In my vision, Real Estate 3.0, the brick and mortar office will serve as a hub, bringing together our buyers and sellers with our community. Our offices will become a facility for merchants to display and merchandise their products."

Tony continued, "Consider this: on Saturday morning a local kitchen renovation or interior design merchant might hold a demonstration on how to re-tile a backsplash or choose curtains for your home. Our real estate office can provide the demo space, and both parties can send out invitations to their clients as well as the public. Ideas like this will be the basis for utilizing the real estate office as a hub to celebrate homeownership. The merchant gains access to new potential clients, and real estate agents establish their offices as a place for the public to view them as a holistic environment that cares for their home needs before, during and after the sale of a home." Here's a link to my complete interview with Tony Vitale.

As a boutique, full-service brokerage, you can and should position yourself as a pillar of the community. Show that you care about your neighborhood and join a philanthropic cause.

When I asked leading social entrepreneur David Ament how a brokerage can engage its salespeople in volunteering, he suggested, "The firm could say, "we would love you to participate in a charitable cause. Go out there and put something together for the community." It's great PR, and it's not necessarily costing you a dime. The agents get to put their face out there, which is a big part of their job as independent marketers and salespeople. And, of course, if they're hanging their shingle under your brokerage, they're getting you good press. That one decision, to request agents to participate, yields an exponential return on investment and benefits society. You'll all enjoy lots of positive attention." Read the full David Ament interview by clicking here.

The new kids on the block—non-traditional real estate firms

You knew it would happen. The internet is transforming all other sectors of the American economy, and it was just a matter of time before it took aim at the traditional real estate brokerage model. Thanks to an explosion of investment and technology, a lot of smart people are working to transform how we buy and sell homes.

According to Forbes, investment in real estate technology skyrocketed from a meager $33 million in 2010 to $5 billion in 2017![18] That's a lot of money in a very short time.

Let's take a look at some of the leading tech-driven real estate companies: Redfin, eXp, Opendoor, Real, and Purplebricks. Whether you're an agent, broker, or executive, it's important to understand these companies because they're sure to transform the real estate marketplace in the coming years. Each of them takes a somewhat different approach to reduce costs and to accelerate and automate the sales process. All of them are a departure from the traditional brick and mortar brokerage model.

As you know, technology and business are constantly changing. You should investigate and confirm everything for yourself, as these businesses are likely to be different by the time you read this book. Contact them with questions; they all have great customer support.

Redfin was founded in 2004 and is an online brokerage with a remarkable web portal. A lot of folks enjoy Redfin's site even if they aren't using the brokerage since it's easy to use and has lots of great neighborhood, pricing, and home information. Redfin appeals to consumers with its discounted fee structure and innovative website.

As an aside, I had a great experience with Redfin's web portal. For some reason, they seem to have new listings a few hours before some other sites. One day, a property which was part of an estate sale popped up in an email notification from Redfin. It was dramatically underpriced. The listing agent was out of town and didn't have a good feel for local market conditions. I contacted my traditional agent (Redfin didn't actually service this property), and we put in an immediate below-asking offer on the house sight-unseen! The seller accepted. I made a sweet deal that day!

Redfin's agents work collectively, particularly when you buy. You can book home tours online and they'll assign you to an available associate. That allows Redfin a nimbler response to tour requests, but buyers have to be comfortable working with multiple agents. I didn't mind that since I enjoyed the different perspectives, but I can see how some folks might find that unsettling.

A key Redfin feature is that agents are paid a salary (with benefits) rather than a commission per sale. They get bonuses for high customer satisfaction, but not for moving each individual home. I like that model for buyers since each agent is encouraged to be more of a consultant rather than a salesperson.

I walked into a property with a Redfin agent who said: "Forget it! You don't want this place. Here's why." I appreciated that.

Here's what Bridget Frey, the brilliant Chief Technology Officer (CTO) of Redfin had to say about the company: "Redfin is unusual in that our agents are employees of the company. They receive a salary and a bonus based on how satisfied a customer is at the end of our transaction." She continued, "We invested in technology to enable our agents to handle three times as many happy customers as the traditional real estate agent. They're just far more productive, and that means that we can offer our service at a lower cost. We charge 1 percent in most markets to list your home versus the traditional commission of 2.5 to 3 percent." The full interview with Frey appears here.

On the seller side, I think the lack of a commission is a bit more problematic. As a home seller, you might worry that your commission-free agent might be a little less hungry to pull out all the stops and sell your home.

Redfin is also experimenting with the iBuyer process, which we'll discuss more below.

Currently, Redfin has limited use of part-time associates. While I'm glad they're making use of part-time employees, I hope they'll expand the practice. To me, the Redfin model is ideal for stay at home parents or folks working other jobs but who would like to work in real estate for a set schedule each week to supplement their income. By expanding the use of part-time employees, Redfin will recruit many fantastic agents that are squeezed out of the hyper-competitive commission-driven real estate world.

Next up is **Opendoor**. Opendoor is sure to be a disruptive player in the market and is one of the initial iBuyers. They recently raised an eye-popping $300 million from investors and are now worth over $3.8 billion![19]

Opendoor streamlines the process of buying or selling homes. According to their website, Opendoor will make you an offer with the press of a button. A home seller jumps on their site, enters some information about the property, and Opendoor's computer algorithm generates an offer price. If the seller accepts, the company sends someone to inspect and confirm the property. Sellers even have the option of leaving the repairs to Opendoor.

The process is so fast, the home can close in just a few days! No staging, no repairs, no advertising, no wait, and <u>no need for a real estate agent</u>.

Buyers can use Opendoor too. Opendoor owns hundreds of homes in each of the markets they service. Buyers can let themselves into the homes using the Opendoor app without an agent. They call it the All Day Open House. Prices are transparent, and the homes close quickly. Buyers acquire the homes directly from Opendoor. Opendoor knows the properties and they provide the buyers all the inspection reports. In addition, each home comes with a 30-day guarantee.

Opendoor makes money on fees. In exchange for an ultra-fast and hassle-free process, they charge sellers fees ranging from 6-13 percent, with an average of 6.5 percent. According to Opendoor, sellers on their site will typically pocket more money since they're avoiding real estate commissions and the costs of staging and holding multiple properties. Opendoor claims that they pay a fair market price for homes, but some agents dispute this. The trouble, of course, is that there's no way to know what the home would have scored on the open market.

As of this writing, Opendoor actively transacts residential properties in 20 major cities, including Dallas, Las Vegas, Portland, Los Angeles, and Atlanta. With their new infusion of cash, they're sure to be coming soon to a city near you.

If you sell with Opendoor, you really don't need an agent at all. Their website and customer support team handle everything.

While you can buy with Opendoor without an agent, the buyer must be willing to select from the company's still rather limited inventory. Opendoor does work with agents on the buy side when agents introduce their clients to Opendoor's homes. In that case, the agent does make some commission. In a sense, it would be similar to a buyer's agent showing their client a home from Redfin.

What does all this mean for the real estate marketplace? Well, in the short-term, the impact of Opendoor is still limited. They're only active in 20 markets and each one only has a few hundred homes. But, they're sure to grow. They have lots of money and powerful investors. I wouldn't be surprised if they reshape the market. Particularly with folks accustomed to immediate online purchases like the Millennials, the rapid and transparent Opendoor process will hold a lot of appeal. They'll wonder why they shouldn't be able to buy and sell a home immediately, just like they can with everything else. The traditional process will seem so SLOW.

When that shift happens, agents and real estate firms will be displaced. Selling agents will be hardest hit. Many homeowners will prefer the speed and simplicity of selling with Opendoor rather than the whole rigmarole of preparing a home for sale.

On the buy side, Opendoor's impact will be more muted. My sense is that they will always want to entice buyer's agents to show their properties, so they will probably cut good deals for salespeople in the foreseeable future.

Ultimately, Opendoor is just another example of how times and technology are changing. Savvy real estate agents will need to reinvent themselves and continue to prove that they add value as a trustworthy consultant. You need to show prospects that their experience will be better with your human touch rather than an algorithm.

Hopefully, Opendoor will give the real estate community the kick in the pants it needs to speed up, simplify, and streamline the transaction process. Over the years, it has become too complex and far too opaque. Many companies are now working on this worthy goal, and I applaud their efforts.

By the way, Opendoor is not alone in the world of iBuyers. Other companies joining this emerging industry include Offerpad and Zillow Offers. Even traditional real estate brokerages like Keller Williams and Coldwell Banker are experimenting with iBuyer offerings. All have slightly different rules and approaches to how they partner with real estate agents.

Experienced CEO and angel investor Nav Athwal JD believes that some iBuyers like Opendoor may be "trying to eliminate the role of the agent in the deal. A seller can come to them and say, 'I want to sell my property,' and within 48 hours, Opendoor will have an offer for them, and they can close the deal without agent involvement, without a showing/staging, without any of the hassles that usually come with the sale of a single-family home. Opendoor essentially becomes the buyer of that property, which means that they have to have a substantial balance sheet. Whether or not they're going to be able to scale that to every market we'll have to wait and see. That model involves tremendous risk. If the housing market corrects, Opendoor is left holding the bag."

Athwal is still bullish on the need for real estate agents. He said, "Real estate agents are so integrated into the sales and purchase process for real estate that I think it's going to be hard to displace them completely. If they are ever displaced, I think it's going to be 20 years down the line."

Another player, **Purplebricks**, is a big hit in Europe and is making waves in the United States. As of this writing, they will sell a home for a flat fee depending on your location. They manage these savings while using local real estate agents whom they call *Local Real Estate Experts*. Buyers using Purplebricks earn cash back at closing.

Currently, there are reports that Purplebricks might be transitioning to a more traditional commission model,[20] and only time will tell where they settle. However, it is clear that innovative companies with new real estate models will continue to appear and likely flourish.

As with all real estate firms, Purplebricks shows listings on all the major portals, including the MLS and Zillow. The company tends to attract DIY-type clients who still want help from a human real estate agent. As Purplebricks grows, it will be a potent competitor to Redfin and Opendoor. It's not a startup. Purplebricks will draw on their European experience to race across the country. Expect to see them soon in a market near you!

eXp is the big new kid on the block. They're an online brokerage with a really cool virtual world! They make it fun to "come to work." If you haven't seen some demos of their virtual office, hop online and check it out.

eXp's costs are very low as they don't maintain offices and employ minimal staff. That allows the company to focus on technology and charge their agents less. In fact, there are no desk, royalty, or franchise fees. Their website claims that agents keep 80-100 percent of their commissions. eXp has a pathway to allow agents to become company shareholders. They have a great leadership team, agents love working with them, and the company is expanding all over the country.

Suzy Truax, a member of the board of directors of eXp World

Holdings, described the company this way: "eXp Realty is a 3-D cloud immersive national real estate brokerage." She explains, "eXp World encompasses all the services you would expect at a real estate brokerage (legal, marketing, broker assistance, education, payment processing) but without the inefficiencies and without the costly overhead." You can read the full interview here.

Truax finds eXp to be "more collaborative than a physical office because, with an office, you're limited to the people who show up. I can go into the cloud campus today and attend a class with someone who was the number one agent in all of Coldwell Banker teaching how to do a listing presentation. Bricks and mortars can't scale this kind of collaboration."

Real is an Internet-based brokerage which leverages a powerful platform and low overhead to save their agents money and time. The company has no offices but uses human agents to transact houses the traditional way—in person. They allow their associates to earn equity in the company, which is a real selling point for many agents. As of this writing, Real is available in 22 states and growing. Click here to read my full interview with Poleg, the CEO of Real.

Home Bay is an internet-powered brokerage. Their real estate agents help buyers and sellers remotely, which allows the company to pass huge savings on to the client. Although relatively new, Home Bay is catching on fast! As of this writing, they've already transacted over 1,000 properties and sold over $330 million in real estate.

Home Bay works by empowering homeowners to sell their own houses. Home Bay's team of experienced agents is available for remote consultation to guide sellers through the entire sales process. Homeowners hold their own broker's tour, open houses, and showings. Buyers can book house tours through Home Bay, and their agents handle the offers and negotiations.

This model may not appeal to all clients since it requires a high level of motivation and drive. But, for the right people, Home Bay is an innovative way to make the system more efficient and save significant transaction costs. Why would buyers who already know what they want to incur the expense of a traditional real estate firm rather than go to Home Bay?

It's easy to see how a company like Home Bay can capture entire segments of the market: knowledgeable buyers and driven sellers of standard properties. For these folks, the value proposition of paying a traditional agent a 6 percent commission just isn't there.

I asked Home Bay's executive chairman Ken Potashner what impact the public's easy access to data and the MLS will have on real estate brokerages. He said, "There's tremendous transparency now in terms of data flow. Zillow provides a great deal of data. People go in now with a preconception of what their house is worth. They're able to see comparables in a way that they weren't able to years ago. We're in a data information-rich environment. In the distant past, you would have had to rely on your broker and trust your broker to steer you through valuation. Therefore, given the existence of the information, the brokerage needs to define differently what value add they're providing to the equation. They need to either look for different ways to add more value or change their value proposition from a cost perspective to align with how much data is flowing freely to the consumer."

The ubiquitous and transparent MLS makes it easy for folks to research homes on their own. Zillow, and startups like Neighborhood Scout, take most of the guesswork out of choosing homes and locations. It's just a matter of time before most people find homes on their own and just need a real estate agent for consultation and negotiation. Home Bay shows us how this model can work.

Top real estate coach and author Tom Ferry believes that, regardless of technology, real estate agents will remain essential. He said, "Century 21 was the first real estate franchise. And the second one? It was a discount broker that was basically looking to get rid of real estate professionals.

The reason I bring that up is this: the only people who are nervous about this are agents who should leave the industry anyway. Good agents will never be replaced by technology. Good agents always have that fiduciary responsibility to walk you through the process, make sure you make the right decision and feel good about the decision, and that you have someone to talk to through the range of emotions that take place inside a real estate transaction."

Ferry continued, "So, do I think real estate agents will be here in five years? I would bet everything I own times a thousand that they will be. Then I would go out 10 years, 20 years, 100 years, and I'd say the same exact thing.

Now, what might change is model and compensation. There is plenty of room for new models and changes in how agents are compensated, but somebody's still going to be there guiding and directing. Did WebMD get rid of doctors?"

It is also worth noting that technology itself might ultimately reduce the power of all brokerages. I asked blockchain and Bitcoin expert Ragnar Lifthrasir how digital currency and a distributed ledger might impact brokers. He said, "The power is going to be much more in the hands of the owners of the real estate because the owners will be able to eventually create a digital deed for themselves. They (agents and brokers) are going to have to realize that their role as middlemen is going to diminish over time, so I would say it's prudent to start being in front of that."

Equip your agents with technology

"Technology is not about replacing people; it's about making people more efficient. And the scarcest thing we have in this world isn't money, it is actually time. Every second that goes by is a second that's lost, that you can never get back. So, if you can leverage technology to be more efficient with your time, you're going to be far more productive, and you're going to be able to do more of what you want to do," said leading venture capitalist and real estate industry expert Matt Murphy.

How do you get cutting edge technology in the hands of your real estate agents? Murphy continued, "One successful example is Climb, a real estate brokerage based in San Francisco that was recently purchased by NRT. Climb has a very interesting approach. Mark Choey, one of the founders and the chief technology officer, fully embraces technology. He doesn't fully build it; he creates an ecosystem around his brokerage where he brings these technologies to his agents. Then he speaks at events and showcases the technologies on the agents' behalf as an advocate. That's a phenomenal way of putting yourself at the center of innovation, as well as improving your brokerage."

"A home is the biggest thing that you purchase in your lifetime. The average person buys maybe two, three homes over the course of their life. By comparison, the next biggest thing is probably a college education, then a car. Because of that, you still want someone guiding you through the transaction of this largest asset."

"Yes, there's a lot of data online where people can do their own research. But at the end of the day, that's not how homes are transacted yet. It still is two people representing a buyer and a seller, negotiating a transaction, writing up the paperwork, and handing over the keys."

"But," Murphy added, "I do think that the next generation will see tech-enabled brokerages, like Compass or Reside, leverage technology to streamline their day-to-day operations. But, humans are still involved in that process." Here's a link to the full Murphy interview.

The tech companies can advertise directly to agents: "Buy my CRM! Use virtual staging! Sell houses with blockchain! Use artificial intelligence to sell houses!" But, that's a painfully slow process. It's nearly impossible to reach all agents with an advertising campaign. More importantly, how many real estate salespeople have the time to learn about and test the avalanche of new technology? Not many.

To stay up to date with the latest innovations, agents and brokers should check out my three favorite sites for the latest in real estate tech: Inman News, Realty Times, and The Real Estate Flash, my daily show on Alexa. We'll discuss The Real Estate Flash and voice technology later in this chapter.

Ultimately, I believe that the real engines for discovering and distributing technology are you, the real estate companies and brokerages. You have the resources to locate and test new tech. You should have a chief technology officer (CTO) whose job is to investigate the new products. Your CTO needs the time to meet with sales reps, play with the new tools, and try them out with actual houses. In addition to a CTO, you might want to partner with a technology consulting company like Stefan Swanepoel's firm, T3 Sixty. They specialize in helping brokerages master technology.

"I think most agents don't have the time to learn all this stuff because it is complex," said Darren Johnson, co-founder of Agent Zip, as part of an interview here. "Learning it takes a lot of money and involves trial and error as you get up to speed."

You need to evaluate the newest CRMs, lead generation tools, and virtual reality options for your agents. Companies like RoOomy use impressive augmented reality to wow your clients and help your agents win business. Investigate how predictive AI can identify future customers before even they know they're going to sell. The technology is out there. Explore!

Once you find a great product, you need to spread the tech throughout your organization. This isn't easy! Here are four ways of distributing technology to your associates:

• Purchase and integrate the best products right into your platform. Their use will be seamless, but you need regular updates and deep training.
• Subscribe to the best stuff and make it available free to your associates. You act as a curator of technology.
• Negotiate a deal with the providers to offer the tech at a discount to your salespeople. Use your size as leverage.
• Publish a regular bulletin with your recommendations about the best products. You're only providing advice; the agents are still on their own.

You'll have to figure out what method of distribution works best for your organization. Doing nothing and leaving the discovery of new tech entirely to your agents is not an option. You must do *something*! It's a mistake to leave the associates on their own without any support and guidance. Empower your agents with technological tools that will keep them at the top of their game and help them impress their clients. If your salespeople don't use modern technology, your competitors will!

Half of all agents feel their brokerage should offer more technological services.[21] Associates want your help! Appoint a CTO, review the latest technology, and share your expertise. You'll recruit and retain the best salespeople. Harness the power of cutting-edge technology to crush the market!

Voice technology

Encourage your associates and brokers to stay up to date. One of the easiest ways to learn about the latest in real estate is via voice technology. I founded The Real Estate Flash on Amazon's Alexa in early 2018. The idea is that real estate professionals can listen to these brief flash briefings each morning while they prepare breakfast, brush their teeth, or drive to work. Everyone has these free moments, why not use them to learn?

The Real Estate Flash delivers daily doses of real estate news, important industry trends, marketing tips, and useful tidbits. We regularly feature insightful interviews with top CEOs and leading real estate innovators.

There are a lot of great real estate flash briefings out there. Encourage your agents and colleagues to give them a listen. Let them know about The Real Estate Flash and a great show by Jason Frazier, The Agent Marketer Flash. Keeping up with daily flash briefings is a simple way to get an edge on the competition.

Your agents can now create their own flash briefings. David Bramante and Kayla Jane's impressive startup, My Home Agent helps real estate pros start and maintain their flash briefings. A branded flash briefing with useful information about local events, restaurants, and houses for sale is a fantastic way for agents to establish themselves as a local authority and trusted expert.

Voice is big, and its value extends well beyond flash briefings. Folks are using their Alexa and Google Home for everything, including searching for houses. Your salespeople need their listings on these devices! The innovative company Voiceter Pro, led by founders Miguel and Amitai Berger, allows users to search for homes via their voice assistants without lifting a finger. Prospective buyers conversationally describe their dream home features, and Voiceter Pro will show them homes that match their criteria. It even shows images of the home, sends results by email, and allows users to instantly determine their own home's value. What a perfect way to attract new Millennial and tech-savvy clients!

Don't get left behind by the explosion of voice technology. Imagine if you were early into video and YouTube. How great would that be right now? You and your agents must experiment with this medium now, before all the top voice real estate is gone. Voiceter Pro and My Home Agent are easy ways your brokerage can get your salespeople up to speed on voice.

While I'm bullish on voice, there are some other cutting-edge tech tools you should consider rolling out for your associates. Porchd lets real estate agents anonymously post home pictures online for review. Folks across the country can check out the pictures and provide feedback. Your salespeople will quickly learn which pictures look good and which to ditch. Plus, we all need a reminder to put the toilet seat down before taking a home photograph! Get feedback from the crowd and end the scourge of bad listing pictures forever.

Ultimately, you want your agents to help clients figure out the right home for their lifestyle and budget. You want your clients satisfied that their new home will work for them. To that end, I'm a big fan of TLCengine. They help your clients objectively consider critical factors like the commute, neighborhood amenities, and long-term costs when choosing a house. Happy clients create better reviews and more referrals.

The future and the endless struggle to add value

There is nothing permanent except change.[22] Our system of real estate firms, brokerages, agents, and 6 percent commissions is long in the tooth. Each level of the chain is ripe for disruption from technology, easy availability of the MLS, online ratings, and educated consumers. The general public (led by tech-savvy Millennials)[23] is rising up and challenging the assumption that transacting houses needs to be so much more expensive, time-consuming, and difficult than any other kind of purchase.

At the same time, elite real estate agents realize that they hold the keys. Their success is plastered all over the web, and anyone with a computer or smartphone can locate their town's top agent in minutes. They don't need your brokerage nearly as much as you need them, and they know it.

You also need to figure out how to address the rise of the internet and tech-based brokerages as well as the looming specter of the future real estate agent pipeline drying up. Storms are brewing on all fronts.

As a real estate brokerage, you must fight harder than ever to add value, both for your agents and the transacting public. You cannot rely on tradition or brand. Find success by recruiting and retaining top agents, winning the technological arms race, innovating new ways to leverage your existing offices, and capturing the long tail.

Hurry. The time to move is now.

Interview with Anthony Vitale, consultant, real estate tech expert, and president of Talk2Tony

Gregory Charlop: You have a lot of experience in real estate. Tell us about your background

Anthony Vitale: I started my real estate career serendipitously. I originally owned a company called Real Soft which developed MLS (Multiple Listing Software) for the then new Macintosh computer in 1987. We had a vision of providing a graphical interface for real estate brokerages instead of the current Windows DOS Systems. We experienced a little success selling to MLS Boards throughout New England. Unfortunately, as Windows 95 grew in popularity the larger boards felt safer with Microsoft than Apple, and we were unable to gain traction.

However, in doing research for the development of that software, I acquired a real estate license and began working in a residential real estate office. One thing led to another, and soon I owned that office and expanded from there. When I finally ended my real estate brokerage career, I and another partner had accumulated over 22 offices servicing Long Island's North Shore.

I stress my background in technology to illustrate my unique perspective of the industry. Early on, I found myself alone among my fellow local brokers. Most of my competition condescendingly considered me an outlier, a geek obsessed with technology which they considered lacking a "human" touch. This provided me with an advantage in the marketplace. I was soon positioned at the forefront of a rapidly changing industry and not afraid of implementing new technology.

Gregory Charlop: As you know, it's my theory that large legacy real estate companies are essentially stuck with nonproductive overhead, like fancy offices, expensive conference rooms, photocopiers, etc. I believe that most buyers really don't care about these offices and that the companies are wasting precious resources maintaining them. In other words, I think most buyers or sellers are happy to meet an agent online, and then perhaps encounter them at Starbucks. But you feel differently. Why do you think that internet brokerages are the wrong way to go?

Anthony Vitale: You're correct. I do feel differently. It is not so much about buyers not caring about offices, rather It is about the brokers and the agents who care about brick and mortar real estate offices—and for a number of very good reasons. I'll provide just two.

Issue number 1: One goal of most brokers is to own their own brick and mortar. After all, they are real estate agents. Who better to understand that by accumulating real estate they can cut down on taxes, hedge against rent increases, control a growing equity- based nest egg to sell or lease back when they transition out of real estate? They have the ability to sell the buildings as part of the sale of their business or keep the brick and mortar and rent it back to the potential buyers. After all, what do brokers really have to sell after their many years of hard work building a company? It's a financial safety net for them in an industry that doesn't provide much security.

Issue number two is maybe more relevant.

In my role as a real estate broker, I was frequently involved in discussions about what the real estate offices of the future were going to look like and how we should be preparing for it. We sat through seminars at national conferences taking notes while listening to predictions and theories about the "future." Real estate gurus were all predicting that we were going to access our buyers through the internet. Therefore, in theory, all we would need to provide was a nicely decorated greeting and conference space between three to five hundred square feet in which our agents would meet their customers and clients, fill out the necessary paperwork and solicit offers. We even discussed sharing those spaces among the competitors using high tech software capable of scheduling and reserving room times. At this point, it might pay to remind you that about that same time, we also expected to have totally paperless offices by the year 2000. Neither of those scenarios materialized Here's why.

Our data proved that the interaction between agents in a secure family-like atmosphere was an important factor in boosting real estate transactions, especially the more highly profitable "in house" sales.

We came to better understand that the agents were our real customers—not the buyers or sellers—and we began competing for the top agents. So, instead of cutting back on brick and mortar offices, we began to enhance it, creating a more dynamic atmosphere where agents would want to come and have a productive dialogue with their colleagues. We became invested in building a culture in our offices. Many of us would go on to reverse the dynamics and floor plans of a typical office. Formerly, the front end (that customers inhabited) was elegant, and the back office or bull ring (the agent space) was stark and utilitarian, typically over-populated with lopsided metal frame desks and motivation posters covering the bland-colored walls.

Instead, I and many of my competitors invested in reworking our agents' space to provide a welcoming, cozy environment. For instance, I—with the enthusiastic input of my agents—retrofitted those environments with new high-quality household furniture, artwork, luxury bathrooms, fireplaces, etc. Always investing in the best office equipment and phone systems and, in my most recent office, even a Barista bar and, on Fridays, a pop-up free nail salon. Combining a careful balance of a nurturing and motivating environment for our agents, we could achieve a very successful dynamic business "buzz." That was, and still is, what I have termed Real Estate 2.0.

So, now as we move into our next operating cycle, Real Estate 3.0, the question becomes: how can we maintain the benefits of having an office and still compete with the advent of lower commission brokerages?

Gregory Charlop: Right. You view using offices in a whole new way. You call it Real Estate 3.0. How should real estate companies and brokerages reconfigure their offices to make them useful in today's internet era?

Anthony Vitale: I see a perfect storm building where a confluence of technologies matures to a state where even a local one-office real estate broker can utilize new technology—for the first time in a long time—to provide a new source of revenue. Think of the new office as a HGTV, Houzz, and Angie's List combined.

For example. As you know, every home we sell affects roughly 40 local businesses—cleaners, landscapers, painters, carpet stores, kitchen renovation centers, handymen, swimming pool installers, deck people even doctors, dentists and attorneys. You get the picture.

We real estate agents have the first contact with new residents coming into a community, and our connection is valuable. As the industry enlarged, it left behind that valuable relationship. Real estate agents once provided the community a conduit between the new homeowners and local business owners —the "Welcome Wagon" of the Real Estate 1.0 era.

We once again have an opportunity to monetize all those valuable warm and fuzzy connections in a new and potentially highly profitable way. In my vision, Real Estate 3.0, the brick and mortar office will serve as a hub, bringing together our buyers and sellers with our community. Our offices will become a facility for merchants to display and merchandise their products.

Consider this: on Saturday morning a local kitchen renovation or interior design merchant might hold a demonstration on how to retile a backsplash or choose curtains for your home. Our real estate office can provide the demo space, and both parties can send out invitations to their clients as well as the public. Ideas like this will be the basis for utilizing the real estate office as a hub to celebrate homeownership. The merchant gains access to new potential clients, and real estate agents establish their offices as a place for the public to view them as a holistic environment that cares for their home needs before, during and after the sale of a home. The residual effects of that will result in more interest in our real estate company, real estate agents wanting to be associated with us, and local businesses promoting us will join. In the future we can see a time when we will curate those businesses and monetize their participation.

Gregory Charlop: In other words, the real estate office wouldn't be just for someone to buy a house, but it would also be a place they could learn about remodeling their house, meet local contractors or vendors, and come up with design ideas.

Anthony Vitale: Correct. Buying a home is much more than purchasing a physical space. It is a sanctuary to build and nurture a family. Offices can, and, in my opinion, should be a meeting place for the community and its residents focused through the home as a basis. The potential is larger than we are discussing here.
I used the offices as showcases for decorators, furniture stores —even artists—to set up displays at our site. With a little imagination you can see the potential for revenue from purchases of home accessories, appliances, etc., etc.

Gregory Charlop: Essentially, what you're describing is converting a real estate office into a positive asset. You're turning it into a destination, a place people want to go and spend time. Is your goal to attract better real estate associates, or to attract more prospects, or both?

Anthony Vitale: It's both. It's a symbiotic relationship. If we are bringing prospects to the office, agents will want to be there. In Real Estate 3.0 agents will be able to jettison a highly negative aspect of residential real estate (the association with the dysfunctional mortgage and title business) and benefit from their association with the positive aspect—caring for a family home.

Their skill set will revert to their talent of presenting the possibilities of a property in a favorable light rather than shoving a mortgage down their customer's throat to please their broker.

Gregory Charlop: Your model is an alternative to my expectation of the future, which I expect will mostly be internet-based brokerages. How will this type of destination office compete with the discount internet brokerages?

Anthony Vitale: As far as competing financially, think of our clients as raw data. We now have control of their data. We can massage and anonymize it, using that data to put merchants and other recipients together. We will have the ability to provide curated third parties with access to that data for a fee.

Gregory Charlop: Who do you envision would be particularly drawn to these offices? Would they be buyers, sellers, older folks, do-it-yourself types—everybody?

Anthony Vitale: If we're smart, we'll get almost everyone—both buyers excited to begin the next romantic chapter in their lives by fixing up their homestead, to sellers looking for ways to enhance the salability of their property. As well as financial people interested in the benefits of particular types of renovation, mortgages, home insurance, elder law, etc.

Think of the HGTV demographic. Young couples watch these channels and love them, but they don't necessarily connect that with a real estate agent. They go out, find a house to buy, and then they start getting into fixing up a kitchen, doing all those things homeowners do. The real estate agent was excluded from benefiting from that revenue. Now, once again, we can be involved.

Gregory Charlop: Earlier, you mentioned seniors. That's an area I'm very passionate about. I think your idea can work very well with seniors. How would seniors benefit from these hubs, or these destination real estate companies?

Anthony Vitale: Greg, that certainly is a noble cause, and I commend you for your effort and involvement. Here's how my vision can benefit not only that demographic but can be adjusted for other local niche markets as well. Think veterans, first responders, etc. It's not hard to see how we can be instrumental not only in helping them transition into a senior facility or dealing with the sale of their home, but also providing a space for their needs. We can help their children and caregivers who are responsible for helping them to transition by providing handicapped access to our office's "Senior Centers" located in communities with a large population of seniors. These centers carved out of our facilities can not only provide access to literature and resources, they can provide a neutral space for professionals such as elder attorneys, financial managers and even health care professionals to hold meetings or seminars on important topics to seniors.

Again, it's reaching out to the community to bring people in through that hardscape, through that brick and mortar, and use it in a much more effective way. These, and many other initiatives we are unable to delve into here, can serve as a new blueprint for Real Estate 3.0.

Gregory Charlop: Thank you so much for joining us. You provided a great counterpoint to my theory that internet brokerages will dominate the market, and you show a way that traditional brokerages can leverage the assets they have to not only compete but perhaps even open up entirely new market segments.

Interview with Nav Athwal, Angel investor, Proptech enthusiast, and Co-Founder/CEO of District

Gregory Charlop: Nav, you have a very impressive resume. You were an electrical engineer, went to law school, you even studied business. Tell us about yourself.

Nav Athwal: I started my career in technology as an engineer. I worked for a firm in Oakland, California doing infrastructure design work and work as an electrical engineer. I was there for about a year. The company was called Earthtech. While I was an engineer, I also got my broker's license. I grew up in a real estate family, so I'd always been exposed to the asset from a young age. But getting my broker's license was my first foray into real estate on my own. So I started selling homes and helping people get financing, moonlighting while I was working as an engineer.

I decided after a year of doing this, to go to law school, and I knew going into law school that I wanted to do real estate law. So, after graduating, I worked for a law firm in San Francisco called Farella Braun + Martel, LLP. I practiced there for about three and a half years in the real estate and land use group. My practice mainly entailed helping large institutional real estate clients acquire assets, lease assets and get entitlement and development rights for new ground up projects in San Francisco. This last piece of my practice was the most interesting and challenging as it was highly political, and San Francisco is notoriously difficult for development.

While I was a practicing attorney, I started buying real estate, mainly small-cap multi-family and single-family homes. During that process, I realized just how broken and inefficient the process of raising capital was, both on the debt and equity sides. That was what prompted me to start RealtyShares, which is really a marketplace to connect capital from passive investors that want exposure to real estate to real estate operators and developers who want a much more efficient way to raise capital. So I left my law firm job in late 2013 and from then until November of 2017, I served as the Founder and CEO of RealtyShares. We had humble beginnings, but eventually achieved strong scale, helping raise over $800 million of capital for over a thousand projects around the U.S., in multifamily, retail, office, industrial, and self-storage. RealtyShares focused on a broad swath of different products, including debt and equity. While I was there as CEO, we were growing rapidly, having raised over $60M in venture capital and doubling how much we were funding every year. We were the leading platform of our kind. It was an amazing ride.

In November 2018, I stepped down as CEO, and the board brought in a new CEO who formerly was the CEO of Cushman & Wakefield, a very seasoned executive. After leaving as CEO, I remained on the board while taking a much-needed break and thinking about what was next for me.

One thing I realized during my time at RealtyShares is that (i) I love building software for large, slow-to-change industries to make them more efficient, and (ii) I love the early stages of companies. So RealtyShares over the last four years was a lot of fun, and I especially enjoyed the earliest stages of it when we were 10-20 people in a room trying to build a business from nothing.

Gregory Charlop: Many of our readers are, of course, interested in the real estate industry, either as brokers or agents or executives. Does RealtyShares work with agents or brokers?

Nav Athwal: RealtyShares did historically work with brokers to source deals. We worked with both transaction brokers as well as Mortgage/Capital markets brokers. At RealtyShares we funded both debt and equity in commercial real estate. Brokers participated by referring clients for both, although we saw more traction with brokers on the debt side. Brokers are a key part of our ecosystem; we've broadened the relationship we have with brokers and agents, both on the mortgage and the transaction side.

Gregory Charlop: Could a real estate agent or broker approach RealtyShares to see if they'd be interested in funding deals?

Nav Athwal: Yes. Agents actually can refer deals to us and also get paid for those referrals. We have a business development team that handles all of our deal sourcing efforts, and that team's email is bizdev@RealtyShares.com. The best way for agents to get in contact with RealtyShares is to shoot an email to our biz dev team describing the opportunity, and we're typically back in touch with the agents/brokers within 24 hours.

Gregory Charlop: Can you tell me how RealtyShares determines which properties to invest in? Does it use a computer algorithm or artificial intelligence? What is your secret to figuring out how to invest?

Nav Athwal: RealtyShares historically did things quite manually with respect to deal analysis and underwriting. We had a team of underwriters that came from the traditional real estate industry reviewing the deals in detail to ensure they were a good fit. Of course, over time, we sought to automate many aspects of this human driven underwriting. But when I left as CEO, things were still human driven. RealtyShares is a curated marketplace and very selective with respect to the deals that get accepted onto our platform. The hit rate is less than 10 percent.

There are a couple of criteria that right off the bat will exclude a deal. RealtyShares does not fund ground up development or deals with entitlement risk. Also, they typically look for transactions where the fundraising required is at least $1 million. RealtyShares doesn't provide capital for single-family residential projects…only commercial projects, so the capital needs are usually well above this threshold number. They also pass on deals that are offered by operators that are not seasoned. So, if this is your first deal or your second deal, and you don't have an established track record and successful exits, we're usually going to pass on those sponsors/deals.

Once RS determines a deal passes its initial sniff test, their seasoned underwriting team does a deeper dive. This team has experience across multiple real estate and private equity firms, such as BlackRock, Hines, Goldman Sachs, etc. The team reviews specifics around the deal, such as pro forma projections, to determine if the return that the sponsor is projecting is achievable. RS does a pretty thorough analysis to determine if the deal is a fit. Some of that's pure analog underwriting, and some of it's based on data and technology. So, it's a good mix of old tried and tested and new fast and efficient.

Gregory Charlop: If a real estate agent or broker came to you for advice about investing, what would you say?

Nav Athwal: Get to know your market. I think one of the biggest strengths that agents possess is knowledge of the local market. So, the stronger that local knowledge is, the more a value add that agent is to their client. They're going to be able to find the right properties for the client, price them correctly, price them to sell, price them so that they're not listing it at a discount to what the property's worth. So, having that local market knowledge can add value and, ultimately, add a lot of value to the client.

The second thing I encourage agents and brokers to do is leverage technology to their advantage. Whether it's winning the right deals, finding the right clients, making the transaction process more efficient or less costly for their clients, or just as a way to avoid being left behind.

Gregory Charlop: You're an expert in both the technological and the legal aspects of real estate. One of the emerging trends now are iBuyers and other companies that disintermediate

Real Estate at a Crossroads

real estate agents. What are your thoughts about this trend? Do you think it represents the future of real estate?

Nav Athwal: Great question. Real estate agents are so integrated into the sales and purchase process for real estate that I think it's going to be hard to displace them completely. If they are ever displaced, I think it's going to be 20 years down the line. I just don't think it's going to be any time soon. There are some interesting companies, Opendoor being one of the largest, that are trying to eliminate the role of the agent in the deal. A seller can come to them and say, "I want to sell my property," and within 48 hours, Opendoor will have an offer for them, and they can close the deal without agent involvement, without a showing/staging, without any of the hassles that usually come with the sale of a single-family home. Opendoor essentially becomes the buyer of that property, which means that they have to have a substantial balance sheet. Whether or not they're going to be able to scale that to every market, we'll have to wait and see. That model involves tremendous risk. If the housing market corrects, Opendoor is left holding the bag.

I think charting 6 percent commission, regardless of what type of market you're in, is going to erode away slowly. In markets like San Francisco, where you're very supply constrained, and the transaction sizes tend to be larger, six percent is very expensive. Those homes typically start at $1M and are going for $1,000+ a square foot. I think taking 6 percent of that transaction doesn't really make sense, and the value the agent brings doesn't justify it. Whereas, that same type of transaction in a market like Phoenix or Dallas does make sense, because the size of the deal is smaller, and the supply/demand balance works much differently than in primary markets like SF or New York.

There are startups now, such as Unlocked. They operate in the San Francisco Bay Area. They're are changing that aspect of brokerage, and I think we'll see plenty more emerge to do the same in other markets. But, again, I don't see agents being eliminated from the transaction process any time soon because they are so ingrained within the home buying process, and most sellers are not comfortable doing such a large transaction without an expert helping them along the way.

I go back to the question you asked before: what advice do you have for agents? Agents who know their market well and can leverage technology will bring value to the transaction, and that, in turn, will make them a critical part of the deal. Agents who are expecting 6 percent in markets like San Francisco, where they often have multiple offers as soon as the property is listed, are taking advantage of the market dynamics and aren't really adding enough value to justify that cost to the client. They're going to slowly be disrupted.

Gregory Charlop: If you were advising someone in college who was debating whether to go into real estate or not, what advice would you give them? Would you say, become an agent, don't become an agent, or go into some similar field?

Nav Athwal: Well, it depends on a few things. First, I'd ask them, "Do you like sales?" Because being an agent is a lot about sales—selling yourself, being able to sell a property, being able to sell an offer from a potential buyer. Sales is a key component of being an agent. So, if you hate sales, hate making phone calls, hate client outreach, if you hate marketing yourself, I think it's the wrong industry—no matter how much you like real estate as an asset class.

The second thing I'd say is, yeah, if you love sales, you love real estate, it can be very lucrative. Because, if agents are good, if they know their market, if they're able to market themselves, if they're good salespeople, they can potentially make a really good living, especially in markets like San Francisco, Palo Alto, New York, Miami, Austin, Los Angeles, etc. If you like sales, if you like real estate, you want a flexible schedule, you want to be your own boss, I think it can be the right career for you. Those are the questions you need to ask yourself beforehand. But, you also need to understand that the market is very competitive, and you need to do what you can to differentiate yourself. Think outside the box, and there, technology can help.

Gregory Charlop: What are your thoughts about some of the emerging technologies in real estate? I'll mention two: virtual reality and augmented reality.

Nav Athwal: I think virtual reality and augmented reality are very interesting. I think it's getting a little crowded and a little saturated, but I think the reason it's so exciting for real estate is real estate is a physical asset. I mean, you have to walk the property, really get a sense of the neighborhood, the property interior and condition, etc. And often it's hard to get out to view the property. That's where I think VR and AR can help. Also, let's assume you have raw land that you want to develop into apartments or a hotel, and before undertaking the construction process you want to visualize what it could look like. Typically, that's through one-dimensional plans, but if you can create a virtual tour of that property, you could actually market it before you put a single stick in the ground. So, I think virtual reality, augmented reality, can have a really interesting application to real estate, especially given the tangible, physical nature of the asset.

Gregory Charlop: I think a lot of Millennials may start to expect to use virtual and augmented reality since they're playing video games that use that. How about artificial intelligence?

Nav Athwal: Absolutely, and I'm very excited about AI's application to real estate. Real estate is a very data-rich asset. There are thousands of data points involved with a single deal, with respect to the deal itself, the financials of the deal, etc. Given the data-rich nature of the asset, I think it's especially susceptible to artificial intelligence. So, I think things that are very analog today, like underwriting and deal sourcing, could be driven by AI in the future. The next Blackstone will be highly dependent on technology and AI for their investment decisions.

So, I do think AI is going to make big waves in the real estate market. It's going to create a lot more efficiency in real estate while reducing human error and allowing for predictive sourcing and underwriting that isn't possible today under the traditional model.

Gregory Charlop: What about Bitcoin? That has attracted a lot of attention recently. What role do you see for Bitcoin, or, more generally, blockchain in real estate?

Nav Athwal: Well, first and foremost, I'm annoyed I didn't invest in Bitcoin seven years ago. I would be a lot richer than I am today. But beyond that, I think Bitcoin's applications to real estate will be limited. The reason I say that is because Bitcoin is treated more like an asset than a currency.

Blockchain can be very interesting. I think blockchain is still a very immature technology. It's going to be a decade or more before it's truly adopted within real estate as something that can change, for example, title, and how title is recorded. Compare the analog way it's done today vs. what it can be with blockchain. I think that blockchain will be a much broader application to real estate than Bitcoin itself. However, I'm not that well versed on blockchain technology. I'd call myself a novice at best. I do know that there are some very interesting companies emerging that are promising to use blockchain technology for real estate transactions, specifically in the world of title. However, I do think it's going to take some time before it's adopted because it requires the existing title companies to get on board, and they are usually very slow to move.

Gregory Charlop: Any other hot, new technologies that you see on the horizon?

Nav Athwal: Proptech is completely transforming so many aspects of real estate that it's hard to pinpoint just a few, but I'll try. Appraisals is a prime example. Companies like Bowery Valuation and HouseCanary are automating the appraisal process, making it cheaper and faster.

Companies like Airbnb and WeWork changed the way we think about how we use space. Airbnb has created the largest hotel company in the world, yet it owns no real estate. WeWork is doing the same for commercial office space. A lot of office leases are very rigid; they have five-year terms, and there's no sense of community or "fun" in those spaces. But, with WeWork, landlords are rethinking how they've been marketing their spaces and structuring leases. I think that's going to continue to change as WeWork and Airbnb continue to dominate their respect markets and grow larger in size.

Gregory Charlop: Another interesting company like that is Peerspace. They help you rent out conference rooms and even entire restaurants for meetings and events. I used them to host my first real estate conference, the Real Estate Tech Expo.

Nav Athwal: Breather is another. It's essentially an Airbnb for office space.

Gregory Charlop: What advice would you give to real estate professionals who are looking to improve their understanding of technology? Are there any particular books, conferences, podcasts or websites that you recommend?

Nav Athwal: MetaProp, FifthWall and NXR are three VC Funds that put out a lot of thought leadership on the proptech space, so I'd suggest following them. They may even have a newsletter for those interested in the real estate tech space. I also actively contribute to Forbes and Linkedin on the topics of real estate and tech. Here are links to my blogs on Forbes and LinkedIn.

Interview with Matt Murphy, venture capitalist and general partner with Montage Ventures

Gregory Charlop: You have an impressive background, Matt. Could you tell us a bit about yourself?

Matt Murphy: As I look at the choices I've made in my career, they're all rooted in a personal passion for leveraging technology to evolve traditional industries. Whether that's financial services, education, healthcare, logistics, or real estate. My first role was with Etrade back in the early days. At first, it was via the telephone. Then it turned online once the internet came about. I had a blast running media advertising for Etrade for six years, creating this challenger brand concept to benefit the consumer.

Then, I was the chief marketing officer of Chegg. We thought textbooks were too expensive. A lot of students were unable to buy textbooks and had to go to the library or just not have a book at all. We innovated a textbook rental concept that cut prices by 70 to 80 percent. We were able to help students get the books that they needed to do well and stay in school. That was a micro-innovation that had a major impact on the educational landscape.

After that, I started Lemon Wallet with a group of amazing entrepreneurs which ended up becoming one of the early Bitcoin wallets. I headed up the U.S. operations at Renren venture capital, which included a large portfolio of health tech, logistics, and tech disruptive companies.

Gregory Charlop: Many of our readers are real estate professionals or executives. What is your connection to the real estate industry?

Matt Murphy: During my time at Renren, we invested in many financial technology companies which touched real estate. We realized the real estate agent was consistently the key customer influencer in mortgages, financing, and property management. We looked at how mortgage companies were able to target agents. Regulations like RESPA or CFPB made it very challenging.

We wanted to make some investments in the real estate/tech space. This was several years ago, so we were very early. We ended up incubating a company called Chime Technologies. They started as a CRM system built to help agents manage their time, manage their sales funnels, and create better relationships with their customers. Chime really helped get me deep into the real estate space, interact, and create friendships with a lot of real estate agents across the country.

Gregory Charlop: You mentioned that you were the chief marketing officer of Chime. Would you tell us what a CRM (contact management system) is and who should be using it? Is that something every real estate agent should use, or just the experienced ones, or just the new ones, or...everybody?

Matt Murphy: Every real estate agent uses some form of CRM today. Some use the address book on their cell phone, others use Microsoft Excel or Word. Some have invested in professional-grade CRMs. But at the heart of it, a CRM is really software that helps you organize and run your business. It's not just about keeping track of your contacts, it's more than that. A good CRM has workflow management systems, sales pipelines, and really helps you turn what you're doing into a business.

That's what a good CRM does, and I truly believe that every real estate agent should use a CRM because it will help them be more efficient with their time. There are a lot of CRMs in the marketplace, and CRMs can be complicated. A number of them are built on a mobile device, which makes them simpler. But at the end of the day, the best CRM on the market is the one you actually use.

Gregory Charlop: Are there some other technological tools that you feel real estate agents should be using regularly but, perhaps, aren't using to their full potential?

Matt Murphy: Lead generation is more than just running ads on Facebook. It's about the follow-up, follow-through, and the consistency of being in front of people, showing them why you're the best agent to represent them in their home purchase or home sale process. So, technology solutions that help with lead generation and lead follow-up are very important. You'll see a lot of advertising companies in that space. A lot of chatbots come in that space to be that first contact when you buy a lead on Zillow or on Facebook. If you're not getting back to them within one to two minutes, you're losing that lead, because someone else is following up with them. Or, more importantly, they're forgetting they actually clicked on your ad.

Immediacy is critical, so technologies that help create that immediate contact are important. CRMs help with relationship management, workflow management, things along those lines. I tell agents, when you're picking technologies, make sure you invest your time into learning and using it.

We're living in a mobile-first environment. All good technology should have a mobile application and really be built on the mobile device first. That brings a lot of efficiency shortcuts, ease of follow-throughs, one-click actions—things along those lines. You'd be surprised how many of the "leading technologies" in real estate do not even have a mobile app. Since agents are out and about in the market at all times, having a mobile experience is critical.

Gregory Charlop: You've written extensively about blockchain. Can you tell us briefly what blockchain and Bitcoin are, and whether you think that they'll have a major impact on the real estate industry?

Matt Murphy: Blockchain is a public, distributed ledger that many different entities can write into and validate transactions in a public fashion that's distributed across many different devices around the world. It takes away the centralization of authority, the centralization of decision making and control, and provides a public interface to store and move data and information in a secure fashion.

Bitcoin is one of the innovations that's been on top of the blockchain, as is Ethereum, or Litecoin, or various different ICOs (initial coin offerings). Each one solves a different problem or is used for a different purpose. Bitcoin is probably the most well-known. Its goal is to become a global currency. So that no matter where you are in the world, you can transact, you can move money, exchange value between people, store value amongst yourselves. Its goal is to replace what a bank, payment processor, or a transaction system does.

Gregory Charlop: Do you think that will have any meaningful effect on the real estate
industry? And, if so, how could real estate agents or companies prepare for that or take advantage of it?

Matt Murphy: Real estate is a little slower to move into new technologies due to the size of the dollar amounts that exchange hands. For example, with all the wire fraud that we're seeing in the space, the industry is slow to enable new technologies because there is such financial risk in all of the transactions based on the size. But I do feel that there are aspects within the real estate industry, sub-sectors, that could benefit from blockchain and Bitcoin.

For example, when you go into a typical real estate brokerage office, there still are file cabinets. And in those file cabinets are purchase contracts that are being stored for three years to seven years. All of that could be digitized online. There are companies like DocuSign that are helping with digital signatures and digital file storage. But that can also happen on the blockchain. The title and the escrow space, title records, are currently stored on a local level, on a city-by-city basis. So bringing that online, digitizing that, storing that in a public, secured ledger could unlock a lot of value in the data that's hidden within those documents and open up a lot of innovations within the real estate sector.

I'm also seeing innovations with smart contracts. Every real estate transaction starts and ends with the contract of selling or buying something. Those contracts can be done via smart contracts on the Ethereum network, stored on the network, secured on the network.

Gregory Charlop: You wrote a great article for VentureBeat about artificial intelligence, which is also a passion of mine. It's a big topic these days. Can you tell us how artificial intelligence (AI) impacts the real estate marketplace and how you think it might shape the future of the real estate industry?

Matt Murphy: At the core of artificial intelligence is big data. And big data is just the massive amount of data that's being created on a per-second basis—publicly and privately generated data, blog posts, video content—things along those lines. The challenge is that there's so much data out there. Interesting companies like HouseCanary or Cape Analytics are doing some really powerful things, leveraging AI to process that data and extract insights.

We have so much data, it's more than a human can feasibly make sense of. So you really need artificial intelligence to make sense of it, extract valuable insights and conclusions from it. That's where I see a lot of value from an AI perspective.

Another area in real estate is the life cycle of consumers. People are born, get educated, get their first job, usually they have kids, maybe they get married, maybe at some point they retire and pass away. And you have this kind of very generic pathway of what human life looks like.

But there are a lot of interesting insights available in social media, in public datasets, that can help you, as an agent, determine when someone is going to sell their home. What attributes have people made public that you can use to figure out if a family is going to sell their home this year? It's almost impossible for you to do that unless you have a relationship with those people. But, leveraging artificial intelligence and big data, you can actually determine the chances that they're going to sell their home this year.

From there, you can reach out to them. Or you can start running ads against them and be in front of them, creating that relationship before they even know they need it.

Gregory Charlop: Do you mean, for example, if people post on Facebook that their last kid has just graduated college, and they're happy to have an empty nest, that person is likely to put their home on the market?

Matt Murphy: Yeah, or they live in a small one-bedroom in San Francisco, and they just had their first baby. Most likely they're going to rent another place or buy a place because that's a little too small for a family of three.

Gregory Charlop: That's brilliant. Do you think that, ultimately, big data and artificial intelligence will eliminate or reduce the need for real estate agents? I mean, will computers be able to do most of what real estate agents do? Or do you still feel that we'll need a human touch for the system to work?

Matt Murphy: I truly believe that a home is the biggest thing that you purchase in your lifetime. The average person buys maybe two, three homes over the course of their life. By comparison, the next biggest thing is probably a college education, then a car. Because of that, you still want someone guiding you through the transaction of this largest asset.

Yes, there's a lot of data online where people can do their own research. But at the end of the day, that's not how homes are transacted yet. It still is two people representing a buyer and a seller, negotiating a transaction, writing up the paperwork, and handing over the keys.

But I do think that the next generation will see tech-enabled brokerages, like Compass or Reside, leverage technology to streamline their day-to-day operations. But humans are still involved in that process.

Gregory Charlop: One of my favorite topics is augmented and artificial reality. What are your thoughts? Are they ready for prime time? How should agents or real estate companies use these tools, if at all?

Matt Murphy: We saw Google Glasses come and go, Snapchat spectacles came and went. There still is hope to bring real-time information or augmented information into the visual eyesight, to transform the experience.

The coolest companies I've seen are Matterport. RoOomy actually lets you transform an empty space, furnishing it via augmented reality. Not in front of your eyes, but on a computer. What's cool about that is, while you're evaluating multiple apartments, you can overlay furniture in your style and design sense. You can really bring it to life and see if that is what your home should look like.

Matterport is doing a lot of really cool stuff with 3D modeling, rendering, and virtual reality tours that help bring a place to life. They also help people do more research online before actually going to see the house, because, typically, real estate photography is all about the angle. You can hide a lot of things in the angle. People show up in person to go view homes because that's where you can get the true picture.

With virtual reality, you can minimize some of that traveling. That will help buyer-agents because much of their time is spent taking buyers to countless homes. When I bought my first home here in California, my poor buyer-agent was with us every weekend for nine months. I felt horrible for her—and thank God she made a commission—but that's just the nature of the beast. I think virtual and augmented realities really can help streamline those processes. If you're moving to a new market, it also helps; if you're an international buyer or moving from one state to the next, it helps speed up that process.

Gregory Charlop: If the executive team from a major legacy real estate company asked you what they can do to make their firm more competitive, what advice would you give them?

Matt Murphy: It's a great question that I've actually been asked by some of the largest brokerage firms and franchises in the country. One of the things I told them was: really embrace technology, don't run from it. Because it's coming, and the faster you adapt to it, the faster you get ahead and the faster you meet the needs of your clients.

Secondarily, technology is not about replacing people; it's about making people more efficient. And the scarcest thing we have in this world isn't money, it is actually time. Every second that goes by is a second that's lost, that you can never get back. So, if you can leverage technology to be more efficient with your time, you're going to be far more productive, and you're going to be able to do more of what you want to do.

Technology delivers time-savings. But a lot of real estate brokerages have taken that advice to the extreme and try to build technology in-house. My response to them, and to every great entrepreneur is: be focused and know what you do well. And for things that you don't do well, outsource it or partner. In general, real estate companies at their core are not technology development firms. They are service-based real estate industries. Can they transform to it? Yes, there have been a few that have been able to, but there has also been a lot that hasn't been able to.

One successful example is Climb, a real estate brokerage based in San Francisco that was recently purchased by NRT. Climb has a very interesting approach. Mark Choey, one of the founders and the chief technology officer, fully embraces technology. He doesn't fully build it; he creates an ecosystem around his brokerage where he brings these technologies to his agents. Then he speaks at events and showcases the technologies on the agents' behalf as an advocate. That's a phenomenal way of putting yourself at the center of innovation, as well as improving your brokerage.

Gregory Charlop: Climb is an interesting example of the exception to the rule. In my mind, one of the biggest problems these large legacy brokerages have is that they're decentralized and fragmented. Everybody is essentially an independent contractor rather than an employee. That makes it tough to bring technology throughout the entire organization for every agent to use.

Matt Murphy: It is. Compass is probably doing the best job at that, but Compass is starting from scratch with technology, and they're also hand-selecting their agents and teams. So, those people are coming into the business knowing it's a tech-enabled brokerage, which is very different than someone who's worked for a traditional brokerage their whole career.

Many agents think they've done things their way and had a great career, so, "Why would I change when I only have five to seven years left before retirement?" And that's a very valid argument. But, if you're just starting your career, or you're midway through with another 20 years in front of you, you better jump on technology very quickly.

Gregory Charlop: Well, executives, you heard it here first. Matthew Murphy will turn you folks around. So, contact him with your technological questions! How?

I have one last question. You're highly experienced with start-ups. If a real estate professional came to you with an idea for their own startup, what advice would you give them to get off the ground?

Matt Murphy: It's a great question. My current role is a venture capitalist and general partner with Montage Ventures. We focus on investing in seed-stage and series-A companies in fintech, real estate tech, health care, and the future of retail. So, I meet with a lot of early-stage starters who really just have an idea. Maybe they have something built, but they don't really have much. We may put that first institutional check in with their business, giving them $500,000 to really kick start them to the next level.

I have met with a lot of real estate agents who see a problem firsthand and want to build a company around it. The advice I give them is: if this is keeping you up at night, and you can not live another day without focusing on this, then focus all of your energy on this problem. If you don't want to give up your day job, and you want to do this on the side to see if you can make a run at it, don't do that. You need to put in 100 percent, if not 150 percent, of yourself to really find success.

It's funny, but most folks don't want to tell me their ideas. They want me to sign a non-disclosure agreement. And I laugh because I was that guy once. I tell them that no idea is that great. It's really all about the execution. I've probably seen your idea five times before because I see hundreds of ideas every day. What differentiates ideas is a passionate founder with amazing skills to execute, build, transform, and not turn away from challenges or defeats to do something against all odds.

That's a high order, but that's what it takes to build the next billion-dollar business that innovates a critical industry like real estate. If they say, "Yes, yes, yes, I'm ready," then the next thing I tell them is to have a good technical co-founder. Because a lot of times, if you're a real estate agent, maybe you studied engineering in school, maybe it's your side gig, but chances are you're more of the idea and the marketing person. So you really need a strong technical co-founder next to you who's just as passionate about this, has equal equity, and is 100 percent dedicated to it as well.

Because, in the seed stage, we're not so much betting on the idea, we're really betting on the people. Especially in the seed stage, because most entrepreneurs need to be willing to pivot many times over—pivot big, pivot small. So, we're really betting on you as the founder and creating a relationship, a long-standing relationship with you. So, finding a good co-founder is key, and really being 100 percent in is critical.

Interview with Darren Johnson, marketing expert, co-founder and CEO of AgentZip

Gregory Charlop: Darren, thanks for joining us. You started in the mortgage industry, then you went on into real estate technology, and then you created Top Agent Connection and AgentZip. Can you tell us a bit more about your background and how you became interested in real estate technology?

Darren Johnson: I started as an inside sales agent. I was on a dialer, cold-calling title leads to find opportunities from homeowners interested in refinancing. My job was to sit on the phone system, call 300-400 homeowners a night and get them essentially to say, "Yes, I'm interested in refinancing." If the answer was affirmative, I would next gather all their pertinent information—like a mini 1003 loan application—and get their social security number. That's what would constitute a lead at that position. From there, it would be transferred to the loan officer to take a full-blown application and hopefully get their loan for them.

At the time, call center workers were making $10.00 an hour, plus maybe $5 in bonuses each hour, which is pretty good for a high schooler. I think the minimum wage was $6.75 at the time. But I saw that the loan officers were making some serious money at that time and I, of course, wanted to advance my career. So, I made a deal with a top producing Loan Officer. We agreed that I would call for him for free and get him leads in exchange for him teaching me the essentials of the loan officer job. That's how I started doing loans. After a few months of that, I learned how to originate a whole loan, and then I was on my own as a loan officer.

When the market crashed in 2008, I left the mortgage business. I always had a knack for marketing and advertising, so I went to San Diego State to study marketing and learn media buying. My marketing professor said I had a gift.

From there, I got a job with Homes.com as a sales rep. Essentially my job at Homes.com was to cold-call real estate agents and sell them on either a website, impression-based marketing or social media management. In our first 30 days in training, I outproduced the entire floor of reps. I brought in more revenue than the 70 other sales reps who were selling the services. I just had a passion for it because I'd been studying marketing. I understood the value of exposure, leads, having the right website, and the right presence. I tied it to my experience with real estate. It just brought together technology and marketing with real estate. I think it was at Homes.com that I figured out that real estate marketing was my passion.

Next I worked for several other Real Estate Tech and Lead companies. I joined a startup, and, with my help, they grew from a tiny single room operation to millions in funding.

After leaving that company, I was a bit rattled but motivated to start my own company. So I took the leap and founded Top Agent Connection. It was kind of like a hybrid of what I did at Homes.com and what I did at My Agent Finder. Top Agent Connection matched agents with buyers/sellers based on the best fit. Does someone want to sell a home in this zip code, in 90 days, and need staging? We're going to then match them up with an agent who fits that criteria. In exchange for us finding that lead, we would then collect a referral fee if they successfully connected and sold with that client.

From there, AgentZip filled a void that Top Agent Connection had, which is Top Agent Connection can only work with the top 5 or 10 percent of agents because if we're matching people with the best of the best, we're leaving out the other 90, 95 percent of agents. AgentZip allows any agent to sign up, take their zip codes, and pick their city. Then, we do all the Facebook and Google marketing. We take care of all the funnels and get them exclusive leads.

Gregory Charlop: You've gone from apprentice to entrepreneur. As an expert in real estate technology, what kind of tools should real estate agents be using?

Darren Johnson: I think agents need to utilize technology for organization and automation. They need a website with a feed of homes that will give them analytics on what homes and features their prospects are searching through. The MLS is no longer a physical book; you need your own website that is very intelligent. Pair it with a good CRM and you have a solid foundation. I get mind blown when I hear agents say they don't have a website.

Secondary to that, they need to have lead sources. Some agents just want to work referrals, and that's fine. Some agents want to work referrals, do lead gen, have people calling, collect data. They are building a real pipeline and future database, and, as such, need to utilize automation and drip marketing. If they have a contact, someone who was interested in a home six months ago, there should be drip marketing campaigns on email. There should be text messages going out to those people. They should have a chatbot or be following up on home searches or market trends. They should be tracking all of the behavior of their leads, and their CRMs should be updating those behaviors and nurturing them accordingly.

As far as websites, I think every single agent needs to utilize retargeting. If you go on Nike's website and you start looking at shoes, you're going to start seeing those shoes follow you on other sites. Through Google display ads, through Facebook—that's all retargeting. I notice many agents don't retarget their visitors. I think it's one of the most underused tools out there and it has the highest rates of conversions.

I think agents need to emulate what all the top companies are doing, which is having very well-structured CRMs. They need automation built in to replace the busy work, and they need retargeting marketing on Facebook and Google.

Gregory Charlop: Many of our readers probably aren't that experienced in setting up technological systems themselves. How should someone who's not that technologically savvy do this? Should they hire someone to do it?

Darren Johnson: Yes. Some companies do everything for them. You can go on Craigslist, on Fiverr, on Upwork and find people who do it. Some companies do it. Local whiz kids do it. If you even start Googling how to set up a Facebook ad for real estate agents, you'll just start getting ads from these marketers saying, "Hey, I can do it for you." If an agent is tech-savvy, there are tons of resources online to set up retargeting and create Facebook ads. There are great YouTube videos and groups on Facebook for advertisers.

I think most agents don't have the time to learn all this stuff because it is complex. Even learning it takes a lot of money and involves trial and error as you get up to speed. If this is too risky for you, it makes sense to hire someone to do it. A thousand dollars paying an expert marketer will get you higher immediate results than a thousand dollars learning it yourself. An expert's always going to do a better job and knows how to get more clicks, more leads, better results because they've already gone through the experience. If an agent has time, yes, learn it. However, I would hire a professional to do it because it will save me time and money, and they'll get me better results.

If you want me to do some of these functions for you, I can be reached at GetDarren.com

Gregory Charlop: What are your thoughts about technological products on the horizon? Any particular products you're excited about?

Darren Johnson: Yes. Alexa, which was a data reporting company before Amazon acquired it. People have these devices at home, and they are logging all the conversations people are having and pulling keywords. Big companies are going to be using this technology to sell leads to agents.

If an agent is a marketing expert or hires someone who is, these opportunities are huge. If they want to learn it on their own, learn on your own, I think a lot of this new technology is impressive. It will know when a husband and wife are talking about selling their home. You are going to be able to put yourself in front of the people who just talked about that. It is going to be another big opportunity.

All the data collection with supercookies is getting better and better. I think agents need to understand that it's not just Zillow anymore, it's not just the portals. Google, Facebook, Amazon, these companies already know who is looking to buy a house and who is looking to sell. You can skip the portals and go directly to them. You can have your own website, funnels, and landing pages. I think that'll be the key for agents to get leads.

Gregory Charlop: I can imagine it must be a little spooky if you're speaking to your spouse about moving and then the next minute you get an email or a message about new houses. Maybe we'll just start to accept that?

Darren Johnson: They have already accepted being targeted on Facebook, Google and other social media they regularly use. It is becoming common and acceptable to most people. You don't get an email or message about it, it's just that ads start coming up. I saw a video about this. Someone just kept saying cat food, cat food, cat food into their phone and they start getting ads for cat food. If you keep on typing in cat food on Google, you're going to start seeing ads. They don't know exactly why it's happening, but I think people are pretty used to the ads that they see online. The commercial they see before they watch a video on YouTube. It's all stuff that they've been looking up and they're interested in.

It's crazy that I sit on my computer and I'm always typing in buying or selling a home. I'm always looking at keywords. I'm always looking at real estate stuff, and I get ads from companies like my company that sells leads. I very rarely get ads from the individual agent. If I'm looking at selling a home, I should be getting ads from local agents too. I should have this virtual billboard in front of me. It's almost insane that agents are spending money on bus benches and billboards when the online ones are so much more effective. You drive by a billboard; you're not stopping to write down their phone number.

Online, I click on their ad and go to their website. I feel out a lead form. I should start getting email drips and text message drips from that agent. I should get retargeting ads. I keep seeing that agent over and over. At that point, it's a no-brainer which agent I'm going to hire because I keep seeing them everywhere. That kind of technology will help agents crush it. The brokerages aren't doing that for them; the agent's responsible for doing it on their own.

Gregory Charlop: It seems like the agents are leaving money on the table.

Darren Johnson: A lot. It will weed out a lot of the old-timers. It's like commuting with a horse in 1956. Just get that Chevy already.

Gregory Charlop: What are your thoughts about virtual or augmented reality in real estate?

Darren Johnson: VR will be big. Think of the overseas investor. He doesn't want to fly and see a bunch of different homes. If he can conduct virtual tours of all the homes, he's saving himself plane trips. They're already using virtual tours like Matterport. Imagine looking at 30 open houses and not leaving the comfort of your home. Then, you can pick out the ones you really want and see them in person. The buyer's agent role will be completely redefined when VR hits the market and people are receptive to it and using it a lot.

Gregory Charlop: Do you think this is going to hurt buyer's agents? Do you think it will decrease the need for them?

Darren Johnson: It's hard to say, but I think it ultimately will. The bigger VR gets, the more it'll hurt agents. If everyone is into VR and putting on those headsets, you don't necessarily need a buyer's agent to show you all these homes, just an agent to show you the homes you really want. I think people need to still physically tour a home because VR's not going to give you the smell, the sense, the feeling you get once you're in a home. It can save a lot of time driving around to open houses, which I don't think agents enjoy anyway. It will cut out a big-time factor.

Not getting too sidetracked, but I think there are 2 million licensed agents right now, and there are 6 million homes sold a year. The numbers are already screwed up there. There are already too many agents. Imagine what happens when you add VR into the mix and enable people to tour homes on their own. What's the need to hire a buyer's agent to show you 50 properties when you end up finding the one you want, and an agent just shows you three properties and then helps you negotiate the offer?

Gregory Charlop: I think that there are a lot of companies now that are heading in that direction. They have very minimal agent involvement, and they essentially help with the paperwork and negotiating the deal. Those companies don't need many agents. I think the need for agents will decrease and probably just the best ones will survive. Those top agents will vacuum up most of the business.

Darren Johnson: Something like 90 percent of agents fail their first year. A lot of people get into real estate thinking it's all glitz and glamour and an easy job. Then they find out how hard it is. Technology will make that a lot easier. The existing agents are going to need to stay very up to date with technology, immerse themselves in it. I think we'll see a lot of tech people enter real estate because they understand the technology aspect.

Gregory Charlop: If a real estate agent or broker approached you today and wanted to start a real estate tech startup, what advice would you give them?

Darren Johnson: That's a tough one. First, become a lifetime learner because the pace of change is insane, and it will not slow down, Be personally resilient. Get ready to fail a lot. Embrace your failures and learn from them. Don't let them discourage you. You don't need to have a perfect plan, but it always needs to be a work in progress. What may be working today may change tomorrow, so get ready for that. Assemble the right team. Have the right roadmap. Have the proper roles defined. Have a clear vision for what you offer and where you want your growth to be. With technology, things change quickly. Many entrepreneurs fail several times before they find their niche, but you will learn from those failures and some of those failures turn into wins.

Interview with Suzy Truax, Board of Directors, eXp World Holdings

Gregory Charlop: You're an agent and member of the Board of Directors of eXp. Can you briefly tell us about eXp and what makes them different from other real estate companies? Some of our readers may not have even heard of eXp before.

Suzy Truax: eXp Realty is a 3-D cloud immersive national real estate brokerage, and historically, the fastest growing. Unless a state requires it or an agent wants to open their own, we do not have a brick and mortar location. Like Amazon, Netflix, and Airbnb, you don't go somewhere to get it. You go on the internet to shop for real estate services. We have a 3-D cloud campus (EXP World) where agents and staff interact in real time, every day to replace the brick and mortar experience.

People have said it's like The Sims or Second Life. Built on the VirBELA platform, it's secure and agents have a full experience psychologically—just like if you were playing a video game, but a truly interactive video game. eXp World encompasses all the services you would expect at a real estate brokerage (legal, marketing, broker assistance, education, payment processing) but without the inefficiencies and without the costly overhead.

Gregory Charlop: Is the idea to get the benefits of an office—like working with colleagues, advice, and mentorship—but without the cost?

Suzy Truax: Collaboration, mentorship. Yes. Yes.

Gregory Charlop: Great. That's a good idea because I think that a lot of real estate agents are stuck with overhead that may not be covering its costs.

Suzy Truax: The profit margins are very thin on real estate brokerages. Glenn Sanford came up with the idea from launching a brick and mortar brokerage in 2008. And we all remember what happened in 2008 to the real estate industry. This iteration minimized overhead and continued to operate as a real estate brokerage, but with this unique concept of collaborating in the cloud that's mind-blowing. That's what makes us unique.

EXP World is way more experiential than your typical webinar. It's more collaborative than a physical office because, with an office, you're limited to the people who show up. I can go into the cloud campus today and attend a class with someone who was the number one agent in all of Coldwell Banker teaching how to do a listing presentation. Bricks and mortars can't scale this kind of collaboration.

Gregory Charlop: Why would an agent choose to work with eXp rather than a traditional firm? Sounds like eXp has excellent networking opportunities.

Suzy Truax: There are so many reasons, Greg. eXp appeals to entrepreneurial, smart agents who understand that they own a business. Number one is the compensation model. The compensation is extremely fair. It's a super low capping model. The monthly fee delivers high-value tech tools, that if an agent were to purchase on their own, the cost would exceed $600 a month instead of $85.

Then there's the technology. Everyone claims to be a technology company, but we actually are a software company that is in real estate. Here's an example. I'm an agent who was not native to technology because of when I was born, but I've adapted because I've seen that it's critical to survival. My very first weekend at eXp, I took some on-demand training. We have thousands of hours of on-demand training around different technologies for obtaining leads. So, that first weekend I learned how to make a squeeze page. I couldn't learn that at any of my other companies unless I paid for the training and went to a class that was two hours away.

Another reason for joining eXp is that we're trying to set our agents up for retirement. When I met Glenn Sanford in July of 2017, I asked him, "What were your thoughts when you started this company? What drove you to create this model?" He said he wanted real estate agents to have a way to be able to retire when they were done working their 30, 40, 50 years in the business. Hence, the agent equity program was born.

The program rewards agents for their first closing, capping, introducing a colleague to eXp on the colleague's first closing. We give agents the ability to purchase stock, like all the Silicon Valley companies. Agents can invest 5 percent of their commission to buy stock at a 20 percent discount.

Finally, eXp offers a revenue share or wealth-building opportunity. There's no mandate; it's just the cherry on the sundae if you'd like to take advantage of it.

Gregory Charlop: How do you see technology transforming real estate?

Suzy Truax: Its effects will be twofold. Number one, it's going to take some real estate agents out of the business. There will be Redfins, Real, Reali, Faira, Offerpad. They're going to take over the real estate sales that don't really require a human touch. I do think technology is going to shrink our industry, absolutely. Those platforms are going to take a big bite. And there will be commission contraction.

On the other hand, agents who adapt to technology will attract more business and increase profits through leveraging technology as they'll work more efficiently and optimize lead generation.

Technology has created an opportunity for me to build an agent group across the country. The REO business is almost entirely tech-optimized now. Look at Hubzu and Auction.com. Where no relationship is required, the real estate agent is a redundancy.

However, I don't think any of these discount models that are tech-optimized are going to be able to compete in high touch situations.

Gregory Charlop: If I understand you correctly, you think that the discount or flat rate brokerages will probably capture a lot of the routine transactions and REOs. Successful agents will do very well with the rest of the deals by using technology. You suspect we'll probably have a lot fewer agents in the future than we have now.

Suzy Truax: Yes.

Gregory Charlop: Do you think technology will replace agents or augment them? It sounds like you think it'll do both. It'll help some agents who are good with it and probably replace or reduce the need for others.

Suzy Truax: Yes. I think that agents who adopt and utilize technology in their business will end up crushing the part-time agents. There is going to be a lot of consolidation into teams. That's because some people won't get out of the business, but they'll gravitate to someone who knows how to use technology to generate leads and run their business. Then, other people are just going to be left in the dust.

Gregory Charlop: What are your favorite technological tools other than eXp's platform itself?

Suzy Truax: For team management, I love Trello. This tool offers workflow/project management and doesn't require a phone call, or a text, or hunting for an email. Here's what needs to be done; here's who is supposed to be doing it, move it along in its path.

We are using kvCORE for CRM and also as an SEO website. It's an all-in-one business and lead management tool provided by eXp. Literally the Bugatti of CRMs.

One of the other things that I love for collaboration is Workplace by Facebook. It's specifically for business. If I'm not in the cloud campus, I'm able to interact with the 18,000+ agents that we have across the US and three provinces of Canada. Instead of calling into the office, I can call directly via Workplace chat. I can call another agent. I can call Transaction Services. It's so efficient, it's crazy.

People ask me when they first join, "Who do I call? What number do I call to get assistance with X?" Whatever it is—accounting, marketing. A phone number is unnecessary. Just go into the Workplace app and hit the phone icon. I try not to email anymore, because it's just so much faster to use the instant message feature.

Gregory Charlop: Amen to that. One last question. If a traditional real estate company called you into their boardroom to ask for advice on how to improve their business model, what would you say?

Suzy Truax: There's a culture that exists in traditional real estate brokerages that needs to change. It's the concept of standing/chatting around the water cooler at the office. Some think that's being productive. That's *not* productive time when you're an entrepreneur. I'd advise them to get the agents out in the field meeting potential customers rather than spending their time chatting with fellow real estate agents.

The number one objection from agents exploring the eXp model is that they want to go to the office, be around other real estate agents. In my experience, really productive agents work with their office door shut because they're lead generating and conducting business. The unproductive agents are typically standing around the water cooler, avoiding doing the one thing that's going to make them more money. Eliminate the water cooler culture from your office. Have that socialization need met in some other way. Because when people are standing around the water cooler avoiding making calls, avoiding door knocking, avoiding networking, it's costing the brokerage owner money.

CHAPTER 3: ELITE AGENTS

Make more money, improve efficiency, and stay at the top of your game

Congratulations! You are a top agent. You close the biggest deals. You crush the competition. You own this town. Clients want to hire you, and your competitors want to be you.

The trouble is, all the other agents want to topple you.

You already know what you're doing. You are one of the elite few with unparalleled social skills, business savvy, and a great organization. You work hard and out-hustle the competition. You're a winner. What you've been doing has worked—so far.

Every day, young and technologically adept upstarts are trying to knock you off your throne. I'm going to teach you how to defeat them. I will show you how to make even more money and close more deals. Believe it or not, it can be done.

To keep crushing the competition, you need to maximize your most precious resource: time, negotiate the most advantageous deal with your brokerage firm, and keep up with the latest technological advances.

This chapter is intended for top real estate agents and anyone who wants to hire them. If you're an executive with a real estate company, I suggest you read this chapter carefully. Signing premier salespeople to your team will be a key to your survival. You may also find some great tips you can use in your business.

If you're an associate but not yet part of the elite, read this chapter to get an early jump on how to succeed.

Time—your most valuable resource

You enjoy the biggest sales in the neighborhood and everyone sees your wins when they check Zillow or Realtor.com. Your massive sales volume propels you to success on real estate agent search site Homelight. Your customer satisfaction rating is off the charts, and buyers will take note of your acclaim on Yelp.

Every new house you sell will generate more positive buzz for you online. Your improved web presence will draw even more clients your way. You'll benefit from a self-perpetuating virtuous cycle of success with each new transaction.

You hardly need to advertise at all. Your acclaim grows organically.

So, what's holding you back from even greater success? I'll give you a hint. It's not lack of advertising or brokerage support.

It's a lack of time.

There is only one of you. You can't squeeze more than 24 hours out of a day. You have so many requests from prospects that you can't accept them all. You turn those prospects down or pass them off to your associates—and take a financial loss. You're losing business that you deserve, and it's frustrating.

No, don't even think about working more! Devote your free time to things that bring value to your life: family, exercise, eating right, sleeping well, and giving back to your community. Looking back, nobody ever wishes they spent more time working at the expense of their family and friends.

So, the question becomes, how can you become more productive while spending the same (or less) time at work?

One strategy is to use virtual assistants (VAs) any way you can. Check out the Virtual Assistant and Chatbots chapter. It includes interviews with leading real estate VAs manufacturers who offer some great suggestions about how to put them to work. Remember, your goal should be to meet with prospects, create a strategy, and negotiate and close deals. Everything else is a waste of your precious time.

"The highest and best use for a virtual assistant is doing all of the administrative stuff that, 1) you don't like doing, 2) you're probably not that good at, 3) it doesn't pay the most," said Daniel Ramsey, CEO of MyOutDesk, as part of a longer interview. "So, you're not good, you don't have time to do it, it doesn't pay the most, and that means you should outsource it. Hands down, that is the barometer."

Delegate! It's the next best thing to cloning yourself. And you can start doing it today.

Clear your mind and focus

You're offloading routine tasks to software programs and virtual assistants, but you still want to make the best use of your own time. What can be done to improve your focus and increase your productivity?

A lot!

Everybody says to work smarter, not harder. Well, you can work **better** by taking care of your body and mind. How? With meditation, improved sleep, morning rituals, and strategic caffeine.

Meditation

Why are we talking about meditation in a book about real estate? Because meditation improves focus,[24] and the more you focus during your work hours, the more you will accomplish. Meditation even improves memory and test performance.[25] If you take an interest in meditation or mindfulness, there are a lot of great books on the subject.

Tim Ferriss, the brilliant author of *The Four Hour Work Week* (a must read) recently wrote *Tools of Titans*. *Titans* is a collection of interviews Ferriss conducted over the years with the most successful folks in society, including elite athletes, business and political leaders, top writers, and famous scientists.

And what common habit did Ferriss observe with most of his interviewees? They meditate. In fact, many of the leaders credit meditation as one of their most important habits. If it works for them, it could work for you.

Don't know how to meditate? No problem! There are apps for that. (This is a technology book, after all!)

Ferriss recommends the meditation apps Calm and Headspace. They're both easy to use and available at the App Store. They're like having a private meditation coach. They both have free features to start out and an option to pay for increased functionality. Download one or both of them today and let me know how they work for you.

You can also learn about guided meditation (meditation in response to a teacher) from books, classes at local community centers, and gyms. It's easy to try.

In addition to meditation, I recommend the daily practice of gratitude. Gratitude is intentionally feeling thankful for what you have and what's going well in your life. It can be big or small. You can verbalize it, think it, or WRITE IT DOWN in a daily journal. For example, you can write "I'm thankful I saw my daughter for lunch today, I got a nice compliment from my coworker, and I finally finished that home remodel." You just take a moment to appreciate what went right during the day.

The daily practice of gratitude improves physical and psychological health, increases empathy, and improves sleep.[26] It's so easy to do, give it a try!

Meditation, mindfulness, and gratitude combined with a healthy diet, exercise, and proper sleep will clear your mind and supercharge your day.

Get some sleep

More restful nights produce more energetic days. And, more energy equals more sales!

To start, you probably aren't sleeping enough. Adults need 7-9 hours of sleep per night, according to the National Sleep Foundation.[27] Are you even approaching that much?

How you sleep is almost as important as how long you sleep. Sleep hygiene is the medical term for proper sleep habits. Here are the basic rules of sleep:[28] [29] [30]

• Avoid caffeine, nicotine, and alcohol (!) close to bedtime. I know, alcohol might help you fall asleep faster, but it disrupts your sleep later at night resulting in low-quality slumber.

• Exercise regularly, but don't engage in strenuous exercise right before bedtime.

• Try to catch some rays during the day, but make sure your bedroom is dark at night. Consider blackout curtains.

• Establish a regular bedtime routine. Do the same things every night; go to bed and wake up at the same time each day.

• Make sure your bedroom environment is comfortable. Buy a good mattress, keep the room cool, and consider eye shades, ear plugs, or white noise machines if those help you.

• Avoid computer/phone screens before bed! The blue light from those devices can wake you up and make it tougher for you to drift off. If you must use your phone before bed, try features like Apple's Night Shift which reduces the blue light emitted by the screen. If you like the sci-fi look, there are special glasses[31] you can wear to filter out blue light at night.

• Don't watch TV, work, or read in bed. Your bed should be for sleeping.

- If you take naps, take them earlier in the day. Don't nap close to bedtime.

- Take a warm shower and meditate before bed. Don't check email or agitate yourself right before you turn in!

Morning rituals

Establish a morning routine and stick with it. Try these suggestions:

- Don't read email or anything annoying when you first wake up. Why start the day agitated?

- Consider buying an alarm clock. They're making a comeback! That way, you won't need to look at your phone as you fall asleep and when you first wake up.

- Try to get some sun as soon as you can.

- Wake up at the same time each day. Yes, even on weekends.

- Do a quick 2-minute exercise routine right when you first wake up. I stole this idea from Tim Ferriss. I've started doing one set of pushups as soon as I get up and I love it. Find a brief exercise you enjoy and do it every morning. It will pump up your day and build some muscle!

- Enjoy a healthy breakfast, although you don't need to eat it as soon as you wake up. I am usually out of bed around 5 am, but I don't eat breakfast until 9 or 10.

Strategic caffeine

Despite its bad rep, it is okay to drink coffee. In fact, it might be more than okay, it appears to be healthy! Currently, the weight of medical evidence indicates that black coffee is good for most adults.[32] Your cup of Joe might reduce your risk of heart disease, diabetes, and cancer.[33] Recent research suggests that coffee might even reduce the risk of death.[34] So, go ahead and drink up!

But, do it the right way. It turns out that downing that latte the size of an oil drum first thing in the morning isn't the best way to do it. You need to be strategic. Here's how.

Instead of blowing your mind with a massive jolt of caffeine in the morning, you should gradually drink sips of coffee (or tea) here and there throughout the day.[35][36] In other words, you need to dole out your caffeine and drink some when you're starting to feel sluggish. Have just enough to reclaim your pep, and then drink some more the next time you're feeling foggy.

The trouble is that if you drink a massive amount of coffee all at once, you'll be coming down from your caffeine high just as your body is starting to get tired as the afternoon wears on. If you drink smaller doses here and there, you can use the caffeine to counteract the natural lows you feel throughout the day. If you want, get one of those fancy coffee mugs that keep your drink warm (or cold) throughout the morning.

And for those of you who exercise, (and I hope that's all of you!), you can enjoy some coffee or tea before you go to the gym or set off on a run.[37] Caffeine will supercharge your workouts and shave time off your races. If you're anything like me, you only have a few hours per week to hit the gym. I don't want to waste that precious time moving like a sloth from one exercise to the next. I want to get results! So enjoy a little coffee or espresso before hitting the weights, and your biceps will thank you.

One caveat. The coffee is the healthy stuff, not all the garbage you add to it. If you're mixing in a bunch of sugar, artificial flavors, or processed creamers, you aren't doing yourself any favors. Try to stick with black or iced coffee or espresso as much as possible. Use a little Stevia, organic soy milk, or cream if you have to - but don't go overboard!

The value of efficiency—sell one more house a month.

Why are we spending all this time discussing virtual assistants, meditation, sleep, and strategic caffeine? So you can be more productive: close more deals without spending any more time. If you can squeeze a little more juice out of your work hours, you could enjoy extra vacation time and make more money. Not a bad goal.

Small changes can make a significant difference. According to a recent survey, over 60 percent of agents spend at least an hour a day on marketing and advertising.[38] Moreover, most people spend between 1.5-3 hours of the workday not doing work.[39] If you fit right in the middle, you squander 2.25 hours or 135 minutes each day.

Now, imagine if your new real estate VA took care of your marketing and advertising. That saves you at least an hour a day. And let's assume that your improved sleep, strategic caffeine, and meditation enhance your focus and decrease the amount of time you waste by 25 percent a modest assumption. Your enhanced concentration will yield you at least an extra half-hour of productivity daily. Therefore, a VA who handles your marketing combined with the other techniques mentioned here will save you at least 1 1/2 hours a day or 7.5 hours per week.

And that doesn't even count the time you'd save by outsourcing document filing to VAs, transferring inbound leads to chatbots, and handing off client management tasks to a real estate CRM!

Let's assume that you spend 40 hours on average per client.[40] If so, you'll be able to serve almost 10 more clients per year just with these simple changes! No extra time, no lost vacation, just more money. Not bad!

The proper use of chatbots will also help you reclaim your

time. Michael Lam, CEO of Kaydoh, told me: "Without a chatbot, you, as an agent, would have to say the same thing over and over. While you're doing that routine stuff, you're taking time away from your existing clients, hosting an open house, or speaking with a potential buyer." Click here to read the full interview with Michael Lam.

What would you do if you closed up to 10 more homes per year? Retire early? Buy a new car? Travel around the world? Donate extra to charity? The possibilities are endless and the choices are yours.

You benefit from massive organic inbound marketing. Without even placing one ad, customers will flock to you based on your history of successful sales and good reviews. All you have to do is find the time to help these people, and your income will soar.

Seniors need your help

Seniors are in trouble. With a fixed income and limited savings, many of our parents and grandparents are unable to afford a safe and comfortable home for retirement. Retirement communities are often too expensive and can rob seniors of their dignity. They are frequently prohibited from having overnight guests, pets, or even watching loud TV at night. Sadly, we often strip away an adult's autonomy in their golden years.

Many older adults plan to age in place so they can stay in their familiar home and neighborhood. The trouble is that the elderly often become lonely and isolated as friends and neighbors move away or die. And many homes are not suitable for folks with disabilities. Stairs and inaccessible bathrooms and kitchens can turn a home into a prison.

My company, Dignified Housing is working to change all that. We want to match seniors with affordable housing that preserves autonomy, ends isolation, and is appropriate for the disabled. We also help people age in place the right way, by preparing their homes for potential illness and disability.

As a top agent, I'd like to invite you to partner with us. We need your talent, drive, and enthusiasm. If you're interested in helping seniors, please reach out to me directly or visit Dignified Housing and join our network. We can make a difference together.

Top agents and their firms

As a top agent, clients seek you, not your firm. Here's a personal example.

I sold my San Francisco Bay Area home a couple years ago. It was a good house, and I felt that if it was marketed properly, I could score a killer deal.

I needed a real estate agent, and I wanted the best.

What did I do? I jumped online and reviewed who sold the homes in my town over the last 6 months. It turned out that two or three salespeople were rock stars. Everyone else wasn't even in their league! I picked one of those super agents, and I was off to the races.

How did I decide on my agent?

I cared about his successful track record. I cared about his marketing plan. I cared about our interpersonal relationship. I did NOT care about his brokerage firm.

The house sold beyond my expectations and my agent certainly earned his commission.

Just to repeat: I picked a salesperson based on his track record. I did NOT care one whit about his firm.

My experience is not unusual. These days, homebuyers and sellers seek out top talent. They do their own research on internet portals like Zillow, review sites like Yelp, or matchmaking services like Homelight. The client zeros in on potential agents based on a salesperson's track record and history of stellar reviews. In short, clients will find you.

Real estate expert and CEO Kim Hughes agreed. She said, as part of a longer interview, "A buyer/seller does not care what your brokerage is or who your franchise is. They care about what you're going to do for them. Being part of a brokerage can be a plus or a minus. Home buyers and home sellers care about who the agent is and what that agent is bringing to the table."

Here's Tamir Poleg, the founder of Real, on the importance the public attaches to your brokerage: "I think in most states they do not care at all. People don't care who your broker is; they care about you, the agent. They want to know that you helped a friend buy a home. They want to know you through social engagement. They want to receive content from you. They want to see your face on yard signs. This is how people evaluate an agent, not through who the broker is. Obviously, there are exceptions, maybe in the high-end market, maybe in New York, but in average America, people couldn't care less who your broker is."

So, if you're a top agent, you hold all the cards. You bring in the sales. You are funding your broker's vacations and boosting your firm's stock price. Your hard work and success are paying for the whole show.

Your firm needs you much more than you need the firm.

Your brokerage is lucky to have you, and there is no reason for you to stick with a company that isn't meeting your needs.

What are your needs?

· **A fair commission split**. You're bringing in the business, so you should keep most of the revenue.

- **Technological support.** While you and your VAs should probably do most of your own marketing, you may want your firm to create and manage your web page. However, don't overpay for this! If your VA will do a better job for less money, have your VA do it instead. Bonus points if your firm can offer you technology that has a high acquisition cost, like virtual reality tours and Matterport cameras. All real estate firms should have a CTO whose job is to research new technology and share it with the group. Look for that in you firm since evaluating all the new real estate tech is a full-time job.

- **Help with unusual or tricky situations**. You know your stuff, but occasionally you'll find yourself in a challenging ethical or legal situation. You want to be backed up by a broker or lawyer who can help you when you're in a jam.

- **Human support.** You want an assistant to run errands, make arrangements, assist with open houses, etc. Again, many of these tasks can be outsourced to a VA, so make sure you're not overpaying your firm for these services. Consider taking on a mentee for these jobs!

TOP AGENTS HAVE ALL THE POWER

TOP AGENT

TRADITIONAL AGENCY

- **Access to training and lifelong learning.** I'm a big believer in this stuff. These services don't have to come through your brokerage, but it would be good to be part of a group that places a strong value on continuous personal growth. (More on how to continue your education later.)

• **Referrals** and access to off-MLS deals.

What you don't need from your real estate brokerage

• **An unfair commission split.** Your split should be radically more favorable than that of your newer or less successful colleagues. They need the firm's help. You don't.

• **Firms that spend a lot of money on advertising** for their brand. Clients don't hire you because of your firm. They hire you for you. If your firm is spending a lot of money on its brand, then the firm getting most of the benefit.

• **Lavish offices**, fancy conference rooms, expensive coffee machines (well, maybe you do want the expensive coffee machine!). But seriously, you don't need this stuff.

You probably spend very little time in the office, and your clients could care less about your conference room. These days everyone meets at a coffee shop or at the client's home. Besides, they have better espresso machines. Click here to read Tony Vitale's counterpoint to this argument.

• **Mandatory floor time** or excessive meetings. Time is your most limited asset. Your firm should protect your time, not demolish it.

The truth is that you are an independent contractor. You really don't need all that much from a real estate firm

You might want to consider a different type of brokerage altogether. Your reputation (and targeted advertising) bring in the business. You really just need a brokerage for compliance and regulatory reasons. Check out some of the other brokerage models mentioned throughout this book. At the very least, you'll understand your worth and improve your negotiating position with your firm.

Reading/lifelong learning

This book is all about change. The old ways of doing business are falling by the wayside as modern technology, fresh blood, and energetic entrepreneurs shake up the marketplace. You're at the top of your game now, but it won't stay that way forever unless you keep learning. Your best investment is in yourself.

I know, I know. You're busy, and I just told you that you shouldn't cut into your sleep, exercise or family time. That's all true, but self-improvement is worth carving out dedicated time. To kick your brain into overdrive, consider reading some of the books recommended here.

Books bring expertise to you

Brilliant people with expertise in business, real estate, art, history, psychology, economics, science, and technology spent years consolidating their knowledge into something you can hold in your hand. With a few hours of your time, you can learn from someone's lifetime of experience. How awesome is that?

Have you ever wished you had an outstanding mentor? Someone who mastered advertising, started a successful technology business from scratch, or dedicated their career to the study of psychology and buyer behavior? You can. Just pick up a book.

Every town has a library and you can browse to your heart's content. Don't want to leave the house? You can have an actual, physical book delivered to your home within two days, and sometimes within an hour thanks to Amazon. If that isn't fast enough, nearly any book is available instantly using your phone, Kindle, or Nook eReader. You can also try my favorite: kick back and let Audible.com read books to you. I listen every day in the car. Why not put that time stuck in traffic to good use? Audible has some fantastic narrators, and you can control the speaking speed to suit your taste.

What books to read? Here are some of my favorites. Most are also recommended by some of the most successful people in the business. Don't focus exclusively on real estate books. Afterall, there is much more to life than houses! I broke them down into categories: Real Estate, Business, Technology, Psychology and Persuasion, and Great General Knowledge. If you read these 18 books, you'll be way ahead of the pack.

Category	Title and Author	Greg's Take
Business	*The 4-Hour Work Week: Escape 9-5, Live Anywhere, and Join the New Rich* By Timothy Ferriss	My favorite business book. A classic about the value of time and work. Reminds me of the importance of free time, creativity, and thinking different. Love Tim Ferriss!
	The ONE Thing: The Surprisingly Simple Truth Behind Extraordinary Results By Gary Keller	From the founder of Keller Williams, learn how to focus on what matters—and forget the rest.
Psychology and Persuasion	*How to Win Friends and Influence People* By Dale Carnegie	A classic! Life is so much easier when people like you.
	The Paradox of Choice By Barry Schwartz	The inspiration for my first startup, Visionary Remodels. We are overwhelmed when faced with too many useless choices. Better to have a few good ones.
	Influence	How to use tools like

Real Estate at a Crossroads

	By Robert Cialdini	social proof and reciprocation to get people to do what you want.
	Pre-Suasion By Robert Cialdini	Learn the power of word choice and how to prime people to accept your ideas.
Real Estate	*Zillow Talk: Rewriting the Rules of Real Estate* By Spencer Rascoff	Don't buy and sell real estate with your gut. Use the data! Written by the Zillow brain trust, this is a fun look at the random facts that can make or break a sale.
	The E-Myth Real Estate Investor By Michael E. Gerber	Top investors Than Merrill and Paul Esajian team up with the incomparable Michael Gerber to explain how to create systems for real estate investing. It's all about finding the right process.
	Loopholes of Real Estate By Garrett Sutton, Esq.	Brilliant real estate lawyer Garrett Sutton pulls back the curtain and reveals the cool legal tricks and tools the rich use when investing in real estate.
Technology	*The Fourth Transformation* By Robert Scoble	Phones will be replaced by visual headsets, and virtual reality will dominate our lives! An exciting look at the enormous implications of new technology.
	Rise of the Robots: Technology and the Threat of a Jobless Future	We may soon reach a point where robots and artificial intelligence

191

	By Martin Ford	can do nearly all jobs. How will we prepare?
Great General Knowledge	*Stein on Writing: A Master Editor of Some of the Most Successful Writers of Our Century Shares His Craft Techniques and Strategies* By Sol Stein	Fantastic book on writing by one of the most famous editors. Easy to read and very useful if you write or create content.
	The Black Swan By Nassim Nicholas Taleb	From one of my favorite authors, *The Black Swan* will help you understand probability and how seemingly random events shape and transform the world. All his books are great.
	"Surely You're Joking, Mr. Feynman!": Adventures of a Curious Character By Richard P. Feynman	Hilarious and insightful book by a Nobel Prize winner in physics. Lessons in life and relationships.
	How Will You Measure Your Life? By Clayton M. Christensen	A leading economist and business expert tackles the meaning of life. A must-read for anyone wrestling with goals and priorities.
	Sapiens By Yuval Noah Harari	One of the most authoritative (and interesting) books about the history of mankind. One of the most recommended books by top professionals.
	The Slight Edge By	How to use small daily habits to your benefit.

| | Jeff Olson | The idea of spending two minutes each morning doing push-ups is a Slight Edge technique. |
| | *Being Mortal* By Atul Gawande | Exposes the plight of the elderly. It was one of the main inspirations for my company, Dignified Housing, Inc. A must-read for anyone growing older! |

Great new books are published all the time. I'll share my latest favorites on my LinkedIn page or my Alexa show, The Real Estate Flash.

Conferences and courses

The National Association of Realtors has some good online courses[41] in addition to their conferences. And state affiliates, such as The California Association of Realtors, also provide useful online classes.[42] Beyond the topic of real estate, colleges and universities, including Harvard[43], UCLA[44], and Stanford,[45] offer stimulating courses for folks of all ages and educational backgrounds who want to expand their horizons.

Reading, conferences, and continuing education keeps you sharp and current. It may seem daunting to fit classes and books into your already jam-packed days, but you need to invest in yourself. Your brain is your main asset; you need to nourish it.

Flash Briefings

Flash briefings are one of my favorite ways to stay up to date with the latest news. There are a lot of great flash briefings out there from leading real estate agents, marketing experts, and news sites. Learn about the various real estate shows and add them to your daily routine. It's an easy and fun way to keep up with the world of real estate.

If you have an Amazon Alexa device, you can check out my daily flash briefing, The Real Estate Flash. I also recommend Jason Frazier's show, Agent Marketer Flash.[46] He's a brilliant guy and knows the real estate and mortgage industries like the back of his hand. Jason is also a sought-after speaker and key influencer.

I'd encourage you to check out all the various real estate shows and add them to your daily routine. It's an easy and fun way to keep up with the world of real estate.

Mentorship

The new world of real estate is leaving behind its newest members.

Please find some time to mentor the new folks just starting out in the real estate industry. They need your help now, more than ever.

So many young people have dreams of making it in real estate only to have the harsh reality of the market crush their hopes. New real estate associates fail far too often. You can help them, you can teach them. You can give them a fighting chance to make it in this tough industry.

If your brokerage doesn't offer mentorship opportunities, check out the local chapter of your Board of Realtors. Most schools have established programs to help folks looking to mentor. And LinkedIn is experimenting with a career advice feature.[47] NAR offers some great community mentorship programs.[48]

Whichever path you choose, you'll feel great knowing that you're giving hope to folks just starting out in an exciting new world.

Interview with Kim Hughes, CEO of virtual assistant firm Kim Hughes & Co.

Gregory Charlop: Tell me a bit about you? How did you get into the real estate virtual assistant, VA, business?

Kim Hughes: My experience goes back to 1983. I always knew that I was going to go into real estate. I went to real estate school, college, and also worked in the real estate industry in Dallas. In Dallas, I was working with mortgage lenders and then went to work for some of the top real estate developers. After that, I went into commercial leasing and did consulting work. Then, I took time off to have a family. By the time I was ready to revisit the real estate world, the internet came about. I knew that I could do something with the internet involving real estate, and that's where the idea of a real estate virtual assistant started.

The real estate industry itself was still new to the world of technology, and the virtual assistant industry was also new. I was able to witness the merge of two worlds and was one of the first to determine that real estate agents needed help learning how to maneuver the technology being thrown at them.

At the time, there were only 25 to 50 "professional virtual assistants", and we all were trying to figure out how we could assist all industries. I was quickly becoming proficient in the area of technology and, because of my extensive knowledge of real estate, I decided to create a niche and work exclusively with real estate agents and offices. That's how the virtual assistant industry started, by finding that niche, determining what you're best fitted for, and making that your focus. That's how my business started.

I knew real estate, had the background, the education, and I knew what agents needed. I was one of those people who

Gregory Charlop

really hustled and got my name out there. I attended conventions, conferences, and because I was the only one doing it, real estate agents showed interest in my business. Michael Russer, Howard Brinton, Allen Hainge, are some of the top names in the industry at the time. They all came together and supported the real estate virtual assistant concept. It is because of the hard work, dedication to learning, and discovering what agents needed, that my expertise became invaluable, and I was able to build a business that is now going on 20 years.

The one thing that I have been very passionate about, over the past 20 years, is that "virtual assistance" is a great alternative for real estate agents. Agents need to be very aware that the experience the virtual assistant brings to the table is unique, because working in real estate is completely different than working with any other industry. If you think about it, real estate has its own language, rules, and laws. Every state is different, every brokerage is different, and every agent runs their business differently.

Virtual assistance allows for a great deal of flexibility. You may not need an assistant full-time or even part-time. You just may need assistance on special projects or to handle a specific area of your business. Agents need to be very aware of what that assistant can bring to the table for them. An agent should always know the experience background of the person they're bringing on as a professional virtual assistant—get references, interview them, and do their due diligence when hiring someone.

Gregory Charlop: Kim, many in our audience may not be familiar with virtual assistants. What is a real estate virtual assistant, and what types of things can they do?

Kim Hughes: A virtual assistant that specializes in real estate can do just about anything for an agent. An assistant can act as an agent's business manager by running the entire business for them or can just do one or two tasks. For example, an assistant can handle an agent's bookkeeping, build their website and manage it, market listings, work as a transaction coordinator, create your daily office procedures, create those systems that go with the daily business, and more.

A virtual assistant can help agents perform 99 percent of the details of handling a listing. They can make the phone calls, advertise, prepare the direct marketing, internet marketing, and input the listing into the MLS, with restrictions. There are restrictions on MLS, so I'm going to put a little asterisk by MLS. It depends on how your MLS is set up to give access to your virtual assistant. Agents would need to work that out. If you are thinking about hiring a virtual assistant, make sure you talk to your MLS if you want the assistant to have access, because there will probably be some paperwork, fees, etc.

Assistants can also do transaction management. Once a property goes under contract, they can take that transaction all the way to the closing table. Then, of course, if you are representing the buyer, the virtual assistant can help you make sure that you are updating the criteria, staying in touch with the buyer, and confirm that everything goes smoothly. In transaction management, you can have a transaction coordinator on both sides. Then, once the property closes, they can assist with a past client campaign.

Connecting with past clients is very important and is one of the things I encourage my agents to do. I started out as a virtual assistant and have built my company from there. I now have 10 virtual assistants who work with me, enabling me to branch out in the area of real estate coaching. A lot of virtual assistants should be able to help you think outside the box. When you interview a virtual assistant, I would ask them, "Well, what skills do you have to help me grow my business, or help me be more organized, or help give me more time in my day?" They should be an asset to you. A lot of virtual assistants who excel in their niche will bring ideas to the agents. Our philosophy is that the agent doesn't need to be spending time researching all the greatest things that are out there. The agent needs somebody to tell them these ideas, and then they can decide if it's something that's going to work for them or not. That's what we do. We're not just virtual assistants. We take it to another level.

The big thing in the industry today is that agents need help with all aspects of their business. Some of the key areas we are asked to assist with are marketing listings, transaction management, and client relationships. A virtual assistant is not somebody who's going to do lead generation. I don't do that. My company does not do that. I believe that if an agent gets a lead, they should be the one calling that lead. It provides them an opportunity to connect and capture that lead.

In the years that I've been doing this, I have clients who have been with me for over 18 years and others who have been with me two years or less. Everybody's a little bit different. The main thing is to make sure that your virtual assistant can help you in the areas that you need help with.

Here are some tips before you start looking for a virtual assistant. First, I highly recommend that you sit down and make a list of everything that you feel you do not have time to do, don't want to do, or don't know how to do. Then, look at that list, and pick the top three to five things that take you away from doing what you enjoy. Now you've got a good idea of what you need help with, and you can be very specific with that virtual assistant. Then, that virtual assistant will be able to say, "Yes, I can help you with that," or, "No, I can't help you with that." That way, you have an idea of where you need help and who can take over and run that business for you.

Gregory Charlop: Kim, what's the difference between a licensed and an unlicensed virtual assistant, and what can each of them do?

Kim Hughes: It's really not relevant, but a licensed assistant can have more conversations with the agent's clients and can even show a property if they're local. They can negotiate on a contract if the agent wants them to. Those are a couple of things that are beneficial but not necessary. An unlicensed assistant is not going to be able to negotiate or relay things to the seller/buyer that must be legally explained by someone who is licensed. That's why I recommend, when looking for a virtual assistant, you make sure that they know and understand real estate. I have seen agents go out and hire virtual assistants at a very low cost because they thought, "Well, I can get the same quality work." You can't do that. You get what you pay for, basically. Hiring someone who doesn't know what they are and are not legally capable of doing can get you in a lot of trouble.

An agent I knew hired somebody who was not licensed and didn't really understand the real estate industry. That assistant went outside the scope of what they were able to say. They answered a question that should've been directed back to the agent, and the client sued the agent because of it. As an agent, you don't want to be put in that situation. So, when looking for an assistant, I would recommend starting with ones who have experience in the real estate industry. I don't want to talk about pricing but be aware that it's not going to be your minimum wage person. If you want somebody who really has a vested interest in an agent's business as a virtual assistant, you're going to have to pay for it. You're paying for the knowledge, the experience. You need to trust them to be your right-hand person and look out for you. They're going to be more than just a virtual assistant.

Gregory Charlop: You mentioned pricing, so I'd like to ask you a bit about that. Obviously, without mentioning specific prices, how do real estate VAs typically charge? Is it usually by the hour, by the project, by the month?

Kim Hughes: It really depends on what you have your virtual assistant handling. For example, if you need a virtual assistant to do marketing for your listings, write the content, label the photos, put it on social media, blog it, do the mail outs, do the whole 10 yards. That could be a package, which is a flat rate fee, or it could be by the hour. It really just depends on the virtual assistant.

If you want someone to create systems for your business, implement those systems, create drip mail campaigns, help you set up your CRM, and other things that are outside of the box, then you're probably going to pay an hourly rate for that. This area differs greatly from agent to agent, so there's no way to streamline it as a package. So, more than likely it would be an hourly rate.

When you talk about transaction management, that is a flat rate fee. You're doing the same thing for every transaction. It's just a repetitive thing, but, at the same time, a good transaction coordinator will take the ball and go with it. They're going to say to the agent, "The only time you need to step into this transaction is when there's a negotiation." Like I said, it just really depends on what your needs are. Your virtual assistant can help you maneuver through all of that when you start interviewing.

Gregory Charlop: Do the rules governing virtual assistants and what they're allowed to do vary state by state? Are virtual assistants allowed to be used in all states?

Kim Hughes: I have clients all over the United States and in other countries. As long as you understand what the laws are and what the rules are for that state or that country, then you're okay to do anything for that agent within those laws or those guidelines. If an assistant is going to offer to work in a specific state or country, they should've already researched what they can and can't do in that state, or even for that brokerage. Some brokerages and franchises have rules about working with virtual assistants. You have to know what those guidelines are. The agent should know what the assistant can do, but the virtual assistant should know more.

Gregory Charlop: Are virtual assistants covered by insurance? Do they have their own insurance, or are they covered by the agent's insurance? How does that work?

Kim Hughes: I can't speak for other virtual assistants, but I'm insured. I would think any business owner would have the E&O insurance. This is where it gets a little tricky working with virtual assistants. I would say 99.9 percent would have a home office. This is not putting anybody down. It's just common sense. A lot of people in a lot of industries—not just virtual assistants—need to make sure that they know what they're doing in their business. Are they a categorized business? My company is an LLC. I have insurance, an attorney, a CPA; therefore, I run a business.

A lot of virtual assistants don't make that investment because they don't really see the need or can't afford it. It takes money to run a business. When I first started, I was doing it just because I didn't know what else to do. As I grew, I realized there were certain things that I did need. I was very lucky that I had people who advised me to get an attorney, insurance, and a CPA. My business is run as a true business, but I work from home.

Gregory Charlop: What type of real estate agent do you envision using a virtual assistant? Would it be somebody who's just starting out, learning the ropes, who has very little business? Or would it be someone who's very busy, who has little free time?

Kim Hughes: That's a really good question, because they're all over the board. It would be beneficial to real estate agents who were just getting their license and coming out of the gate. A good virtual assistant would be able to help them set up their business correctly and then help them manage it. Even though the new agent may not have the budget, they could say, "Well, I can afford X amount per week to get this person to help me get my business started or help me market my business." That would be the perfect solution for a new agent, but we all know they may not be able to afford it because everybody works on commissions. So you've got to keep that in mind.

I have agents who are brand new that come to me. I have agents that have been in the business 10 years who realize that they can't do it all themselves, and they need somebody to help them. Agents may have lost an assistant, and now they're looking at the virtual assistant because it just makes more sense. I have agents who have been in the business 40 years or more and have come to me in a different phase of their career. I have agents all over the spectrum. I have clients that have very large teams, and then I have some agents that have maybe one or two on their team. Some brokers bring me on as the virtual assistant, and then offer the services to their agents. There's not just one particular mold of what I have as a client or what would make the perfect client.

Gregory Charlop: That was actually a perfect segue to my next question: are virtual assistants typically hired by individual agents, or are they hired by a real estate firm, brokerage, or a larger company?

Kim Hughes: I would say 97 percent are hired by a single agent. An agent may work with a franchise or have their own brokerage. It is unusual for a brokerage to hire a virtual assistant to work with all the agents on the team or in their office. To give you an example, I have a team of seven and the agent works for a franchise. He offers transaction management to his team. He encourages his team to give all their transactions to the transaction coordinator. Then the agent pays for that service because he understands that having someone handle those transactions allows the agents to focus on other areas of their business. This agent pays for all of the transactions, and that's not uncommon.

Another client that has a large brokerage with multiple offices and over 100 agents. He offers the transaction coordination services to all the agents, but the agents are responsible for paying me. He does provide an incentive. His top three agents can use me for a set number of hours per month on whatever they need, but they've got to be in those top three. Those top three could change every month, or it may be the same people all year long. It just depends. It is an incentive and a reward to those agents to be able to use me for that service.

Gregory Charlop: I believe that there is a trend for real estate agents, particularly top agents, to move away from high price brokerages with high fees towards either discount real estate firms or online brokerages. Do you feel that real estate virtual assistants will make it easier for these types of agents to move away from the larger high price firms to function more independently?

Kim Hughes: Yes, I'm already seeing that. The great thing is that the agents are going to be able to keep more of their commission, they're going to be able to have more control over what they want to do with their business, and they're not tied into the franchises. The biggest problem is that agents are hesitant to make that change because some think the only reason they're being hired as the listing agent or as a buyer agent is because of the franchise name. That's not true. I tell all my agents: you're being hired because of who you are and what you bring to the table. A buyer/seller does not care what your brokerage is or who your franchise is. They care about what you're going to do for them. Being part of a brokerage can be a plus or a minus. Home buyers and home sellers care about who the agent is and what that agent is bringing to the table.

Gregory Charlop: I completely agree that virtual assistants may give agents the opportunity to be more independent and strike out on their own—particularly successful agents, because they can probably meet a lot of their own transaction needs and support needs without being part of a large agency.

Kim Hughes: Right. I do see that agents are a little nervous about making a transition because they are used to having certain things provided to them through their brokerage. I know it's bold to say this, but you're a real estate agent. You are a community leader. You need to put your big boy pants on and act like one. You need to have a business that runs successfully in the background.

As you know, we live in a world that is self-serving. One of the things I tell agents today is: It's hard to find good customer service anywhere. As a real estate agent, you're in a customer service industry, so you need to make sure that you're servicing your clients all the way. When you get a listing, you need to be able to say, "I am with you till the end, until we close this property, and then I'm going to still be with you." It's all about creating that customer service and building that client connection.

Agents now have to rethink old school strategies. You don't need to pay a lot of money for leads. If you're a good agent, you already have leads in your database. You need to rethink how you work those leads and reconnect with those leads. You need to look at your past clients and nurture them because they are the ones who have already done business with you. They are the ones who are going to come back to you to buy and sell again, and they're going to be the ones to refer business to you. I would rather see an agent spend $500 a month on nurturing their past clients than spending $2,000 chasing leads that may never convert. If you are already an established real estate agent, then you have all you need in your database.

A new agent wouldn't need to pay for those leads either because what they need to do is get out there and do the leg work, go door to door, make those phone calls, meet their neighbors. What friends do you have? What family? It really is a sore topic when I talk to agents and hear that they're paying $2,000 or $3,000 a month for leads, and they can't even convert them. I'm a big advocate of that. A lot of agents get really nervous; they're like, "Well, if I leave this brokerage, I won't get the leads." You don't need those leads. What you need to do is learn how to do real estate the way it's supposed to be done. And don't rely on somebody to give you a lead. That's just my personal opinion.

Gregory Charlop: How do you think real estate agents should be using social media?

Kim Hughes: I am so glad you asked that because I see so many agents just using it to post their listings. I don't care if you live in a town of 1,000 or a town of two million, as a real estate agent you are viewed as the community. As a real estate agent, you should be aware of everything that goes on in your community, and you should be talking about what's going on in your community. You should support your community. Agents are missing out on a huge advantage by not using social media that way.

On Facebook you should have a business page. Your business page should be everything about real estate but also everything about your community. Meaning, talk about the upcoming events for that weekend or for that month. Talk about your local businesses and what's going on in the schools, football games, baseball games, swim meets, hockey games, etc. If there's a 5K run for breast cancer, talk about it. If there is a new restaurant, you don't want to talk about the franchise restaurants, but you want to talk about the locally-owned ones. These are your neighbors and your friends who run these businesses in your town. Talk about them and get to know them. Talk about how they provide a service to the community and, in return, they're going to do the same thing for you.

When you focus on what's going on, it really does make a big difference. People gravitate to what other people are talking about in the community. If something bad happens in your community, be aware of it. Talk about it, acknowledge it, and focus on what you going to do to help. If something positive happens, recognize it, talk about it, and express how you participated in that. Offer to help people. One of my agents saw homes in her community that were run down, and the yards were not well cared for. Of course, that's going to bring the market value down in that neighborhood, right? She was able to approach the people who live in that house and find out why they are not able to take care of their yard, or why their garage needs to be painted, etc., and began to ask how she could help them.

Maybe the person in that home is an elderly woman who does not have anybody to help her. That could be where you, as an agent, could help her and get involved with the garden club or get a landscaper to help her. That will help bring the property values in that neighborhood up, plus the neighbors of that home are going to see that. This person actually goes to homes and asks them, "What can I do to help you with your yard? I would love to do that."

When you ask, "What can I do to help you?" you might be surprised at how much help you get from the neighbors and community. These are little things that agents need to be doing and then could talk about on social media.

Instagram is more visual, so you don't really need to go there to develop relationships. You're going to Instagram to bring awareness. That's where you would do motivation. Or take pictures of your community and put them on there. Your social media, depending on what it is, needs to be more about what's going on in your community and not all about what you're doing. You're a community leader, so talk about your community. LinkedIn is a totally different breed. It's a business to business platform. A real estate agent should be on LinkedIn connecting with local employers and with the communities around them; really get to know those people.

Interview with Tamir Poleg, the founder of Real

Gregory Charlop: Can you tell us about Real? What is Real, and how does it work?

Tamir Poleg: Real is defined as a technology-powered real estate brokerage. The idea behind it is to provide an alternative to the traditional brokerage by providing a lot of value to real estate agents through technology and charging a lower cost. We looked at the market and realized that brokers today are failing at providing value to their agents. The market has changed a lot. Consumers need a different kind of service, but brokers (mainly) and agents in addition, are not really providing the value that the market needs. We tried to understand what an agent goes through every day, from the moment they wake up in the morning until they go to sleep at night. We thought, "Okay. How can we automate all of that? How can we make agents' lives better, both professionally and personally?"

We also realized that agents are in a situation unlike other industries. Regulators required agents to work under the license of a broker. The vast majority of agents are independent contractors, so they do not enjoy the benefits of being employed. On the other hand, they do not really have the freedom of running their business the way they want to because they have a boss, the broker. We wanted to change that. We want to help them run their business the way they want to while providing everything they need to be successful. We think that traditional brokers—and maybe franchises—will not be around in about 10 years. We are offering a technology platform with better service at a lower cost.

Gregory Charlop: Do you have any physical locations or offices?

Tamir Poleg: No. We thought about that at the beginning, but we understood that, in the past, physical locations were one of the brokers' assets. Everything happened around the office: if you as a buyer or seller needed information, you had to come to the office; if you wanted to sign a paper, you had to come to the office. Everything was happening around the office and fax machines. There were no emails, no smartphones. But as technology progressed, the office became more of a liability than an asset to the brokers. When we looked at it, we decided that it doesn't really make sense for us to open offices everywhere. Instead, we can take those savings and give it to our agents by charging a lower split. This is what we decided to do.

Gregory Charlop: When you say the office became a liability to the broker, do you mean that the office became a fixed cost that the broker had to cover, and then they have to make that up by charging the agents more?

Tamir Poleg: Exactly. If you ask brokers about their expenses, about 50 percent of the expenses go to either rent or maintaining the physical space. It doesn't make sense to spend so much money on physical locations because customers do not need it anymore. Nobody wants to drive to visit your fancy or not-so-fancy office. On the other hand, a lot of people also thought: "Hey, the office provides me the opportunity to create social relationships with other agents and to engage." But I think the technology demonstrated that you don't need to be physically close to somebody to feel close. You look at Facebook and other social media. They provide you the opportunity of creating relationships without being physically close to somebody. I think technology today is ripe enough to provide you an alternative to a physical location when it comes to social engagement and productivity.

Gregory Charlop: If you don't have a physical location, a corner location on a busy street, how would customers find your agents? In other words, how do your agents acquire new customers?

Tamir Poleg: Studies show that about 90 percent of home buyers and home sellers today are starting their process online. To market yourself, you have to have some online presence. We thought about it quite a lot and asked ourselves, "Okay. How do we help our agents obtain more clients and have an offline aspect to it?" You need to have the door hangers and flyers and brochures—all those physical things. But I think we can provide an edge with an online presence and digital marketing. Agents do not know how to spend money online, they don't know how to measure ROI. Today, we also cover the offline aspect. So, if someone wants to order business cards, yard signs, brochures, or anything else, they do it through our app.

We also cover the online aspects of it. Agents can define how much they want to spend online every month, and we actually spend it for them. We optimize it for them. We help them create business pages on Facebook. At the end of the day, agents are not digital marketers. We decided that we will do it for our agents instead of them paying somebody else. I think that the offline aspect of the business will gradually decrease and the online importance will only increase.

Gregory Charlop: Do you think that most home buyers or home sellers today care much about what real estate company their salesperson works for?

Tamir Poleg: I think in most states they do not care at all. People don't care who your broker is; they care about you, the agent. They want to know that you helped a friend buy a home. They want to know you through social engagement. They want to receive content from you. They want to see your face on yard signs. This is how people evaluate an agent, not through who the broker is. Obviously, there are exceptions, maybe in the high-end market, maybe in New York, but in average America, people couldn't care less who your broker is.

Gregory Charlop: What type of real estate agents are most likely to work for an internet real estate firm? In other words, do you expect it to be more of the top, already successful agents who have large client bases looking to save commission? Or do you think it will be newer agents who like technology and are just trying to keep their startup costs low?

Tamir Poleg: I think that everybody would be attracted to it. It would be a mistake to think that in 10 years the market is going to look the same as it looked 10 years ago. The moment agents understand that, they would start asking themselves, "Okay. How do I adapt my own business to how the market is going to look in five years? In 10 years?"

There's a long food chain. The consumer pays a commission to an agent, then the agent has to pay a broker, and then the broker often has to pay a franchise. Today, consumers are telling us that they do want the experience of working with an agent, but they want it at a lower cost.

I would bet that somebody along the way would have to give up something. I think that agents are not going away, brokers are not going away. I think that franchisors will need to disappear at some point because consumers are requesting a price reduction, and the agents and brokers wouldn't be able to sustain the franchise cost.

The best-producing agents are feeling fine where they are. They probably have good terms with their brokers, and they're afraid of making any serious change in their business. So, at this moment, the top producers are not likely to join a technology-powered real estate brokerage. I think that beginners are likely to join a company that can train them hands-on for the first year or so. Anyone in the middle would be attracted to a model like ours. I can tell you that the average age of a Real agent is 41, and that's way below the national average. I would say, anyone who's been practicing real estate for about a year knows what they're doing. They know how to write a contract, how to engage with clients. They have some deal flow. And they understand that they're paying their brokers too much and they make too little. They understand the market is changing, and they need to be more responsive and take care of their online presence. Those folks would be attracted to a brokerage like ours.

CHAPTER 4: VIRTUAL ASSISTANTS AND CHATBOTS

Use these powerful tools to engage clients, win business, and improve your quality of life

Real estate is all about seizing the moment. Act fast and sign that prospect. Take too long, and that commission check will land in your competitor's pocket.

Beyond the competition, you need to respond immediately to catch a potential prospect when they're in the right frame of mind: when they're thinking about real estate. Darren Johnson, CEO of lead-generation firm AgentZip, said they send leads to agents in *under 2 seconds*. He recommends that agents contact the leads immediately. Delay, and the prospect will switch gears. They'll move on from thinking about houses and start searching for lunch, dreaming about shoes, or watching a movie. You need to engage the prospect at the exact moment they're thinking about real estate.

But, how can you be everywhere all at once?

Even more vexing, how can you be everywhere 24/7 and still maintain a life, see your family, exercise, eat, read, and sleep?

The short answer is, you need a team. Welcome to the world of virtual assistants and chatbots. With these remarkable virtual tools, you'll accomplish more, follow up on leads immediately, and make your life easier—all while spending less time and money. These tools can help you do it all:

- Respond to prospects the second they message you, dramatically improving the probability they'll hire you as their agent. Most people hire the first agent they interview.[49] You want to be that first agent.

- Chatbots will take all the customer's info and can even start their home search, impressing your prospect.

- Chatbots will screen out prospects who don't match your market segment.

- Chatbots are ALWAYS on the job! They don't get sick, take vacations, or hit the bars on Friday night.

- Virtual assistants can do almost any task for your real estate business.[50]

- VAs will do the stuff you don't want to do.

- Busy now? Add some VAs to your team. Slowing down? Reduce or eliminate your VAs. They're flexible!

- Don't know how to edit videos, use the newest CRM, or update your website? Your VA does! It's easy to find a VA to do or teach almost any skill.

How do they work? They allow you to be in more than one place at a time!

Imagine this. It's a Monday morning and you are an office of one. James, a prospective buyer, visits your website and is excited about that pricey home you're selling downtown. Your chatbot screens him, reviews your calendar, and makes an appointment for you and James to meet at the property at noon. At the same time, Isabella, a prospective seller discovers your optimized Facebook page and wants to meet you. Your bot screens her and schedules tea with her at 4 pm.

Meanwhile, your virtual assistants are preparing documents, arranging pest inspections, and hounding the appraiser to finally deliver that report you requested last week.

And you? You're enjoying breakfast and a leisurely cup of coffee at home with your family. Life is good.

YOUR ASSISTANTS DO THE WORK SO YOU DON'T HAVE TO

- SCREENS PROSPECTS
- MAINTAINS YOUR SOCIAL MEDIA ACCOUNTS
- FILES PAPERWORK
- HOUNDS CONTRACTORS

CHATBOT/VA → YOU

Even with a one-person shop, you can get everything done, convert more leads with quick responses, and still have time to read bedtime stories to your kids—thanks to your friendly virtual assistants and chatbots. The trick is creative outsourcing.

What are virtual assistants?

Virtual assistants (VAs) are licensed or unlicensed professionals who work remotely. They work from their home or in a large office, often in other countries. Those folks can handle all kinds of tasks including internet marketing, lead generation, CRM and database management, office automation, transaction coordination, filing paperwork with the MLS, and hounding those pesky contractors.

You'll be surprised by all of the stuff they can do. Not only can VAs perform routine tasks that you don't like, but they can teach you stuff you never knew. For example, you can hire a VA to set up and maintain your Facebook business page, even if you have no knowledge of Facebook. They can help move you off of your old spreadsheet and onto a much more useful CRM. In fact, you can find a VA to handle almost any task—no matter how technical.

I asked Kim Hughes, CEO of virtual assistant firm Kim Hughes & Company, what a VA can do. She said, "A virtual assistant that specializes in real estate can do just about anything for an agent. An assistant can act as an agent's business manager by running the entire business for them or can just do one or two tasks. For example, an assistant can handle an agent's bookkeeping, build their website and manage it, market listings, work as a transaction coordinator, create your daily office procedures, create those systems that go with the daily business, and more.

A virtual assistant can help agents perform 99 percent of the details of handling a listing. They can make the phone calls, advertise, prepare the direct marketing, internet marketing, and input the listing into the MLS, with restrictions."

Why should you waste your time doing that kind of stuff? Focus your attention on the important tasks that only you can do, like negotiating deals and meeting new clients. Every minute you spend doing routine tasks that can be outsourced is a minute you're not developing your business, sleeping, spending time with family, or exercising. Focus on the important stuff!

In Gary Keller's classic book *The ONE Thing*, we learn the importance of concentrating on one major task or priority. When we let other stuff get in the way, we become distracted and do a crummy job at everything. Multi-tasking ain't good! Let other folks do the mundane work so you can focus on your ONE thing: closing deals and signing new clients (okay, that's two things).

Another great benefit of working with a well-trained VA is that you can learn valuable new skills. Not sure how to market on Facebook? Your VA knows how and can show you. Don't know how to set up a CRM? Your VA knows how and can teach you. VAs offer a great way to learn new skills and get stuff done.

Could you just hire an in-person assistant to take care of this work? Sure, but get ready to pay for it. It costs a lot more to hire staff than a VA.[51] If you have your own staff, you have to worry about all the rules and regulations that come with having employees, like unemployment insurance, workman's comp, etc. With a VA, you don't have to deal with all those headaches. Another advantage: VAs tend to be more flexible than someone you'd hire for your staff. You can use them as needs arise and not worry about them when things are quiet.

Virtual assistants can help provide your business some protection from the unexpected. According to Daniel Ramsey, CEO of top virtual assistant firm MyOutDesk, "losing one person on your team can create mass chaos. Stability becomes the winner of the day. A lot of our folks will be a backup to the transaction coordinator. Or, the listing coordinator will be a virtual assistant, and the operations manager will be somebody who's physically in the office, so you have some redundancy. That way, if somebody's out sick, their business continues. If somebody needs a vacation, he or she can actually go on a vacation. So, at some stage, the stability of having two people capable of doing one job becomes critical." The full interview with Ramsey appears here.

Finding a VA isn't too difficult. In fact, there are several companies that will help you find and hire just the right VA for your needs.

Kim Hughes has some advice if you're considering hiring a VA: "Here are some tips before you start looking for a virtual assistant. First, I highly recommend that you sit down and make a list of everything that you feel you do not have time to do, don't want to do, or don't know how to do. Then, look at that list, and pick the top three to five things that take you away from doing what you enjoy. Now you've got a good idea of what you need help with, and you can be very specific with that virtual assistant. Then, that virtual assistant will be able to say, "Yes, I can help you with that," or, "No, I can't help you with that." That way, you have an idea of where you need help and who can take over and run that business for you."

Chatbots

Nearly three out of every four sales go to the first agent interviewed.[52] You want that agent to be you. Thankfully, you can make that happen with chatbots.

Chatbots are a great automated tool to decrease your work and impress your clients. They're easy to set up and will win you new business. Chatbots are computer programs that utilize artificial intelligence and are designed to engage customers. Many are specifically made for real estate. They immediately respond to prospects, answer questions, screen prospects, and promote your brand.

Here's how they work. Imagine that a potential client visits your website or Facebook page and has a few questions. The prospect asks questions and receives immediate replies. There's no waiting, no delays. The chatbot will answer questions, book appointments, and collect the prospect's information—all without you lifting a finger.

Who do you think prospects are more likely to hire? Someone who is able to answer their questions immediately, or someone they have to wait hours to hear back from? If you're taking hours to reply, prospects are going to just hop over to your competitors who are faster than you are. But, if you can engage these people early, you will have tons of new business.[53]

Dave Phillips, the VP if industry relations with Realtor.com and interviewed elsewhere in this book, says chatbots are one of the top technologies that real estate agents should be using, but aren't. Why not put these automated geniuses to work for you?

Thankfully, there are many innovative chatbot companies competing for your business. Kaydoh and HelloAlex are leading the pack.

Michael Lam, CEO of Kaydoh, discussed the value of chatbots, as part of a longer interview. "The first person to meet a lead generally wins. Prospects usually only interview one agent. So, using a chatbot to deliver quick information to the prospects is paramount. With a CMA, which is a traditional way of lead capturing on a website, prospects put in their address, and then they wait—up to 24 hours—to get a report back through email. And then there is generally no follow up. That person is a lead that the agent should be aware of and immediately speak with that individual. You can use a chatbot to generate the report and deliver it directly to the person via SMS."

"A great thing about a chatbot," according to Lam, "is it's an extension of the agent. It's conversational rather than robotic. The conversation has emojis in it. It's designed to be more natural. Just like you and I would message each other on a messaging app, the chatbot does something very similar, but it captures information while having a conversation. You could have thousands of people speaking to a chatbot, so you, as a salesperson, do not need to take that initial call. The chatbot can handle that initial interaction, including the prequalification, an automated alert, and scheduling."

Natural Language and the future of client engagement

Natural Language Processing (NLP) is a form of artificial intelligence that deals with how computers and humans interact. The goal of NLP is for people to communicate with computers using regular speech, rather than computer code. Chatbots are a great example of NLP at work.

You are starting to see this technology all over the web as the friendly computer-generated bot. While you're shopping for shoes, it offers to help you find the right sandals. Some customers seem to prefer chatting with a robot rather than searching themselves or digging through the FAQs to answer their questions. The interactions feel more natural to users, even if they are chatting with a computer!

As NLP technology improves, chatbots will sound more and more like a real person. They'll increasingly understand idioms, slang, incorrect grammar, and irrelevant comments. The conversation between client and chatbot will feel more and more like texting a friend.

Enhanced chatbot technology will benefit savvy real estate agents and real estate brokerages. Many of these improvements will appear in the background and will make the user experience more seamless without the real estate agent needing to upgrade software. In other words, your chatbots will get better and better, so start using them now!

NLP isn't limited to texting and online messages. New products like Google Duplex are making waves with the spoken word. When we talk to Alexa, Siri, or the Google Assistant, we are speaking to a computer using NLP. We will increasingly turn to these tools to carry out our daily tasks, including complex projects like making appointments and following up with contractors.

In a sense, NLP can become a truly "virtual" assistant. As the technology improves, NLP programs will do more and more of what a human VA does today. They will ultimately be faster and less expensive than VAs. Having said that, I still recommend using human VAs for now. They save you time, teach you new skills, and act as your second (virtual) pair of hands for complex tasks.

We cover NLP and AI in more detail in the Emerging Technology chapter of this book.

Cut the cord

Can you put a price on freedom? If you're smart about using VAs and chatbots, freedom is just around the corner.

Let's face it, you want to cut the cord. You want to leave the office and work entirely from home on your schedule. But, you're afraid to leave those confining four walls because you need to interact with your assistants and coordinators. Perhaps you need to go to work to get up to speed about the latest CRM or marketing tool.

Now, you can do all that from home in ways you never could before. You can kiss the office and all its associated costs goodbye.

Think about it. You hire a team of VAs that takes care of all of your back-office work. They manage your paperwork, expenses, and marketing. On top of that, they know about all the newest techniques better than your office staff—and they can teach you!

Your army of chatbots is handling all your inbound traffic, eliminating the need for a receptionist of any kind. They boost your lead conversion and manage your daily schedule.

There you have it. Everything you need to work autonomously—except for the broker—is sitting right there in your smartphone. You are truly your own one-person shop, but with all the amenities and support you expect from a large company. You pay less and have total control.

If you so choose, you could take all this virtual support and eliminate the overhead. Armed with a team of chatbots and VAs, it might make more sense for you to leave a larger traditional brokerage and switch to a more bare-bones operation with lower fees.

If you own or run a traditional brokerage with high fees, you need to consider how chatbots and VAs will impact your business model. You will find it increasingly difficult to compete with minimalist brokerages since most salespeople won't need you for their routine administrative support. We cover more tips about how your company can remain competitive in the Brokers and Executives chapter.

Gregory Charlop

Interview with Daniel Ramsey, CEO and co-founder of MyOutDesk

Gregory Charlop: Daniel, what sorts of services might a real estate agent ask of a virtual assistant?

Daniel Ramsey: My favorite is operations. The highest and best use for a virtual assistant is doing all of the administrative stuff that, 1) you don't like doing, 2) you're probably not that good at, 3) it doesn't pay the most. So, you're not good, you don't have time to do it, it doesn't pay the most, and that means you should outsource it. Hands down, that is the barometer. If you don't like it, if you're not good at it, and if it's under $10, why would you ever do it?

We have this thing called the Seven Figure Agent Map, which is our brainchild to take a real estate agent from where they are today to where they want to be. Everybody wants growth. Everybody wants to make more money, make a bigger impact on the world. What we do here is we'll snapshot where you are today and try to find out what you're spending the most time on. So, that could be operations, or bookkeeping, or transaction coordinating. It could be marketing all of your listings or your potential buyers or sellers. It could be generating online leads. There's a whole list of everything that's not meeting a client, negotiating a deal, and closing a transaction. You're the only one who can make the relationships, close the deals, and negotiate contracts. That's what you're basically paid to do. Everything else should be done virtually.

Gregory Charlop: Can you give some examples of specific tasks that the assistant might do? Maybe specific marketing tasks, or bookkeeping, or setting up CRMs, or following up with clients or contractors?

Daniel Ramsey: All of that! So, here's what's awesome: 70 percent of all real estate is done by referral. That's the number.

It's been tracked over the last 30, 40 years. It's by referral. And, how you generate those referrals is key to what makes a successful real estate broker versus a non-successful one. There's a lot of work in that. Creating a CRM, creating a follow-up campaign, calling them just once a quarter to thank them for their referrals or their business, creating micro events where you invite everybody to coffee and give them high fives and hugs. Tracking their anniversaries. I mean, all that is just work.

Let's say you're closing 50-75 deals every year. Year three you can't keep up and, also, continue to try to grow your business. The smartest folks in the business go, "What's my highest and best use of time? And, what's my hourly rate?" because your hourly rate is the barometer. So, when we do that Seven Figure Agent Map, we'll outline everything that you do, and then what's dollar productive and what's non-dollar productive. So, non-dollar productive: creating a flyer for a listing, inputting it to MLS. Or, sending an email out to your entire database to say, "This listing is coming soon," putting an ad on Facebook, creating the file and transaction coordinating software, creating the file within all of your QuickBooks and all of the files that you have to do to get paid at the end of the transaction.

All of those things are just not dollar productive. If it's not dollar productive, you shouldn't be doing it.

Gregory Charlop: I completely agree with you. I try to outsource everything I don't need to do as well, because, as you said, the only thing you don't have is time. So, you don't want to waste time doing things you don't do well. People are better than you are at certain things, just let them do it. So, I'm on board. Actually, the book *"The 4-Hour Work Week"* first inspired me on this concept.

Daniel Ramsey: *"The World is Flat"* is another excellent book about how borders are melting, and the opportunity to get skilled people anywhere in the world.

Gregory Charlop: What's the difference between a licensed and unlicensed assistant? What can each do to help out a real estate agent?

Daniel Ramsey: If you're prospecting, certain states have passed laws prohibiting non-licensed people. Texas is a great example. You cannot have a conversation about a home unless you have a license. So, in those states, our virtual assistants are doing a lot of warm calls. Meaning, the calls are to people who are already currently clients, or clients who requested information from that company. Or if somebody calls into the office, they're just transferring to a licensed person or scheduling appointments. So, you have to be careful about what the laws are in your particular state.

That being said, typically if somebody requests information about a home, it's okay for an unlicensed person to call, set up an appointment, answer their questions, and see if they need to meet with a licensed real estate agent or broker.

Gregory Charlop: Say I'm a real estate agent and I'm considering using a virtual assistant, but I don't know the rules in my state, because I've never used one before. How would the assistant know the rules? Is that something that your company and virtual assistant companies would tell them? Or, should the agent research that on their own?

Daniel Ramsey: In my area, there's a local association. You call their legal hotline and just ask, "What can I do with a licensed person versus a non-licensed person?" The reality is if you're in a state that prohibits, like Texas, we have a ton of people who are using virtual assistants for transaction coordination, listing coordination, social media and Facebook stuff. It's pretty incredible the number of tasks that we have to do. I think the standard now is there are over 160 individual tasks every time you list a property. 160. I mean, imagine that? There are systems that automate a lot of those things. But, some just cannot be automated, right?

Gregory Charlop: How can real estate agents keep data and trade secrets safe when using a virtual assistant? What happens if the assistant makes a mistake, or if the agent gets sued on a task involving a virtual assistant?

Daniel Ramsey: I'll start with how we protect our clients. 1) We do an FBI grade background check. It is massively important that it be done in the country where you're hiring a virtual assistant.

So, within MyOutDesk, we're doing all those checks, as well as doing an introduction, "This is what real estate is. This is how you're successful. This is what the expectation is from the client." So, we're doing all this upfront stuff, as well as just checking to make sure that the assistants have high-quality internet, a computer that works, headsets, and a video.

Now, on the client side, we also have expectations. Meaning, you need to train your virtual assistants. When most folks encountered a problem, it was because there wasn't training, there wasn't a process and procedure, and the virtual assistant didn't know what to do. In the beginning stage, what we call our launch or nesting period, it's 90 days. You should not let your virtual assistant do something that could get you in trouble. So, you should be reviewing all files before they go out. There should be a licensee's brain on that file before it gets executed and delivered to the other side.

The 90 days of training are the biggest determinant of success for a virtual assistant. Most agents are like, "Well, I'm too busy to do that." And we say, "Okay, great. Then, you shouldn't be a client of ours." Because, without that, there's just not going to be success. You must set expectations, create a training process, and make sure the person gets all the tools necessary to be successful.

The responsibility of a leader is to create a system and process where there are checks and double checks, especially in mission-critical things like contracts, execution, and closing files. So, you have to create that process and system. If, for some reason, there is an issue, you're E&O will cover them. Unfortunately, we don't cover it in our insurance, because we don't have any control.

So, it's essential that you have E&O, that you make sure that you're controlling the outcomes on the mission-critical things, and that you're nesting ... That 90-day nesting period is super important. Most of our failures, like if a client hires us and says, "Hey, this is hard," or, "It's not working," come in that first 90 days. We coach people through that. You get past that 90 days, and you're golden.

Gregory Charlop: You would have to do more or less the same thing if you hired someone in your office. You'd have to train them as well.

Daniel Ramsey: We constantly get people who call us and say, "Look. I need to hire somebody, but I'm in LA. I can't find somebody for under $70,000 a year." We're around $20,000 a year. So, they say, "But, I don't want to train them." I'm like, "Well, you're getting somebody at 20 grand a year versus the $70,000 that you're going to pay for somebody who also has no experience, but they just happen to be local."

If you're reading this book and you're considering making this move, there are two places for you to kill it or get crushed. Those two places are choosing the right person, and then onboarding them correctly in the first 90 days. That's it. We've done this 4,000 times, and every single time I can typically tie it back to one of those two things.

Gregory Charlop: When a real estate agent hires someone through you, do they keep working with the same person or do they cycle through different people?

Daniel Ramsey: Our business is a one-to-one model. So, if you're a broker or an agent and you need leverage, and you've identified the things that you should not be doing, or you don't like doing, or isn't the highest and best use of your time, we'll group them into functional areas. You have sales, marketing, and operations. Those are the three functional areas that we support as a company.

Once we group those tasks, we'll go after your outcomes. Typically, sales are more listings. Typically, marketing is getting more eyeballs on your listings. And operations is doing all of the paperwork required to get paid. Those are the three things. It's not rocket science. It's a very simple process. With 1.2 million real estate agents in the country, nothing is new in this space. So, those are the three typical areas that we support. The biggest thing that you can do is get very specific on what the outcomes are within those three areas and then hire to those outcomes.

Gregory Charlop: Without getting into specific prices, how do virtual assistants charge? Is it by the hour, by the month? Can it be by the project or by the property, or are there different models depending on what you're trying to do?

Daniel Ramsey: I would say there are three or four models. There's a per transaction virtual assistant. So, you could get somebody just to do your transaction coordination or your listing coordination. Then, some services are by task. So, I need my marketing set up from zero to 100, and you can pay a fee to have all of that done. New cards, new website, all that stuff. There are task-specific needs like, "I need a new website designed," and somebody says, "Oh, I can do a website." And, those people can get together for a per project cost.

There are staffing companies like ours. When we hire a client, and we really view it like hiring a client, we're creating a match. Our goal, the vision for the company, is for those matches to be forever, a client for life. The reality is, when you're growing, your biggest obstacle is finding talent. And, that's what we do for people. That's our value proposition: we find great talent.

So, those are the four or five different models out there. If you're new, you probably ought to do a per transaction thing, and a per project thing until you generate enough business where you can handle a full-time person.

Gregory Charlop: How can hiring a virtual assistant provide more stability for an organization?

Daniel Ramsey: One of the biggest challenges in the real estate space is, once you've reached a particular size—let's say you're doing a couple hundred transactions—losing one person on your team can create mass chaos. Stability becomes the winner of the day. A lot of our folks will be a backup to the transaction coordinator. Or, the listing coordinator will be a virtual assistant, and the operations manager will be somebody who's physically in the office, so you have some redundancy. That way, if somebody's out sick, their business continues. If somebody needs a vacation, he or she can actually go on a vacation.

So, at some stage, the stability of having two people capable of doing one job becomes critical.

Gregory Charlop: One of the premises of this book is that technology, including the transparency of the MLS, enables the top real estate agents to leave these larger firms and, more or less, strike out on their own. They would potentially go to very low cost, or internet-type brokerages that charge low fees and provide few services. After all, they've already got a great client base. They're excellent agents. They don't need much help. So, what they want is to keep most of their commissions.

My feeling is that more and more we'll see a lot of these top agents leave and essentially strike out on their own, as much as legally possible. Do you feel that virtual assistants make that process easier? In other words, a top agent could say, "Listen, I don't need this office anymore. I'll just have a virtual assistant. I'll go out on my own and enjoy more independence."

Daniel Ramsey: What I love about what you're saying is there's a transition going on within our industry. Brokers used to control 80-90 percent of the business because you needed a brand. Associates needed recognition. People were like, "Wait, who are you with?" And, now that doesn't matter.

Through the enablement of technology, relationships have been the winner of the day. If the broker maintained all the relationships with the market, they're winning. If the agent maintained the relationship with a market, that agent has a lot of power. We have several clients who have negotiated with their broker a 98 or a 97 percent split, which was just unheard of 20 years ago.

To answer your question, I think that smart brokers are going to start looking for ways to provide value to their agents, so they stay relevant. A great office is going to matter. All the transaction coordination and listing coordination built in. All the marketing built in. And, you're going to see brokers become the market's relationship. I've seen a lot of this happening, where a broker will create a purpose-based business goal. You know, "We're going to support this orphanage," or, "We're going to do this good work in the community." And then, enlist their agents into that. You have to create some stickiness that is just beyond a name and reputation.

Virtual assistants are just a byproduct of the internet just being so awesome. It's kind of like Netflix. Their business model wasn't streaming stuff online initially. Their business model was to compete with Blockbuster, just doing it through the mail. So, technology changed, and they had to shift. That shift has been great for everybody. I think, over time, our industry is going to transform. It's going to be great for the consumer, it's going to be great for our industry, and everybody will win.

Gregory Charlop: In this book, we've interviewed several executives from online brokerages. I think that this type of technology would be a perfect match for those types of companies.

Daniel Ramsey: Here's what your challenge is: In the real estate space, and I'm sure you've heard this before, it's not an 80/20 rule like in most worlds. It's almost a 90/10.

I mean, 90 percent of the agents do almost none of the business. So, I think your online brokers are going to get all those people. That 10 percent is still very much up for grabs, because the rest of the agents need training, they need business support, they need a brand, they need a purpose-based goal for their business, they need a home. They want to have a business worth owning.

Most real estate companies cannot be sold. Meaning, you can spend 30 years working as a broker and, ultimately, because you've never set up systems and processes, and you never had leverage, and it's all about the broker. That makes it tough to sell your brand. The broker or the team leader is the relationship with the marketplace.

So, a lot of really smart brokers are starting to warm up to the idea of virtual assistants, setting up leverage, and creating processes and brands that aren't centric to them so that they can sell their business. We love that because that's what I did. And, that's what we help people do.

Gregory Charlop: That's an excellent point. Technology and virtual assistants may be a great way of helping you with your business, but it also may be a great way of helping you exit your business when you're ready to retire or move to something else.

I appreciate you mentioning the purpose-based business because we touch on that in this book. I like the idea of philanthropy and the real estate community giving back.

Daniel Ramsey: I got introduced to a guy in Southern California. He's turned into a great friend. We've done some traveling together. He has this tremendous purpose-based synergy around this business where he gives a percentage of every single listing that he gets back into the world. And, they've created a non-profit. Every quarter they give money, and every year they get to choose their three charities. I think it's compelling because the market responds.

You walk into a contract negotiation and the people on the other side are saying, "I'm going to try to get Daniel to sell our property for 3 percent and not take a commission." As a broker, it's like, "How do I get them to give me 6 percent?" Well, you can make that conversation disappear—literally disappear—by having a purpose-based business. We've created our own non-profit called The MOD Movement, and we give back to our community. For example, we support orphans in the Philippines. Last time we were there we had over 120 people volunteering at Boys Town, which is an orphanage in the Philippines. So, when we join with a client, we're not only saying, "Hey, we're going to help grow your business," but, "We're also going to positively impact the world."

Gregory Charlop: That's great. It's good for you, and it's good for the community at large. I'm happy you've mentioned that. I want to switch gears a little bit. One thing people might worry about with virtual assistants is security. Should real estate agents be concerned about the safety of their client information or trade secrets? How do they know that that stuff will be protected if they use a virtual assistant as opposed to someone in their office?

Daniel Ramsey: That is an excellent point. First of all, we are a corporation here in the U.S. So, you and I, Gregory, we would be in a contract. And, we have certain rights and responsibilities as contracted. We're also a corporation in the Philippines. So, we are a legal entity in the Philippines, and we sign contracts with all of our virtual assistants. We have legal representation with all of our virtual assistants. We have insurance. We're doing FBI grade background checks.

So, not only are we taking the precautions, but we've created legal entities. We are holding the bag in terms of making sure that we're finding the best talent. Now, I'm not saying you should give your credit card to your virtual assistant. I'm not saying that. But what I am saying is that they really can't do much with intellectual property or a client list. Think about it like this: If you're a broker and somebody calls you and says, "Hey, I've got a client list of 10,000 people who have bought or sold a property in Sacramento (my home market). Would you like to buy it?" Nobody's going to buy that. You're going to think "fraud" right away. Also, credit cards don't work over there.

We're in real estate; there are no trade secrets. Everybody who's listening or reading this book who thinks, "Oh, I have a trade secret." Reality is, it's been done before. The secret sauce in being a real estate business owner is execution. It's always execution and leverage. If you can figure out those two things, you win. My suggestion is to go slow with your virtual assistant. Get to know them. Don't give them sensitive information on day one. You might want to hold off. We have a lot of title reps, and mortgage professionals, and lawyers, and insurance brokers who have access to all that stuff. You have to have a system to input the information and protect yourself as a company. However, errors and omissions cover all that. You'll be fine, in my opinion.

Gregory Charlop: Do you have any technological tools that you think real estate agents should be using but are not utilizing to their full potential now?

Daniel Ramsey: If you're a new person in real estate, your first thing is a CRM. You should go with a top three. Just choose the largest one that has the most tools. There's a lot of cool project management stuff. SkySlope is an excellent technology for transaction coordination.

I like Listings to Leads, which is, in my opinion, the number one listing-based marketing platform. However, there are a lot of platforms out there. QuickBooks is easier to use for real estate companies. You can get a chart of accounts inside QuickBooks now, for the first time as a real estate broker, which is cool.

There's a lot of stuff going on with lead automation, meaning a lead comes in, they get a text message immediately, there's a task to give them a call, they get a welcome email.

I like what SkySlope is doing. They're building automation into their transaction coordination. They're spending a lot of money on R&D, which is unusual in the real estate space. So, they're a great partner.

I also like Firepoint and I really like LionDesk. I appreciate some of the stuff at Sales DialerThey're an automated follow-up campaign using a phone. You can get a four-line dialer. As a real estate agent, your highest and best use is talking to people. Yet, most people are still dialing with their cell phones. Now, Sales Dialer says, "We can automate that." They'll link up with your CRM. Then, instead of dialing with a cell phone, you're dialing four numbers at once and automatically dropping voicemails for the ones that don't answer and putting you on the phone with the person who does answer. So, you can imagine, if I have 10,000 people in my database and I'm using a four-line dialer, I can get through that entire database in, I don't know, I week. Whereas, if you were manually dialing, it's just an impossibility to get through that.

Interview with Michael Lam, chatbot expert and CEO of Kaydoh

Gregory Charlop: Michael, what is your background and how did you get into chatbots?

Michael Lam: I'm the founder of Kaydoh, a real estate technology company. I got started with chatbots years ago when I was at GoHire. It wasn't a chatbot company to begin with. It was a job board company, and my responsibility was to drive traffic and get people to look for jobs that met their criteria. But people were just bouncing around the website, and we didn't know why. We did everything in terms of best SEO practice, but people were just bouncing all over the page. The homepage was a very simple page. All it had was a search screen.

We put in a live chat and started speaking to our visitors. To our astonishment, more often than not, our visitors would come back with a common problem. They would be more open to speaking with us in long-winded sentences. I would introduce myself saying, "Hi, I'm a recruiter. How can I help you?" I would get replies back saying, "Hi Michael, I'm looking for part-time jobs in Kansas City." All I would do was reply back saying, "Not a problem. Give me a few moments." I would take that and do the search for them. We gave them that link and they were on their way, satisfied.

Then, my co-founder Jonathan Duarte and I thought, "How can we automate this thing?" We were bootstrapped. We couldn't hire anyone, and that spawned chatbots. It was perfect timing because that's when Facebook released an open platform to plug in automated messaging.

Gregory Charlop: We probably have readers who are not familiar with chatbots. Can you tell us what they are and what they do?

Michael Lam: Chatbots are automated messaging systems

that reply conversationally. That's all they are. Often, the media will confuse chatbots with AI, but they're different concepts.

Gregory Charlop: How does the chatbot know what to say? Would the creator of the chatbot need to program in responses for everything?

Michael Lam: There are chatbots out there that can chit-chat with you. They use what's called NLP, natural language processing. Other chatbots are rule-based. You could think of them as a flowchart. They go down a specific path. It may ask, "Are you interested in purchasing this product? Yes or no?" If they say "no," the chatbot may take them to a sale. If they say "yes," the chatbot will present the prospect with a list of the products to purchase.

Gregory Charlop: Would someone employing a chatbot program it themselves or would the chatbot vendor do the programming?

Michael Lam: There are platforms that allow anyone to create a chatbot in five minutes. But, that doesn't mean that it's going to be an effective chatbot. There are platforms that let you can create it mostly yourself. You manually update the responses and connect the pieces as people go through a specific funnel. You use a particular script that you have designed upfront.

A lead capture chatbot generally will solicit five key pieces of information, like, "What's your first name, last name, what's your email, possibly your mobile number, and what product are you interested in?" You need to decide how to ask that and in what order. A platform will allow you to plug in those questions and collect that information. However, you do need to be involved to put the pieces together. Generally, it needs to be put in your own CRM or in your email. Platforms may or may not provide that type of automation. If you're technically savvy and you feel like you can do it yourself, you can use these platforms relatively cheaply. Again, some of them don't require technical knowledge. For example, ManyChat is a good tool you can set up really quickly.

Some vendors have a team to help you. You tell them, "This is what I'm thinking, I want lead capture. These are the five questions that are most important to me and to qualify this lead." Then, have them design a script and put it on the platform you want. This platform could be Facebook Messenger, WeChat, a website as a web chat, on SMS, or even Skype. There are different ways you could use that bot, but then you would have to consider the monthly cost as well as the post-implementation fee.

Gregory Charlop: If someone wanted to use chatbots but they didn't have any idea how to program them, they could hire someone to arrange everything for them—program it, monitor it—and pay them an initial fee plus a monthly fee to do that?

Michael Lam: Yes. Generally, the costs of a vendor are setup, implementation, and maintenance. You have to allocate resources for maintenance. A chatbot is not like software where we can just purchase it and have it automatically work on its own. It's an ongoing project. You can create the script, but then, as a business owner, just like with a website, you always need to figure out how to convert the user. You're making changes to your website. Similarly, with a chatbot, you're looking at the analytics and how people are speaking to your chatbot, trying to figure out a better way to have a better conversation that can lead to a sale—
if that's your goal.

Gregory Charlop: Bringing the discussion back to real estate, how would a real estate agent use a chatbot, and why would they use a chatbot rather than just answering questions themselves or hiring someone to answer questions for them?

Michael Lam: Why would you want to use a chatbot? Most agents will not hire an assistant. That's an overhead cost that most agents will not want to pay, especially if they're starting out. Scheduling an appointment or creating a CMA (comparative market analysis report) is pretty routine. It doesn't take too much to do that. To generate a comparative market analysis, for example, all you need is the address. You plug the address into your system, and it will produce it. A lot of the quick CMAs allow that. Those are great opportunities to have a system to automate, and a chatbot is a prime use for that. You can have a lead capture chatbot that offers a CMA. A product we offer at Kaydoh is called TextCMA.

Gregory Charlop: Could the chatbot do other things like make appointments to meet the real estate agent or answer some questions? Real estate is a competitive market, and the first to meet with a prospect will have the best chance of converting that prospect into a client.

Michael Lam: Absolutely, you made a great point because that's actually one of the statistics from NAR. The first person to meet a lead generally wins. Prospects usually only interview one agent. So, using a chatbot to deliver quick information to the prospects is paramount. With a CMA, which is a traditional way of lead capturing on a website, prospects put in their address, and then they wait—up to 24 hours—to get a report back through email. And then there is generally no follow up. That person is a lead that the agent should be aware of and immediately speak with that individual. You can use a chatbot to generate the report and deliver it directly to the person via SMS. That's actually one of the products that I built at Kaydoh to provide that instantaneous lead. The minute a prospect shows interest in creating a report, the salesperson will get a notification from their chatbot saying, "Hey you got a lead." You have the address and the number, make that call! It's your lead to lose at that moment.

Gregory Charlop: Chatbots allow the real estate agent to respond quickly to a potential lead like you just described, and they let the real estate agent be in more than one place at a time. In other words, the chatbot might be making an appointment with one potential client, while at the same time doing a CMA for another prospect or answering some questions—all while the real estate agent might be driving their kids to school.

Michael Lam: A great thing about a chatbot is it's an extension of the agent. It's conversational rather than robotic. The conversation has emojis in it. It's designed to be more natural. Just like you and I would message each other on a messaging app, the chatbot does something very similar, but it captures information while having a conversation. You could have thousands of people speaking to a chatbot, so you, as a salesperson, do not need to take that initial call. The chatbot can handle that initial interaction, including the prequalification, an automated alert, and scheduling. These are not the income-producing stages. They are in the early stages and are generally done by script, meaning it's going to be routine. Without a chatbot, you, as an agent, would have to say the same thing over and over. While you're doing that routine stuff, you're taking time away from your existing clients, hosting an open house, or speaking with a potential buyer.

Gregory Charlop: Will the client realize they are talking to a machine, or will they think they're talking to a person? If they believe they are talking to a machine, will that bother them?

Michael Lam: Studies have shown that 50 percent of people surveyed are more than willing to speak with a chatbot as long as you don't try to trick them. Some chatbot developers are missing the mark when they try to trick people. Look, humans are very intelligent. We are not at a technical level to be able to create chatbots that are truly human-like where people can't tell the difference between a human and a bot. So don't try to present a chatbot as human. As long as you're honest with people and tell them, "Hey, I'm a chatbot. I am Jerry's virtual assistant. How can I help you?" They will be more than inclined to continue the conversation. The younger generation doesn't pick up the phone to talk, they would rather message. Even if it's not a human, they would rather text message someone to get an immediate response. That's more valuable. If you're able to provide a solution or quickly deliver some results, it really doesn't matter if it's a bot or not.

Gregory Charlop: It sounds like a great tool to reach out to Millennials and younger buyers because they don't want to talk on the phone. They want an immediate response by text or by typing something on their computers.

Michael Lam: That's absolutely right. And to take this drive even further, look at your phone and my phone. If I look at my phone, I see how many missed emails I have. I'm going to be honest. I have 12,600 unread emails. If I look at my messaging, I have zero. Even on LinkedIn, I have zero. As a Millennial, yes, an older Millennial, I don't really call on the phone. There are a lot of studies that prove that.

A recent study done by a Danish company found that the open rate for email was about 23 percent, and the open rate for SMS is an astonishing 98 percent! As a salesperson trying to promote business by spreading the message, sending emails the traditional way just doesn't cut it anymore. That way no longer works because you have marketers spamming the hell out of people. So people don't really look at emails anymore. But, if you send them a text message, you have a 98 percent chance someone is going to open it. Just going through that front door is very challenging right now, and if you can do it through messaging, SMS, that's huge.

Gregory Charlop: The world has changed a lot with technology. If we want to sell to people, we can't fight this change. We have to accept it. Not only has talking on the phone become passé, but email is nearly passé as well. So, if you want to reach people you have to try new techniques.

Michael Lam: I can tell you from my experience with chatbots in real estate, we are getting some promising results compared to email performance.

Gregory Charlop: If real estate agents reading this book wanted to start using chatbots, how would they go about investigating this or getting it set up?

Michael Lam: I recommend going to a vendor and having them give you the lay of the land. The vendors will help you define your scope. You might want to say, "I want lead capture." But there are many variations of lead capture, and it depends on how you want to set up your lead capture. Is it going to be on your website, on SMS, on Facebook Messenger? Generally, good vendors are honest and wouldn't charge you for the consultation. Stay away from vendors that charge you for a consultation.

Gregory Charlop: Who typically purchases products like chatbots? Is it usually an individual real estate agent, a broker, or a real estate company?

Michael Lam: Generally, it's real estate agents. Brokers that I've worked with try to get discounts for the entire team. So, it's both.

CHAPTER 5: EMERGING TECHNOLOGY

Real Estate at a Crossroads

Learn how artificial intelligence, Bitcoin, robots, and virtual reality will reshape real estate

This book is all about technology. Public access to the MLS took a wrecking ball to the traditional real estate firm's role of gatekeeper, while increased transparency—via online reviews and sales records—lifted the veil of secrecy from real estate agents.

At the same time, technology is making life easier for real estate professionals. Facebook, review sites, and custom domains are revolutionizing advertising, while online virtual assistants are saving you time and boosting your sales.

All this technology is here today. Use it.

But even more technology and innovation are on the way that have the potential to completely revolutionize the industry. Learn about these products and companies now so you're ready when they reshape the real estate marketplace of the future.

So, strap on your virtual goggles and let's have some fun!

Artificial Intelligence and Natural-Language (Alexa, Google Duplex)

Ring! A prospect calls.

Your assistant answers with a pleasant "hello!" After some small talk about the weather, your friendly "employee" determines that the caller wants to buy a 3-bedroom townhouse near good schools. Your assistant screens the prospect and sends them a few properties that meet their exact criteria. A few days later, your employee follows up with the prospect and confirms their meeting with you. The only thing is, your employee isn't human. It's your natural language artificial intelligence program!

Computers are now able to speak nearly as well as people due to breathtaking advances in artificial intelligence. Products like Google's Duplex, Amazon's Alexa, and Apple's Siri use natural language technology to hold lifelike verbal conversations. Think of these programs as chatbots on steroids!

Natural-language processing (NLP) systems understand accents, slang, and incorrect grammar. Just like a human, they're able to interpret meaning through context. They're even designed to add filler words like "um" and "hummm" just like a human would. And, these tools are improving by the day. It won't be long before conversations with these bots will feel just like talking to a person. If you're not convinced, just YouTube "Google Duplex" and watch as a computer books a salon appointment and restaurant table reservation over the phone with unsuspecting people at the other end of the line. It's mind-blowing!

How can you take advantage of this technology? The possibilities are endless. It won't be long before companies create customized versions of Amazon or Google products for real estate, just as Kaydoh and HelloAlex created customized chatbots. These new tools will engage with prospects, tell them about your services, screen them, and set up appointments. They can follow up with your contractors and remind them you need your property painted by next week and call your clients to tell them about a new listing or remind them of upcoming appointments. They could even call other agents (or their natural language bots!) to confirm a listing's availability, ask questions, or make an offer.

In short, natural language tools will be your virtual assistants but they'll be less expensive and (presumably) completely trustworthy. Just as you can now ask your Alexa to turn on the lights and play your favorite tune, you'll soon ask her to call your mortgage broker and find out when the funds will be available to close. How cool is that?

Paperless transactions

Remember the days when you and your clients had to FAX 50-page contracts back and forth? Inevitably, the FAX machines would jam or run out of something. Those days weren't that long ago.

Thankfully, we now have electronic document services like DocuSign. The back and forth is easier, faster, and much less frustrating!

But the transformation to an automated documentation system is not yet complete. Agents still have to call around to remind folks to fill out forms and we still have multiple signings. All of these steps create work and risk scuttling the deal. The paperwork is great for printing companies and your local notary public, but bad for the rest of us.

Now, imagine an alternate system. Agents and home buyers/sellers have an app with a dashboard which shows progress toward the goal of the sale. Each step is color-coded for the state of completion—green, red, and yellow could signify projects completed, due, and upcoming. All parties would have their own task list set to a schedule and would know what everyone else has completed.

Even better, most tasks could be ordered directly from the app. Need an appraisal? Tap the app and it's ordered. Time for pest inspection? Order it instantly. Need to send a contract to the sellers? Zap! It's done. Need a lawyer to review the updated contract? Send it while you're in line for your morning soy latte. Easy!

Real estate agents could even have their virtual and office assistants on the app. Instead of having to call to ask them to complete some task, they could instantly delegate projects to their staff.

Best of all, the parties could legally sign documents and transfer funds right on the app. Yes, there would be some regulatory hurdles to jump, but this is already done in other regulated fields like banking and healthcare. Why not real estate?

An app like this would slash escrow time, decrease everyone's workload, and improve compliance and accuracy. Buying a house would be almost as simple as planning a vacation!

Thankfully, the paperless process is coming to the mortgage industry. Rocket Mortgage by Quicken Loans,[54] for example, lets you apply online, gives you a fast answer, and closes within a month. Lenda[55] is completely paperless, answers within one business day, and can often close within 30 days.

The future for this concept app in real estate is almost here. Redfin, eXp, Real, Opendoor, Purplebricks, and other technologically-savvy real estate companies are already working toward the goal of a frictionless transaction process. It won't be long before we're all using a similar system. This is one innovation we can all appreciate!

Virtual and augmented reality

We're no longer bound by the laws of physical reality. As anyone who's used Snapchat knows, we can grow huge ears, sprout mouse whiskers, and sport crazy oversized glasses out of thin air. All you need is a bit of imagination and a good augmented reality program. Scratch that, you don't even need the imagination–the right software will do it for you!

I predict that augmented reality (AR) will create a shockwave in real estate. And soon. Lots of great real estate AR tools are already available.

To start, here's how augmented reality differs from virtual reality (VR). AR is a computer-generated image superimposed on the user's view of the world, creating a composite image of the real and synthetic. In contrast, VR is entirely computer-generated, although it can be based on real images.

Virtual reality transports you to a completely synthesized world. It could either be fictitious or real, such as "walking through" Alcatraz from the comfort of your living room. Imagine playing a game with a headset. You're jumping across clouds and dodging dragons trying to poke holes in your rainbow balloons. That's virtual reality.

It turns out that homebuyers really go for this technology. According to a survey by Coldwell Banker, 77 percent of respondents wanted to take a virtual tour before visiting a home.[56] It is just a matter of time before virtual tours are a standard part of listings.

Augmented reality is great for virtual staging. Companies like RoOomy and Sotheby's make a great product that allows you to virtually populate a room with furniture. The clients aren't sure how their beloved couch would fit in a home? Take out the RoOomy app the couch into the room. No heavy lifting required! Art.com makes a fun app that virtually hangs paintings on the wall. Buyers can see what their artwork would look like in a home without lifting a hammer or a nail.

Augmented reality is perfect for open houses and engaging potential renters. Imagine that you're walking through a home wearing an AR headset. As you pass the stove, a little chef materializes to inform you that you're looking at a brand-new Viking range. When you turn your head towards the staircase, an animated tour guide pops up to invite you upstairs to check out the master suite and library. How much better would that make your property tours?!

My sense is that augmented and virtual reality will soon be critically important in selling most homes. As we discussed earlier, Redfin found that 45 percent of Millennial homebuyers in 2017 made an offer on a home sight-unseen.[57] I'm sure that number is even higher today! The buyers relied on pictures, videos, and online information. The fraction of folks willing to rely on technology rather than on an in-person tour will continue to grow as Millennials increase their dominance as homebuyers and everyone becomes more comfortable with video tour technology.

Bridget Frey, the CTO of Redfin, is a fan of augmented reality but she urges some caution. "You can imagine when you're walking through an open house, messages pop up about new appliances or remodeling details. That can be part of your experience of touring the home. I do think that some of the technology is still a little bit early. We're just getting past the Pokemon Go craze. There's still more that needs to happen. When you're selling someone's home, the quality of the video, the photography, the augmented features have to be extraordinarily high. This is a very costly asset that people are trying to sell, and I do think that the technology will have to be quite good before it becomes something standard in real estate."

Artificial intelligence

We've covered artificial intelligence (AI) throughout this book. As the technology evolves, it will replace humans for increasingly sophisticated cognitive tasks including writing news articles and predicting future behavior. In fact, AI is already quite good at understanding human preferences - sometimes better humans are!

Bridget Frey, the CTO of Redfin said, "One of the first features we built recommend homes to consumers. We've always had a feature on the website where you can save a search. You can say, "I'm interested in homes between 400,000-600,000 dollars with two bedrooms." We'll send you an email that lets you know when a new home comes on the market matching that criteria. It turns out that our machine learning recommendation algorithm is actually much better than the customers themselves. The customer is four times as likely to click on a recommended home as they are on a listing that matches their saved search.

We're actually better at producing homes clients might be interested in than they are themselves. That's incredibly exciting." The complete interview with Frey appears here.

Think of how good this technology will be in a couple of years...

Robots

Imagine this: your prospects have just walked into your rental listing in a tony part of town. They're greeted by a robot! The cyborg invites them into the home, takes their contact information, and escorts them around the property. It points out the magnificent views, sun-drenched patio, and Sub-Zero refrigerator. They're wowed by the home and fill out your rental application with the robot. No human required!

Zen Place offers just such a robot. While security and user-acceptance still need to be worked out, it's easy to see how an army of friendly tour-bots can work wonders with home showings.

Blockchain and Bitcoin

Along with artificial intelligence and virtual reality, blockchain and cryptocurrencies like Bitcoin are technological innovations that could reshape the real estate marketplace.

The **blockchain** is a list of linked records secured by cryptography. The records, called blocks, are time-stamped and distributed throughout the internet. As a result, they are considered relatively secure and resistant to tampering. Theoretically, they can be used to record property deeds or even create smart contracts.

Matt Murphy, a partner at venture capital firm Montage Ventures, sees great potential for blockchain with real estate. "When you go into a typical real estate brokerage office, there still are file cabinets. And in those file cabinets are purchase contracts that are being stored for three years to seven years. All of that could be digitized online. There are companies like DocuSign that are helping with digital signatures and digital file storage. But that can also happen on the blockchain. The title and the escrow space, title records, are currently stored on a local level, on a city-by-city basis. So bringing that online, digitizing that, storing that in a public, secured ledger could unlock a lot of value in the data that's hidden within those documents and open up a lot of innovations within the real estate sector."

Bitcoin is a form of cryptocurrency (there are many, but Bitcoin is the most popular). It is recorded on the blockchain. There is no central bank and Bitcoin is not regulated by a central government. Some users prefer Bitcoin over conventional currency because it offers more privacy, can be transferred instantaneously, and has low transaction costs. Bitcoin can be used to buy and sell properties if the seller is willing to accept Bitcoin as payment.

One of the world's leading experts on blockchain and Bitcoin with real estate is Ragnar Lifthrasir, interviewed here. He described Bitcoin this way: "Bitcoin isn't a company or an organization or a government. Bitcoin is simply software. It's an open-source protocol that anyone can look at, can view, can try to adapt. It's an open-source protocol, just like we have an email protocol. All email applications use the same email protocol. That's why you can have different email addresses. You might have Gmail and I have Yahoo, but they can talk to each other. Why? Because everyone is using the same protocol, and anyone can build an application on top of the email protocol. That's what Bitcoin is. It's an open source protocol to transfer value."

Lifthrasir said blockchain replaces or reduces the need for third parties across lots of real estate applications, such as title transfer, chain of title, money currency transfer, and certain contracts. Blockchain allows users to "make things more peer to peer, replace middlemen with code, basically," Lifthrasir said. "With money (transfer) you have bitcoin. You don't need the intermediary of a bank."

While there is a lot of excitement about Bitcoin, some are urging caution. Nick Bailey, former President and CEO of CENTURY 21®, said, "Cryptocurrencies are certainly gaining a lot of attention, but right now, there are many risk factors that could impact the success and security of a transaction, for example, the volatility of Bitcoin and the current timing associated with the various steps in the real estate transaction."

Will Bitcoin take the place of cash and will the blockchain replace contracts? In my view, neither of these technologies is ready for prime. However, any savvy real estate agent and brokerage would be wise to stay ahead of this trend so they're ready to hit the ground running if/when the blockchain breaks out.

Real Estate at a Crossroads

Interview with Bridget Frey, CTO of Redfin

Gregory Charlop: Bridget, you're the CTO of Redfin and Jani, you're the SVP of Communications. [Author's note: Jani Strand is no longer with Redfin. She is the former SVP of communications for Redfin]. Redfin is one of the most internet-savvy real estate companies. Thank you for joining us for this book.

One of the central premises of the book is the transformative power of the internet on how folks buy and sell homes, which is obviously something you understand very well. The easy availability of the MLS in people's living rooms or on their phones is fundamentally changing the entire real estate sales process in America. My first question: are most people these days using the internet to search for homes? Or is it more of a niche group of buyers?

Bridget Frey: The vast majority of buyers are using the internet to look for homes, find homes to tour, and see prices. Survey data tells us most customers are actually using multiple websites during their search, and they become quite savvy at using data.

Jani Strand: Data shows that more than 90 percent of people search online.

Gregory Charlop: Wow. Very impressive. Do you think they're using it just to kick the tires? Or do you think they're actually seriously looking at homes with the internet?

Bridget Frey: There's a broad spectrum. On one end, you have people checking out the value of their friend's new house and real estate enthusiasts browsing homes for fun, or people interested in their own neighborhood trends. On the other, you have people using technology to find homes quickly and compete in a fast market, organize their open house schedules, and figure out what price to offer.

Jani Strand: We actually see people using technology from initial search all the way to making an offer. Our latest data shows that one out of three home buyers made an offer on a home sight unseen.

Gregory Charlop: That's a very impressive statistic. What do you think customers are looking for when they check out homes on the internet? Do you think they're just looking at pictures or do you think there is any particular information that customers are looking for?

Bridget Frey: First of all, today's real estate consumer really wants to be informed. They want the data to be transparent. They don't want those old days when you had to drive around to a number of different real estate offices and look through binders of homes for sale. More recently, we see consumers demanding speed and instant gratification. It's what we call the on-demand economy, where people expect to be able to go to a website and book a table for a restaurant. They expect to be able to place an order and have some things show up on their steps the next day. This is a major focus at Redfin, as we look at problems like automatically scheduling tours, something that we've invested in over many years. We want to make it as easy to tour a home as it is to order a pizza.

Gregory Charlop: That sounds like a millennial thing; The desire for immediate satisfaction.

Bridget Frey: Certainly, people who've grown up with technology have come to expect this, but we're seeing demand for that type of thing across all of our demographics. Convenience is something that, really, everyone can get behind.

Gregory Charlop: Absolutely. How do you think real estate agents should use technology to reach these internet-savvy customers? Are they doing enough?

Bridget Frey: At Redfin, we build technology for our agents and for our customers themselves. The amazing part is link-ing the two together. That's extremely powerful. Our agent-facing technology helps our agents be extremely efficient and knowledgeable, arming them with data to give the best possible advice. We automate everything that a computer can do better than a human, freeing our agents to spend their time building relationships with their customers and helping them win.

If you think about it from the customer perspective, what do you want your agent to do? Do you want them to fax documents and paste things into PDFs, or do you want them to be there to talk with you, to walk through homes, to answer a question, to get to know you so they can provide really personalized advice? I think that technology helps an agent to do more of that personal advice, and less of the faxing and document management and all those other things.

Gregory Charlop: Some readers may not be very familiar with Redfin, so can you briefly describe Redfin—the process and how it works and what makes Redfin different from a more traditional real estate firm?

Bridget Frey: Absolutely.

We are a technology-powered brokerage. We are using technology to make every part of the real estate transaction more efficient and also less costly. Our goal is to have the most successful customers in the industry. Redfin is unusual in that our agents are employees of the company. They receive a salary and a bonus based on how satisfied a customer is at the end of our transaction. They also get comprehensive healthcare and paid time off. Why should a customer care? Because this culture of partnership between our agents and engineers creates a better service for customers. An agent whose interests are aligned with the customer's is very different from the traditional contractor-based commission model. That also means that we can train those agents, and we can have them use our technology and get all of those things onto the same platform.

Next is our investment in technology, which I think you well know. We have invested in technology such that our agents are able to handle three times as many happy customers than the traditional real estate agent. They're just far more productive, and that means that we can offer our service at a lower cost. We charge 1 percent in most markets to list your home versus the traditional commission of 2.5 to 3 percent. We also offer a refund to our buyers at the end of the transaction. You get full service, the best tech, and you pay less. That's what technology should do.

Gregory Charlop: You had mentioned an interesting stat, that your agents are able to handle around three times as many customers as a traditional agent. Certainly, the Redfin agents I've worked with have all been excellent and really very experienced, probably because they handle so many transactions.

Bridget Frey: That's right. You can become a local expert in the real estate market very fast if you're doing so many transactions in a very small local area.

Gregory Charlop: Does this technology and the efficiency that you're able to achieve mean that there are fewer real estate person hours required for each transaction? And if that's so, do you envision fewer real estate agents being needed in the future? In other words, will you need as many real estate agents to sell the same number of homes in the coming years?

Bridget Frey: We think about it in terms of which part of the job does a real estate agent need to do, and what parts can be handled either by technology or through a team. In the case of our agents, like I said, most of the time they're meeting customers. Our agents don't need to be cold calling or prospecting as traditional agents soften have to do, especially when they're starting out.

All of our agents, from day one, have a team to support them. That's something that only top-producers enjoy in traditional real estate. Having a team of transaction coordinators and tour schedulers and folks answering the phone or going on tour when they are already booked with another client. This is something Redfin agents have on day one. We look at the combination of the agent, the technology and the team, then use that to make the entire experience amazing.

For example, Fast Offers is a new technology for the agent that makes writing an offer much faster and more accurate. Starting from when a customer says, "Hey, I want to buy this house." Now the agent needs to pull together a packet of paperwork, let the listing agent know about the offer, any disclosures, any estate forms, and all the rest. That can be quite a time-consuming process that varies from market to market. But figure an hour or two, maybe even a little longer for a new agent. Fast Offers automates everything that can be automated and pulls together all the data based on the home and the customer.

We take information the customer has given us online, automatically paste that into the PDFs and all the documents and staple them all together. We get the electronic signatures and all the rest. That means that even a new agent can do this in a matter of minutes. That really increases the efficiency of that agent without sacrificing service and practice. In fact, it's better for the customer if you can get that offer onto the listing agent's desk before anyone else. That's where technology can really help to make the agent more efficient.

Gregory Charlop: One of the developments I've seen lately in the real estate business is these two-dimensional immersive tours. The kind of things you might film with a Matterport camera or a GoPro or something similar. They almost appear three-dimensional as though you're walking through the house. What are your thoughts about this type of technology?

Gregory Charlop

And do you see this type of thing as a future standard?

Bridget Frey: We love that technology. We're early adopters of it. Anytime we put a home on the market, anytime we list a home for sale, we actually take a 3D scan of that home and put it on our website. For any Redfin listing, you can get that experience, where you can kind of walk through the home as though you were there. This means buyers can get a sense of what it's like to be in that space before going on a tour, or maybe not need to tour at all. Our sellers just love it as well. We believe this is something that consumers are going to come to expect over time.

Gregory Charlop: In a similar vein, virtual reality and augmented reality are capturing a lot of attention in the press. They certainly caught my eye. There are a lot of new phones out now that have some great VR and AR features. What are your thoughts about virtual reality and augmented reality in real estate sales? Is that coming soon or how do you think something like that could be used?

Bridget Frey: We are very interested in augmented reality and some of its applications in real estate. You can imagine things like, when you're walking through an open house, messages pop up about new appliances or remodeling details. That can be part of your experience of touring the home. I do think that some of the technology is still a little bit early. We're just getting past the Pokemon Go craze. There's still more that needs to happen. When you're selling someone's home, the quality of the video, the photography, the augmented features have to be extraordinarily high. This is a very costly asset that people are trying to sell, and I do think that the technology will have to be quite good before it becomes something standard in real estate.

Gregory Charlop: Yeah. I agree. I think it's still probably in its infancy, but it's amazing what could potentially be done with that technology once it's more ubiquitous.

Bridget Frey: Oh, absolutely.

Gregory Charlop: One of my favorite topics is artificial intelligence. How is AI and machine learning being used in real estate? And does Redfin use artificial intelligence, perhaps, to help match buyers and sellers or help people find properties?

Bridget Frey: Absolutely. This is actually a huge area of investment for us. I joined Redfin six years ago to found our analytics engineering team. We built our first big data systems back then to learn what we could do with machine learning to help our customers and our agents. One of the first features we built was to help recommend homes to consumers. We've always had a feature on the website where you can save a search. You can say, I'm interested in homes between 400,000-600,000 dollars with two bedrooms. We'll send you an email that lets you know when a new home comes on the market matching that criteria. It turns out that our machine learning recommendation algorithm is actually much better than the customer themselves. The customer is four times as likely to click on a recommended home as they are on a listing that matches their saved search.

We're actually better at producing homes they might be interested in than they are themselves. That's incredibly exciting, because it means that we can really help customers find the perfect home. We've done a lot of other things with machine learning as well to help our agents figure out ... You know if they have five minutes in between tours, what is the best thing to do at that time? Which customer should they reach out to? We have machine learning conduct that as well.

Where it really transforms things is on our listings business, where we have invested in the Redfin Estimate. It's the most accurate online home value estimate. It's more than twice as likely to be within 3 percent of the final list price as any other online home value estimate. That's an incredibly powerful tool for our listing specialists who use it to figure out how to price a home and come up with a pricing strategy before they walk into someone's living room to meet a homeowner.

All of these examples are a huge frontier for us. We have a ton of data in real estate. It's an industry that's flooded with data. There are so many exciting applications.

Gregory Charlop: Your computer algorithms are better at guessing a customer's interest than customers are themselves.

Bridget Frey: It really shows you how hard it is for a customer to sift through all that data. We talked about the intent of the customer when it comes to all these websites. They're craving information, getting their hands on that first-person perspective on the idea, and yet if we could help them sift through that data through machine learning, it would be much easier for them. That's really very exciting.

Gregory Charlop: I totally agree. Often, people don't really know what they want. They like data, but they get overwhelmed by choices. A computer that could help guide you to make a better choice would be very useful. Sometimes the computer can know what you want better than you might yourself.

Bridget Frey: Absolutely.

Gregory Charlop: Do you have any thoughts about the use of chatbots in real estate?

Bridget Frey: I think that there's a set of questions that a chatbot could answer that are kind of easy to answer. How many bedrooms does this particular home have? A lot of those kinds of questions could be answered by just looking at the webpage for that listing. But interacting with a chatbot might also be a good experience for some customers.

But I think pretty quickly people get to a place where they need to talk to a licensed real estate agent, where they need direct access to that person, and it's beyond what a typical chatbot is able to do with current technology. I think the interesting question will be: how many customer questions can the chatbot handle that are in between the easiest things and what an agent needs to handle themselves?

Gregory Charlop: Could you tell us a bit about your background?

Bridget Frey: Sure. I started programming when I was five with my dad on an Apple 2E in our kitchen. So, I fell in love with technology from a really early age. I majored in computer science at Harvard, and then I've spent my career working at high growth startups like Redfin. I joined Redfin because of the opportunity that we had here to really help customers with the biggest transactions of their lives. Also, the culture of this company is really special. It's a collaborative culture where real estate agents and engineers are working together, where we do our best work to help people to collaborate and come up with the best ideas. I love that environment. I feel like I learn so much every day, and that's how I ended up here.

Interview with Ragnar Lifthrasir, founder of the International Blockchain Real Estate Association.

Gregory Charlop: You're an expert on the blockchain. Tell us what the blockchain is.

Ragnar Lifthrasir: Yes, the blockchain is a protocol for doing a couple of things. It transfers digital value peer to peer without the need or permission from a third party in a censorship-resistant network, and those digital asset transfers create an immutable ledger. You have value transfers with an immutable ledger recording those transfers.

Gregory Charlop: Excellent. What does this have to do with real estate?

Ragnar Lifthrasir: Real estate is about transferring value, whether it's an actual property from one owner to the next, whether it's money for an asset, or whether it's a short-term asset like renting or leasing. Also, obviously in real estate it's very important to keep track of ownership and transactions. In real estate it's important to be able to come to agreements between two parties. So big picture, what the blockchain does is it makes real estate more peer to peer, and it replaces or reduces the need for third parties. And that's across lots of applications for real estate, whether it's title transfer, currency transfer, chain of title, certain forms of contract, and investment. What the blockchain is allowing us to do is to make things more peer to peer, replace middlemen with code, basically.

Gregory Charlop: When you say, "more peer to peer," if I understand you correctly, you're saying it would enable a buyer and a seller of a piece of property to transact more directly with each other without having other parties interfere or be involved with the contract or the payment?

Ragnar Lifthrasir: Correct. For example, let's just look at a

Real Estate at a Crossroads

transfer of a property. Let's say an office building. There are two forms of value there that are transferred. There's the actual building itself, ownership of that, but then there's also money. Someone transfers money, the other person transfers the ownership, so blockchain can do both of those. Obviously, with the money you have Bitcoin, you have other digital currencies, so instead of having to go through your bank, each person can use their blockchain wallet, their Bitcoin wallets, their blockchain software to transfer that value. You don't need the intermediary of a bank. You also don't need the intermediary of an escrow, potentially, because you can do a blockchain escrow with a Bitcoin multi-signature transaction.

Okay, so that's the money portion. That's a currency value transfer that we just made more peer to peer and censorship resistant because you don't have these third parties saying you can't do it. Now, the second part was the actual property, the title. You can create a blockchain token that represents that property. You can create digital assets, so I say this blockchain token is my blockchain deed and I can transfer it directly to you. I don't need to have a lawyer write it up or have the title insurance company write it up and then print it out for us and then look it over. We can use software to do that.

Gregory Charlop: Great, so it sounds like they can make the process of real estate transactions faster and cheaper by removing these intermediaries?

Ragnar Lifthrasir: Yes, faster, cheaper, more secure and, not only that, but with lower friction, and just a completely different experience. I think the best way for people to sort of visualize what the whole process will be like is buying stock, from Apple, for example. You go to a website, you can see all the data in front of you, you can take ownership of that asset by clicking a few buttons and transferring some money, and now you own that asset. That will be where we're trying to get this to. That will be the experience, versus what people currently have, which is much different.

Gregory Charlop: Potentially then, there will be more direct interaction between the buyer and the seller to the exclusion of other parties.

Ragnar Lifthrasir: Correct.

Gregory Charlop: It sounds like this could potentially cause job losses in the mortgage industry, escrow markets, notaries, and other areas. Would you imagine if the blockchain were fully adopted that there would be less need for those job categories?

Ragnar Lifthrasir: Definitely there would be much less need for those job categories. But I would say that those people, those professionals who work in those fields, a lot of them, might be working for the software companies that make the software more user friendly and know how to adapt software to the real world and the laws and requirements for all these things. So, yes, some of those jobs will go away, but some of them will actually transform and probably be more exciting and probably higher-paying too.

Gregory Charlop: If you were speaking to someone who is considering going into escrow as a profession, what advice would you give them?

Ragnar Lifthrasir: I would say there is going to be a long rollout of the technology but start now with hands-on experience. Buy some fraction of Bitcoin you feel comfortable with, and just start playing around with it. Get comfortable with wallet software, watch introductory videos on YouTube. Just start self-educating and start now, because it's early enough to where you can be kind of a leader and have valuable skills, so then as the transformation starts to happen, you're prepared. You don't want to wait five years. I think now is a good time for people in these professions—be it escrow, brokerage, title, others—to just start getting into the new economy.

A lot of people say blockchain is the most important invention since the internet. The internet made information more peer to peer. It made information digital. Well, the blockchain makes value more peer to peer. It makes value more digital, so it's a similar revolution, and just as the internet replaced some jobs, it created a whole bunch of new great ones.

Gregory Charlop: A lot of the people reading this book are real estate agents or brokers or executives with real estate companies. How would those folks, if at all, be able to use blockchain now? In other words, is there any way that an agent or broker or company could incorporate blockchain now into their business?

Ragnar Lifthrasir: Right now there are residential and commercial real estate brokers who are helping their clients accept Bitcoin or pay for properties with Bitcoin. I know several right now. In fact, two residential real estate agents here in Southern California have named themselves the Crypto Realty Group. They're starting to specialize because now there's a lot of wealth floating around in Bitcoin in this area. People want to use that to trade for real assets. Something they could do now is learn how Bitcoin works, buy some Bitcoin themselves, transfer it around, get comfortable with it and just start telling clients, "Hey, I'll help you do it," and then once they find their first client, really figure it out.

I would say "yes" to answer your question. First thing is just get comfortable with cryptocurrency. Don't worry about title and smart contracts and any of that stuff. Just the cryptocurrency; Bitcoin is the first place to start.

Gregory Charlop: Excellent, and I do want to ask you a bit more about Bitcoin soon. But before we get to that, just so I could better understand, it sounds like for now, blockchain would mostly be using something like Bitcoin. But how do you envision real estate agents using blockchain or related technologies in the future, in five or 10 years, whenever you think it might be fully adopted? How do you think that would impact the day to day lives of real estate agents and brokers?

Ragnar Lifthrasir: The power is going to be much more in the hands of the owners of the real estate because the owners will be able to eventually create a digital deed for themselves. They (agents and brokers) are going to have to realize that their role as middlemen is going to diminish over time, so I would say it's prudent to start being in front of that.

Gregory Charlop: If you were speaking to someone considering a career in real estate as an agent or broker, would you still recommend they go into real estate or would you recommend it but make sure they learn about blockchain or do you think it would be a bad idea because there would be a far lower need for real estate agents in the future?

Ragnar Lifthrasir: That's a tough question because I think it will be a long rollout and the world is changing so quickly. So I think it's fine that they go into that profession, but they need to be aware of Bitcoin and blockchain today. Not in three years, not in two years, today. They may not use it, but they need to start being in front of it and setting themselves ahead of the curve for that. So I think it's fine they go into that. They just need to start today by getting their feet wet at a bare minimum.

Gregory Charlop: It sounds like current real estate agents could potentially use blockchain or at least acceptance of Bitcoin even as a marketing tool, if I'm understanding you right, because they appeal to clients who want to use that.

Ragnar Lifthrasir: That's the simplest way. Once they have a basic competency, they feel comfortable moving a hundred dollars of Bitcoin around at a time. They know how to secure it with the right security practices. Then they can start doing that to set themselves apart, and when they do land a client, they could call someone who really is good at it and make it work.

Gregory Charlop: When do you see the blockchain being commonly used as sort of a routine part of real estate practice?

Ragnar Lifthrasir: It's so tough to predict and it's just so uneven. Some things are going to jump ahead really fast. I think cryptocurrency, Bitcoin is definitely coming. It is appealing to overseas buyers, especially the tech crowd, so I see it more in terms of the users, not necessarily the technology. So if you're in an area with more tech-oriented people, adoption will occur faster. If you're in a different part of the country with a less tech-savvy client base, you probably won't be as affected by it. So how I would predict is based more on the sector. There's the divide between residential versus commercial. I actually think commercial will beat out residential first.

Gregory Charlop: It does seem like it might actually fit into commercial transactions more easily. I could see more savvy buyers and sellers in commercial real estate perhaps than you do in run of the mill residential real estate.

Ragnar Lifthrasir: Commercial real estate companies often have a bigger budget. They often have a bigger team. So, they have the budget and the expertise to be ahead of the curve. They have a lot more money to save and friction to be reduced because they're operating at a larger scale, so it's more compelling. Economies of scale kind of thing.

Gregory Charlop: It sounds like you're saying that in the short and medium term, real estate agents could really benefit from understanding and perhaps even using some basics of the blockchain, like Bitcoin, because they could attract savvy customers, particularly in technologically-savvy areas. But in the longer term, it may decrease the total number of real estate agents needed, and probably the ones who remain will need to be fairly competent with blockchain. Is that essentially what you're saying?

Ragnar Lifthrasir: Yeah, that's pretty fair. The best application of the blockchain is Bitcoin. The best application of the blockchain is currency That's why it was first and that's why it will continue to be first, just because of that reason. And also because money is so important. Real estate is so much about money, whether it's a security deposit, a lease payment, a purchase, or whether it's investment in crowd-funding. Money matters so much in real estate, and Bitcoin is programmable money. That's what it can do. Smart contracts, what are you programming? You're programming money to act a certain way, so even though a lot of people talk about title being first, I disagree. I think it's cryptocurrency first.

Gregory Charlop: What is Bitcoin? I think we've all heard it in the news. What does it mean? Is it a thing? Is it controlled by any government?

Ragnar Lifthrasir: Bitcoin is a peer to peer currency, but it also has properties of more than currency. It has properties of an asset, of a commodity, so it sort of acts like a currency and a commodity, and it has aspects of a payment network. It's digital gold, so what is Bitcoin? It's a combination of actually several things, depending on how you use it, but basically what it is is a digital, peer to peer asset.

Gregory Charlop: For many of us, the whole process sounds a bit mysterious, this idea of Bitcoin sort of being on the internet. Is Bitcoin stored somewhere or is it just kept in computer networks, and who's deciding Bitcoin's value and who sort of runs Bitcoin? Does anybody kind of own it or oversee it, or is it sort of an autonomous thing?

Ragnar Lifthrasir: Bitcoin isn't a company or an organization or a government. Bitcoin is simply software. It's an open-source protocol that anyone can look at, can view, can try to adapt. It's an open-source protocol, just like we have an email protocol. All email applications use the same email protocol. That's why you can have different email addresses. You might have Gmail and I have Yahoo, but they can talk to each other. Why? Because everyone is using the same protocol, and anyone can build an application on top of the email protocol. That's what Bitcoin is. It's an open source protocol to transfer value.

Who controls it? That's a great question. Who controls the email protocol? Basically, the users. The people using it. There are software developers who write the code, but then there are users who use it. Probably the hardest part for a lot of people to understand is who controls it, and the answer is no one and everyone at the same time.

Ragnar Lifthrasir: Where is it stored? Bitcoin is also a ledger. That's really what it is. It's a distributed ledger and every single person who runs what's called a node, everyone who runs a node has a complete copy of that ledger going back from day one, back when the very first Bitcoin transaction occurred in January of 2009. So if you run a Bitcoin node, you have every single transaction that's happened since that date to the present. And there are tens of thousands of these Bitcoin nodes around the world. So where is Bitcoin stored? They're stored on tens of thousands of computers that all have the same exact copy of that ledger. So when you're sending a Bitcoin, you are not actually sending anything, you're just changing the ledger.

Person A used to have this amount of Bitcoins and now person B has this amount of Bitcoins because person A allowed person B to send Bitcoins from person A to person B. Bitcoin is a ledger.

Gregory Charlop: It's not a tangible thing, so it sounds like you could never cash out of Bitcoin, per se, like you can't exchange it for gold, or can you do that? Can you exchange it for something and cash out of Bitcoin once you have it?

Ragnar Lifthrasir: You could trade it for anything that someone is willing to take for it. So if I have a certain amount of Bitcoin and you have euros, and you and I agree to it, I'll send you Bitcoins and you give me your euros. Or if I have a certain amount of Bitcoins and you own a house, we could trade one thing for the other as long as we both agree to it. So Bitcoin can technically be traded for anything that two people come to agreement on.

Gregory Charlop: You and I could just agree with each other without having any other party involved, if I wanted to trade your Bitcoins for my house or my euros.

Ragnar Lifthrasir: Yeah. Again, it's digital gold, so I could buy your car with gold or I could buy your furniture with gold. As long as you want my gold, we could do that, same with Bitcoin.

Gregory Charlop: How safe is something like that? It sounds like you're describing something that lives on the internet, that's on everybody's computer. Is that safe or can some clever people, maybe living in their mom's basement or working for a government, hack Bitcoin or just take all of your Bitcoins away?

Ragnar Lifthrasir: The main risk with Bitcoin really isn't hackers so much as the people themselves losing their Bitcoin. Not so much theft but just loss, and they could do that several ways—by forgetting their wallet password or by writing their private key down somewhere and then losing it. So Bitcoin is not safe if you don't do some basic security things, which are actually relatively easy once you've done them and you're in the habit of it. But Bitcoin definitely requires more responsibility though, because there isn't a bank. There isn't someone you call to get your Bitcoins back if you lose them. Bitcoin is great because it's censorship resistant, it's peer to peer, but because of those same reasons, you do have to take more responsibility for it.

Gregory Charlop: You had mentioned that there may be clients looking to buy properties or sell properties using Bitcoin. Why would someone say, today, prefer to use Bitcoin rather than dollars or euros or gold?

Ragnar Lifthrasir: There are several reasons. Some people invest in Bitcoin and the value has gone up dramatically since its inception almost eight years ago. Instead of having to convert that into dollars to buy the property, they might just say, "Hey, I just have this and this is just what I want to use because I have it." It'd be like if you have euros versus dollars, if someone will accept euros, it's easier and faster for someone just to accept the euros than having to change it into dollars first. So the first reason is because some people are just sitting on that much Bitcoin, either because it's gone up in value or they've bought it or they've earned it. The second reason is because, especially for international buyers, it just makes the transaction much smoother, and people don't know this until they do their first Bitcoin transaction.

Try to send your brother 500 dollars who lives two states away. Do that via a bank and then do it via Bitcoin. Once you do it yourself, the question answers itself. It's so much easier and faster, so there's convenience. Also, it costs less because you don't need all the intermediaries. And I think it actually lowers the risk because escrow agents are human, and they make mistakes. They have office hours and they're not always available. Banks, too, make mistakes, and wires can take several days, especially for international transactions, whereas two people can just do it right now. So between convenience, faster, safer, there's several reasons.

Gregory Charlop: How is that different from PayPal? In other words, if I wanted to buy your car, I might PayPal you the amount of money that we agreed to buy your car. Why would I choose to pay you with Bitcoin rather than PayPal other than if I just had a bunch of Bitcoin and I wanted to use it up?

Ragnar Lifthrasir: PayPal is still a form of a bank. You still have to have an account with them. They still charge large fees. They will question a large transaction, like if you try to pay for property in PayPal, they probably won't let you. They're going to flag it and stop it and there will be long delays. So, in terms of friction, cost, and having that intermediary—those reasons. The other thing is, with Bitcoin, it's not just the payment; you can also program that payment. You can do a smart contract in terms of an escrow. You could program the money to only leave after one day or 10 days or 30 days automatically, so you could actually program the money.

Gregory Charlop: You provided me another perfect segue. What is a smart contract and how might a smart contract be used in real estate?

Ragnar Lifthrasir: Smart contracts are one of the most overhyped and misunderstood concepts in blockchain. Blockchain really is just taking code and automating something that was performed manually. Here's an analogy from Nick Szabo, the father of smart contracts He said a smart contract is like a vending machine. Before vending machines existed, you had a human who would have the food behind the counter. You have to talk to him and pay him the money, then he'd get the thing you wanted and hand it over the counter. A vending machine automates that process. You put a dollar bill in the machine and you get your candy bar. Likewise, a smart contract really just takes code and automates an otherwise manual human process.

Escrow is the best example of a blockchain smart contract.

Normally, when you're going to buy a property, you deposit money into escrow. That means a human holds that money in a bank that is controlled by other humans. To release that money, you have to talk to the humans and go through all these steps with the humans in physical space. Whereas a smart contract in Bitcoin just means you could automate that process to where, as long as the buyer and the seller agree, the money can automatically be released on a certain day, for example, after a certain time. Or they could actually lock up those funds in an escrow so that neither of them can access those funds unless they both agree to release the funds. The best real estate smart contract really is what's called a multi-signature escrow.

Gregory Charlop: That sounds like a great idea. Using something like that could, potentially, eliminate a lot of, as you say, friction, and a lot of parties' involvement in making an escrow contract work.

Ragnar Lifthrasir: The reason you don't see it yet is because there's still some volatility in Bitcoin, so if you try to do a 30-day escrow, the price of the Bitcoin will fluctuate. Now, for short term escrow, it's fine, but that is one issue. Another good use, for example, is for a security deposit, like a lease, because a big problem right now is that landlords often take the security deposit and don't give it back or give a portion of it back. That's against the law, but they are able to do that because it takes a tenant taking them to court to get their money back. The tenant could say, "Okay, let's put my security deposit in a Bitcoin smart contract that will automatically release in 12 months, or let's put it in a smart contract where the money will only be released if both of us agree to it. And if we both don't agree, let's have it decided by an arbitrator who has one of the private keys." That would really cut down on all of these small claims court cases of security deposits, for example.

Now, you still have the volatility of Bitcoin, but if you look at the amount of money that most people lose in these things, I think that risk would be worth it for a lot of people, especially if you could hedge that with something.

Gregory Charlop: Earlier, you mentioned land title and owning land title via the blockchain. What does that mean?

Ragnar Lifthrasir: Title is all the rights to something. You take all the title information, the address, the owner, the legal description, anything like that, and you take a digest of that (called a hash) and then you put it on a blockchain token, like a portion of a Bitcoin, for example. And you say, "This token is the paper deed, and if I want to transfer ownership, I send you this blockchain token just like I could send you a Bitcoin, I could send you this blockchain deed using pretty much the same software."

I Imagine: instead of writing your deed on paper, you print it on a dollar bill. You could do that. It's probably illegal but you could do it in terms of technology. Take it a step further. Instead of printing your deed on paper, instead of printing it on a dollar bill, you print it on a Bitcoin. That's what we mean by blockchain title. That's the first part.

When we say real estate on the blockchain, first what we mean is a deed token that transfers ownership. The second aspect is the chain of title, so when someone transfers that blockchain token, the deed gets recorded on the blockchain. Every blockchain transaction is on the blockchain. Every time someone sends a Bitcoin, it's recorded on the blockchain. That's what the ledger is. So if you have this blockchain token that represents title, and it transfers from person A to B to C to D to E, four transfers, each of those transfers is going to be recorded on the blockchain. The chain of title, therefore, is on the blockchain as it went from person A, B, C to D.

Gregory Charlop: If you use the three components of blockchain—the title, the currency aspect with something like Bitcoin and the smart contract—it sounds like you could really roll up a whole real estate transaction entirely through blockchain.

Ragnar Lifthrasir: Exactly. You're putting the pieces together. Where this really is exciting and where I see this going ultimately is blockchain can be a comprehensive platform for the currency, for the escrow, for the title, for the chain of title, for some of the contract stuff. It can all be done on the blockchain, and that's when you cut down the friction, you cut down the cost, you cut down the middlemen, because it's all the same thing.

Gregory Charlop: If and when that ever happens, that would be a radical change from our current system.

Ragnar Lifthrasir: Yes, and that's why I think once we can put those pieces together, that's when you'll get the hockey stick adoption. Progress happens by entrepreneurs, and so there are different entrepreneurs working on different aspects of the problem. There are entrepreneurs who are working on the currency, there are entrepreneurs working on title. It takes time for these different companies, these different investors, to build all those pieces up to where you could say, "We had these two, three, four, five companies that each have built this piece. Now let's all link them together," so it's similar to the internet. First you had to digitize everything, but you needed email, you needed a website, you need a computer. Once all those things came together, everything is digital.

Gregory Charlop: As you know, real estate is a very heavily regulated industry by the government. The government stores title. You have to have everything recorded with the government. The government has very powerful regulations about real estate contracts, and they regulate real estate agents. They really keep the real estate industry and the process of changing title under its thumb. How would a blockchain real estate transaction or a component of the blockchain real estate transaction jive with the strong government involvement with real estate? Would the title functions that the government now serves be replaced by blockchain or would it be folded into the government? How would the government and regulations interplay with all of this?

Ragnar Lifthrasir: There are two variables here. It depends on which application of blockchain you're talking about, be it currency or escrow or title or something else. So first by application and second by the specific government or agency. For example, we could take each of those. Currency: there's nothing restricting anyone from using Bitcoin right now to buy, sell real estate, lease anything. There's nothing stopping people from doing that. You can use gold, euros, dollars, anything of value to trade for assets, so there's no government problems there. You just have to comply with the existing laws. You can't commit fraud, things like that. If you go to escrow, again, nothing prohibits people from doing a smart contract. In terms of title, that's usually where people ask this question because the government is involved in title, and this is where you have to distinguish between conveyance of title and a recording of title.

In the US we're on the deed system, so those are two separate steps. When you convey title, the government does not get involved. That's between the buyer and the seller—the transferor and transferee—and as long as they follow the requirements for what a deed is, address, owner, consideration, those sorts of things, then there's not any law prohibiting people from conveying their property with blockchain. They just fulfil the requirements for what a deed is. Now, in terms of recording, that's where the government gets involved. In most places, recording is not required, but people do it for many good reasons. In that case, we're not going to replace the government for that function, but you can still record a blockchain transaction and take it down to the government office to record it. Consequently, you could have a parallel title system for convenience sake that's on the blockchain that everyone uses to look up, but if it ever goes to court, people will refer to what they recorded down at the county courthouse.

I just talked about the applications. It also depends on the country, because most countries outside the U.S. are not on the deed system, they're on the title system. So in those countries and most of Europe, the buyers and sellers don't convey property between themselves, they go down to the government land records and say, "Government employee, I am buying this property from so and so. Please change the record to reflect that change," so that's different. In that case, again, the government does get involved, so when you're talking about blockchain and government regulations, you have to distinguish applications. Is it money? Is it escrow? Is it title? Is it smart contract? And you have to consider which country you're in.

Gregory Charlop: Alright, very good. How would someone who's interested in blockchain learn more about it? What sources would you recommend—books, websites, blogs or online courses?

Ragnar Lifthrasir: I would go to the International Blockchain Real Estate Association (IBREA). There we have a library of articles, we have events and we do webinars, etc. IBREA is the leading and only organization dedicated just to blockchain real estate education So that would be the first place to start.

Gregory Charlop: Very good. Since you're obviously very savvy about new technology, other than blockchain, are there some other interesting technologies you see on the horizon that may dramatically affect real estate or that real estate agents may want to start looking out for now?

Ragnar Lifthrasir: Yes. It's complimentary to blockchain and it's an important missing piece of blockchain -- distributed file storage. Instead of having data on a single server or even a cluster of servers owned by the same company, like Amazon or Dropbox, distributed file storage distributes files on independent nodes that are redundant. This will become very important with blockchain because blockchain isn't a database, it's a ledger, so blockchains don't store a lot of information, they just store transactions, basically, and some code. Since they're not great at storing large amounts of data, for blockchain to really be useful in real estate, which has so much data, you're going to rely on distributed file storage. So that would be the other technology people need to start looking into. Best example of that is something called IPFS or interplanetary file system.

CHAPTER 6: PHILANTHROPY AND REAL ESTATE

Help your community (and your bank account)

There's one thing that will distinguish you from your competition more effectively than any Facebook advertisement or fancy logo. And at the same time, win the loyalty and admiration of your prospects, partners, clients, and colleagues. What is it?

Social responsibility.

Here's a simple truth: people want something they can rally behind. We all want to feel good about what we're doing. Our purpose must be greater than just making money and closing deals. We all have a yearning for meaning—a thirst for a higher cause.

Here's how to achieve it.

Have a mission. Work for your community. Dedicate yourself to improving society. Care about something larger than yourself and build that into the fabric of your business. When your goal is more than just your bottom line, your good deeds will magically boost your community, self-esteem, and bank account.

As Simon Sinek illustrated in his classic book *Start With Why*, people don't buy what you do, they buy why you do it. Statistics, graphs, and glossy brochures will not create passion or loyalty. Caring about your community will. Your prospects, clients, and colleagues will see the *why* behind the *what*. They'll see the dedication behind the deeds. And, they will respond!

For example, imagine that you're a real estate agent in Austin. Like all other agents, you work hard, hustle for business, and give your best to your clients. You do the usual internet marketing, social events, and occasional speeches. You're good at what you do and you genuinely love real estate.

But, unlike other agents, you're actively involved in your local Habitat for Humanity chapter. You don't just spend a day there over the holidays. You are actively involved. When you're not buying and selling homes, you're helping to build homes for the disadvantaged.

In fact, you're so committed to the cause, you regularly promote Habitat to your peers, employees, your kid's teachers, your hairstylist, your accountant, and your dentist. You mention Habitat to anyone who will listen. You're a true-believer.

Every other month, you organize volunteer days for Habitat. You round up past clients and your entire social network for a cause. Last month, you traveled to the homes of cash-strapped seniors to help out with painting and minor repairs. You and your volunteers improved the lives of those elderly homeowners. You did the chores necessary to help seniors stay in their homes - chores they couldn't do themselves. You and your network made a difference.

When you come home in the evening and reflect on your day, you feel good. You know that your day had purpose.

The next day at work, your secretary is excited about yesterday's volunteer day, and she can't wait for the next one. Your dedication inspired her and her husband to join Habitat as volunteers and they'll help organize the next event.

You never mention your volunteer work in your advertisements. But everyone knows.

The community respects you and your good deeds. The next time someone in your town is looking to buy or sell a home, who do you think they'll choose as their real estate agent? You.

Most importantly, you'll have the satisfaction of a life with purpose.

Leading social entrepreneur David Ament had this to say about the right way to run a business: "It's beyond being profit-focused at all costs and, instead, creating true wealth and true riches in your lifestyle. You get up in the morning, and it's not just, 'let's make another buck.' It's a matter of, 'let's change some lives.' How can we make some money and change lives? The more money we make, the more money we get to put back into our social cause—something that we care about." Click here to go to the full interview with David Ament.

This generation cares

The demographics of real estate customers are changing. Millennials already represent the largest share of homebuyers, and their numbers will keep growing. It is estimated that by 2025, Millennials will represent 75 percent of the American workforce![58] If you want to crush it in the real estate market, you must appeal to this demographic.[59]

It is certainly true that folks from all generations care deeply about society and community. However, Millennials merge social causes and economic/buying decisions more than previous generations. Consider these findings from the 2015 Cone Communications Millennial CSR Study:[60]

MILLENNIALS ARE THE LARGEST FRACTION OF HOMEBUYERS

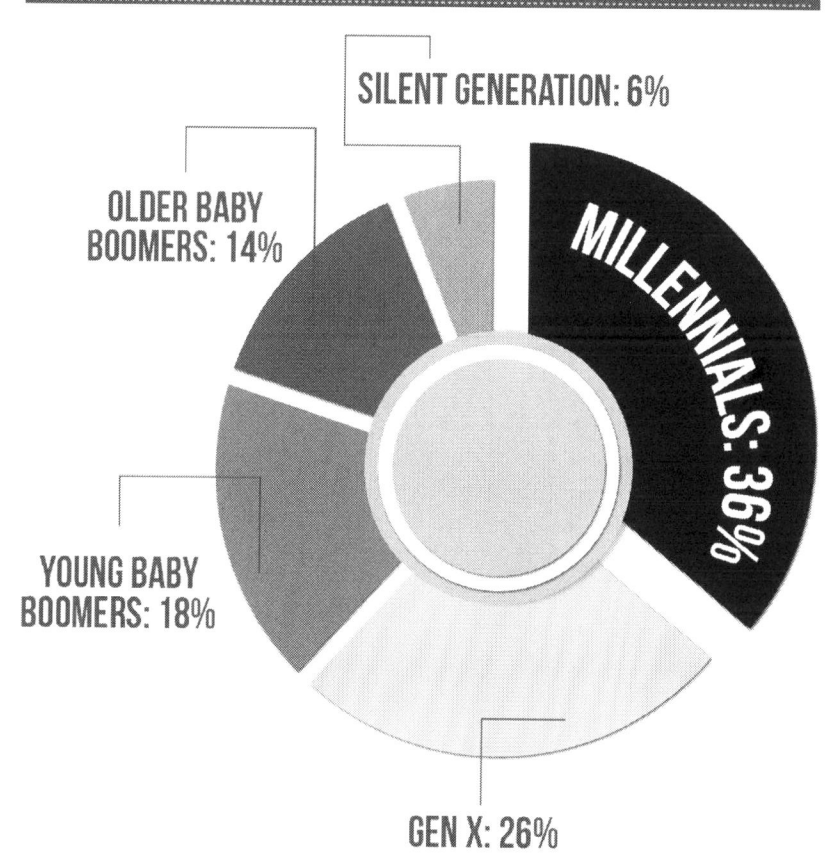

- SILENT GENERATION: 6%
- OLDER BABY BOOMERS: 14%
- YOUNG BABY BOOMERS: 18%
- GEN X: 26%
- MILLENNIALS: 36%

- 87 percent are more willing to purchase a product with social or environmental benefit.
- 82 percent will talk to family and friends about corporate social responsibility.
- 62 percent will take a pay cut to work for a company they consider socially responsible.
- **70 percent are willing to pay more for a product they consider socially responsible.**

If that isn't enough, here are a few more eye-popping stats:

- 81 percent of Millennials expect their favorite companies to publicly commit to good corporate citizenship.[61]
- Millennials want companies to involve customers in their good works.[62] **That means you!**

The simple truth is that Millennials (and most people) want to feel like they're doing some good for the world. They want to help the planet and the less fortunate. So they are increasingly willing to put their money where their ideals are.

TOMS Shoes is a classic example of corporate responsibility winning over the hearts (and wallets) of their customers. Their founder, Blake Mycoskie, noticed on a trip to Argentina that many children had no shoes. So, he founded a company that donated a free pair of shoes for each pair purchased. So far, TOMS has given away more than 10 million pairs of shoes![63] They started from scratch to become a major player in the shoe market—and they've helped many people along the way.

Look around. Today's corporate landscape is teeming with examples of companies founded around a social cause. Whole Foods and Warby Parker are two retail giants with social good baked into their DNA.[64] In a world littered with clone companies, these businesses stand out. Their dedication to social causes benefits their reputation, sales, and employee loyalty. They're doing good for the world AND their bottom lines. They don't have to compete by price and features. They can name their own price because their loyal customers believe in their mission. Would Whole Foods customers switch to Walmart if they knew that Walmart's apples cost 20 percent less? Not a chance!

So, how does all this relate to real estate? How does corporate responsibility transfer to your day to day job as a real estate agent, broker, or executive?

Let's back up for a moment. As discussed earlier, there are far too many real estate agents in the U.S.—more than 2 million. And about 5.5 million existing homes are sold each year.[65] That means that, on average, each agent would sell about 2.3 homes per year. But we all know it doesn't work that way. Top agents will sell most of those homes, and the rest will fight over a limited pool of listings. Most folks entering real estate will sell a couple of homes, tops. That won't be enough to sustain a family, hence the high attrition rate from the profession.

To make matters worse, technology will cull the field even more. Internet brokerages enable one "virtual agent" to do the work of 30 or more traditional agents.

You need an edge.

To stay in the game—distinguish yourself

Unless you're already an elite agent, you need a way to differentiate yourself. And I gotta tell you, your price, quality, or shopping cart advertisement ain't gonna cut it. You need something real, something meaningful that will set you apart from the pack.[66]

Here's your chance.

SOCIAL RESPONSIBILITY: THE BEST DIFFERENTIATOR

SAVES NEIGHBORHOOD PARKS

When you weave a social cause into your business, you set yourself apart from the crowd. Your actions, not just your words, show that you care.

For example, use your real estate know-how to help educate seniors and disadvantaged people in your town. Go to retirement villages and college campuses and teach the folks there the basics of real estate and financial security. Don't do it for leads, do it because it's the right thing to do. You're an authority! Show them how to plan for the future. You'd be surprised how much you can help people just by sharing a bit of your expertise.

Compare the power of a fellow volunteer's recommendation vs a slick Facebook ad. They'll advocate for you because you care about the same principles they do. You could never buy enough advertising to outweigh the strength of true believers. That's why your goal should be to form deeper connections with folks throughout your community by joining with them in a common and worthwhile cause.

Establishing yourself as a pillar of the community will do more than just secure new clients. Your clients' sales are likely to be more successful because of their association with you. For example, imagine that you're known for all the good work you do renovating neighborhood playgrounds. The parents of the kids in town will appreciate your efforts. You'd be a local hero. Then, when they see you listing 123 Main St, potential buyers will have a more positive view of that home because they already admire you. Your client's home will benefit from having a local champion like you listing it.

Remember, residential real estate is largely an emotional decision. Sure, buyers have certain criteria such as a maximum price or a minimum number of bedrooms. But, after that, buyers will decide where to purchase based on gut. Does the smell of the home remind them of their childhood? Can they visualize their kids playing on the backyard swing? The goodwill you generated with the playgrounds will transfer to your listing and will win the hearts of your potential buyers.

Finally, dedicating your free time to worthwhile causes will reverberate throughout the rest of your life and relationships. When you're committed to more than pure financial gain, you'll find more meaning and purpose. Your relationship with yourself and others will improve when you infuse your life with meaning.

Your colleagues and clients will see your dedication to helping others. In turn, you'll be viewed as more honest, caring, and compassionate. People will want to do business with you because they'll trust you and believe in your mission.

It may not even be a conscious decision, but folks will feel more comfortable partnering with a pillar of the community like you. You'll get more deals, better terms, and improved service.

When you feel better about yourself, when you feel like you have a mission, you'll be more productive and happier. Your business will improve because of your renewed internal drive. Your devotion to helping others will improve your self-esteem. Work will feel less like work and more like a cause.

Ultimately, feeling better about yourself and your reason for being on this planet may be the best benefit of all.

To be clear: I don't recommend you support a charity as a slick form of business advertising. In fact, you shouldn't mention your charitable work in your advertising at all! Help the community because it's the right thing to do and because you *want* to do it.

Ways to help

Here are a few ways you can get involved. I'm sure you can come up with many more:

- Become a regular volunteer at an existing charity/group.
- Recruit friends and family to volunteer for a charity.
- Join the board of directors of a charity or organization.
- Join a trade association and steer them toward charitable aims.
- Start your own charity or group.

These ideas are just to get you started. See what appeals most to you and which fits best with your drive and skill set. For example, if you're well-connected, you should consider harnessing your network to volunteer for a group. If you're politically savvy, look at joining an organization and redirecting their focus toward a charitable cause. You know your strengths, use them.

Volunteer at an existing charity: You can start this one today. There are so many great groups that would love to have your support. Consider organizations such as Big Brothers/Big Sisters, the Red Cross, Habitat for Humanity, the YMCA, local churches or synagogues, an animal shelter, the community hospital, an art museum, retirement home, a national/state park, a food pantry, or library. All of these organizations need volunteers like you—and they could put you to work right away. Best of all, there are no special skills required. All you need is a willingness to help.

Pro tip - You'll get the most out of volunteering if you go regularly. Make sure you find a cause you believe in because you're much more likely to stick with it over the long-haul. If you don't like the first organization you join, pick another one until you find the right fit.

Recruit friends and family *to volunteer for a charity*: A lot of wonderful groups need volunteers for big projects. For example, Habitat for Humanity has days where they go out into the community and build or repair homes for seniors or the disabled. Food pantries need tons of extra volunteers for major holidays, snowstorms, and natural disasters. Retirement homes often hold fun events around the holidays to cheer up their residents. For these special days, groups need lots of extra volunteers. If you have a big network, why not mobilize them to pitch in? You'll make life easier for the charities and you'll introduce your friends and family to some great organizations.

Join a board of directors: If you have a skill or interest in a particular area, harness your passion and offer to join a charity's board of directors or leadership team. As a real estate professional, you already know about marketing, managing an office, interacting with people, making sales, and understanding needs. Charities are in desperate need of your skills! Most of these organizations are led by volunteers just like you. You have the talent, now put it to work for a great cause!

Join and redirect a trade association: There are a lot of excellent organizations that can be harnessed to support charitable causes. You're probably already a member of some, like your local or state real estate association. Your real estate firm probably has a charitable arm. You can join the leadership team of these groups and encourage them to support more philanthropic causes.

Most of these businesses and trade groups want to support charities—they just need someone like you to give them direction and energy. If you volunteer some time with your company or organization to promote your favorite charity, you can bet that they'll be willing to back you up.

Start your own charity *or group*: You're an entrepreneur; everyone in real estate is. You know how to run a business and you have hustle. You do it every day. Why not take that talent and start your own charitable group? They're easy to form and many companies will offer your charity discounts on websites, supplies, and support. When you start your own charity, you'll have total creative control. You can support any cause you choose! It's easier than you think—and you already know how to sell it.

I asked top real estate agent and philanthropist JR McKee his tips for agents who want to give back to the community. He suggested "joining a community service organization. Service organizations need support from professionals, as well as regular individuals from every walk of life. As a real estate professional, joining a charitable organization is an amazing opportunity to support the community, to give back, and to get that sense of gratification and sense of balance. It is therapeutic to help by giving back to the community and supporting our children. It balances and offsets the intensity under which we work."

I asked McKee how his philanthropy impacted his business. "It's also good for marketing. I mean, by default I am so visible through my community giving that it reinforces who I am. It does bring me business, but that's the secondary benefit—not my primary goal." Read the full interview with JR McKee by clicking here.

If you have a particular affinity for helping homeless beagles or cleaning up neighborhood playgrounds, go ahead and start a group of like-minded folks and get the job done. In fact, for most causes, you won't even need to create the charity itself. Just start a Facebook or LinkedIn group. You can create a group on one of these platforms in just a few minutes, and you'll be surprised how many volunteers will be willing to follow your lead if you just get the ball rolling.

Use your real estate acumen to help the disadvantaged

Rather than supporting charitable causes after work, how

about helping the underserved *as part of* your work? Poor single mothers need housing vouchers and a safe place to raise their kids. Low-income seniors need assistance in finding affordable (and handicapped-accessible) housing. Folks in blighted parts of town need the expertise to improve their neighborhoods. Recent immigrants need help to navigate our complex housing system.

They need a champion. You. You have the experience and the skills to make their lives better.

My journey to philanthropy

As a kid, my parents and I regularly visited my grandparents in their Florida retirement community. They had a great place to live, lots of visitors, and a home designed for the disabled. As I grew older, I realized that not everyone enjoyed a secure home during their golden years.

When I read *Being Mortal* by Atul Gawande, I learned that the elderly really have it tough in this country. Many cannot afford to own a home. Their fixed income often makes renting difficult. Far too many rely exclusively on Social Security to pay their monthly bills. In fact, almost half of the unmarried elderly rely on Social Security for over 90 percent of their income![67] That doesn't leave much for rent.

Seniors become isolated as their friends and neighbors move away or die, and they lose the ability to drive. Aging in place can go from promise to prison as physical disabilities prevent the elderly from walking upstairs, using their own kitchen, and opening doors.

Now, I do what I can to help the elderly find affordable homes with my company, Dignified Housing. We help connect older adults with real estate pros who share my passion for the elderly. We are a marketplace for affordable senior housing. And, we are a source of useful information to help older Americans make the right housing choice for their golden years. If you're dedicated to the elderly and disabled, I urge you to join our team!

Whatever your philanthropic zeal, find a way to weave your social commitment into your real estate career. Technology can help you do it.

Technology makes supporting a charity or starting your own easier than ever. With a few clicks, you can create a Facebook group to support any cause you choose. Never in history has it been so easy and affordable to mobilize like-minded people to pitch in and help out. Give it a shot, it's easier than you think!

Interview with David Ament, philanthropist, international speaker, business advisor, investor

Gregory Charlop: Can you tell us a bit about your background?

David Ament: Absolutely. For the most part, I collect companies. That's what I do now. I am a business advisor. I love strategy, both domestically and internationally. My companies cross multiple sectors. I have a real estate portfolio—real estate investments in the U.S. as well as outside—a couple of schools, a non-profit, a technology company. I'm actually in the process of acquiring a construction company. I've been in the spaces of renewable energy, imaging business services—it's quite diverse. Businesses are not that different from one to another to another.

Gregory Charlop: You're also a leader of the International Institute for Peak Performance. What is that?

David Ament: That's a school that teaches business and wealth, along with leadership, health, and relationships. The focus of it is personal and professional development. I just happened to have aggregated and curated some of the best teachers in the world to come together in different locales to teach students.

Gregory Charlop: Is that something that the real estate agents and professionals reading this book might be able to sign up for?

David Ament Yeah, they absolutely would be able to. As a matter of fact, we have a new curriculum that is specifically geared toward the real estate professional, both improving their business and getting to the point of peak performance.

Gregory Charlop: You also are a social entrepreneur, and you've coached other social entrepreneurs. What exactly is a social entrepreneur, and what is the difference between a social business and a charity?

David Ament: When I first heard the term social entrepreneur, I thought it had to do with Facebook or social media, but a social entrepreneur means that there's not just a profit, but a social cause behind the goals and the actions of a company. It's tied to both purpose and profit. Profit is one side; the social cause is giving back to the community. It's beyond being profit-focused at all costs and, instead, creating true wealth and true riches in your lifestyle. You get up in the morning, and it's not just, let's make another buck. It's a matter of, let's change some lives. How can we make some money and change lives? The more money we make, the more money we get to put back into our social cause—something that we care about.

Gregory Charlop: I love that. You are both running a profitable business and benefiting the community. That idea really seems to be catching on, and it seems like it gives you a reason to wake up in the morning.

David Ament: Absolutely. It puts a lot more pep in people's steps when it's not just a job. I was working for somebody else and it was a job. Even if you own a company, at some point it can turn into just another job once it gets into the mechanics of money.

But you can attach a social cause to your for-profit interest, such as a separate foundation or a charitable arm of your for-profit entity. And having that piece makes it exciting because you get to look at how you're impacting the community. Maybe it's the world ecology, maybe it's the local school, maybe it's a group of underserved or underprivileged individuals. You get to look into their eyes and see how you're impacting them, see how you bring a smile to their face.

Gregory Charlop: It sure feels good to know that you're helping other people and not just your bank account.

David Ament: Yes. I'm all for the bank account, by the way.

But, I'm also all for building true wealth and a truly rich life. The bank account is great for feeding the stomach, but how are we feeding our souls?

Gregory Charlop: You mentioned that there are different structures one might use to create a social business. It is beyond the scope of this book to discuss all the different structures, but who would someone interested in doing this contact to learn more about these different structures and what would be best for them? Would that be a lawyer? How would someone go about setting up a social business?

David Ament: That's one of the tough parts. If you talk to a lawyer, they'll advise you on the legalities of setting up one kind of entity. As soon as you ask any tax questions, they say go talk to your accountant. The accountant will tell you the same thing—I can answer only your tax questions. So, it's a little bit difficult.

For instance, when I deal with folks, it's more about goals than it is about legalities or the tax ramifications. But the legal side and the tax side are really just part of the ingredients to the legacy that you're creating—both a living legacy today while you're on Earth, as well as something that lives beyond you.

Gregory Charlop: In my view, real estate professionals are ideal social entrepreneurs. They know a lot about their community and they care about it. And they also tend to have large networks. What do you think are some ways that real estate agents or brokers, or even executives, could work to benefit their communities?

David Ament: You're absolutely spot on. I believe that real estate professionals are the right people to have a social cause and infuse that into their brand, into what they stand for. Don't be just another real estate company, another face on a business card, or just another logo hanging on a sign in front of a house. Instead, you're communicating that, in addition to real estate, look at what we're doing over here. We're doing something to solve the homeless situation, build parks, etc.

I recently heard about a real estate agent who sponsors an annual Easter egg hunt at a local market in the Salt Lake City area. He's known for it. So, he's got this great PR. He's doing something that creates his brand. When folks in that area think of him, they don't just think, "Oh, he's just another real estate agent." He has branded himself with the annual Easter egg hunt. That's something that makes him stand out. He's not just another pretty face and logo on a business card or sign.

Gregory Charlop: So it sounds like supporting the community is a great way for real estate agents to differentiate themselves from their competitors.

David Ament: Absolutely. Here's an example. Marc Benioff, the billionaire founder of Salesforce.com, said that while they were founding Salesforce, they want to give 1 percent of profits to a social cause. And, they want to give 1 percent of their employee time to a social cause. So, they ended up paying their employees to do volunteer work. It was part of the fabric that was woven into the entire company. And in record time, it became a multi-billion-dollar company. They created an entire brand and a huge impact.

Gregory Charlop: I'm glad you mentioned that point about weaving it into the fabric of the business. Because I think almost all businesses probably contribute some money to charity at the end of the year before they file their taxes. And, while I think it's great that they do that, I don't think it's the same as defining yourself as working for a social cause. I think it needs to be a bit more than just cutting a check to a charity at the end of December.

If a real estate agent came to you with no business background and had an idea to help the community—say they wanted to help build a park or clean up a neighborhood or help local seniors—what advice would you give that agent on how to get started?

David Ament: Build a team. Find out who else is enthused about what you're trying to accomplish. Depending on whether you're using this as marketing, you might consider bringing in other agents. Maybe you'll bring in other people who are on the periphery of your industry, such as mortgage bankers, etc. and try to get that collaboration going. It's not necessarily a bad thing to include other agents. Many hands make light work.

Let's say you want to build a local park for the kids. Maybe the city doesn't have the money. You and your team can approach local clubs, such as rotary clubs, or service clubs and say, "Hey would you guys sponsor this, would you participate in building this park, this community garden?" Whatever it may be. The parents of the kids in the neighborhood would probably be pretty active participants.

Gregory Charlop: A related question: what if a large legacy real estate company called you into the boardroom, and their chief executive said, "Listen, we're worried, we're losing market share, we're starting to struggle now, and we would like to have a more philanthropic cause." Number one, do you think it's possible that these large, legacy companies can transform themselves into having more of a social mission? And number two, what advice would you give them about how to do it?

David Ament: Number one, the answer is yes, they can tie in a social mission. And number two, how would they do it? Real estate firms have a bunch of independent contractors who work for them, so they're quite unique compared to most businesses. So, any policy they create for independent contractors would not necessarily be binding.

Most real estate agents have extra time on their hands. As a matter of fact, if anything they probably have a surplus of time because it's a boom and bust type of business. There are certain times when you're high in demand and certain times when you're really not.

The firm could say, "we would love you to participate in a charitable cause. Go out there and put something together for the community." It's great PR, and it's not necessarily costing you a dime. The agents get to put their face out there, which is a big part of their job as independent marketers and salespeople. And, of course, if they're hanging their shingle under your brokerage, they're getting you good press. That one decision, to request agents to participate, yields an exponential return on investment and benefits society. You'll all enjoy lots of positive attention.

Real Estate at a Crossroads

Interview with J.R. McKee, philanthropist, founder of Home in Silicon Valley.com

Gregory Charlop: Can you describe your philanthropic background?

J.R. McKee: I started in 1997, attending a few Kiwanis Club meetings, and, by 1999, I had joined the Kiwanis Club of Campbell here in California. Kiwanis is an international organization in every country around the world, some 600,000 plus members strong. The Kiwanis Club of Campbell has about 25 members.

Kiwanis is a mosaic of ordinary people doing extraordinary things to uplift and support children and our community. There's a club virtually everywhere. Our purpose, as individual clubs—beyond community service—is to also establish "SLP's" or Student Leadership Programs at each school and grade level within our club's service area. We have a K-Kids program at an elementary school, and a Key Club (The world's largest high school leadership program) at a local high school, as well as programs for middle school, college, and special needs youth.

We create, sponsor, and teach the students and members of their individual clubs to be club officers—presidents, vice presidents, secretaries, treasurers, sergeant-at-arms, historians, how to recruit, build their membership, create and run projects, fundraise, and how to give back at their grade level, or where they're at. It's a whole process in a very well-orchestrated organization somewhat similar to Rotary, Lions, and other similar charity organizations.

Gregory Charlop: And how do you help the kids? What sorts of activities do you or the club do with the kids?

J.R. McKee: Great question. To give you a little background, we as an organization, internationally, do somewhere around

18 million hours of community service annually. Of that 18 million hours of community service, 12 million is done by our student leadership programs. So most of it is done at the high school level, which is the Key Club. We do many projects, both locally and internationally. Local community service projects become teachable, hands-on learning opportunities for our youth leadership programs. Probably 60 percent of our work is performed by our youth leadership clubs, or Key Club, specifically. Not only are we acting jointly as two clubs, sometimes three clubs—Kiwanis Club of Campbell, Westmont High School Key Club, and Rosemary K-Kids—to make a difference through this community service project, but it also becomes a leadership and training opportunity. We can train these youth on how to run the various facets of whatever it is that we happen to be doing. So it's a win-win. The community benefits, our youth learn, and we as Kiwanians make a difference, completing us and compelling us to be better for it.

We train our youth, they help us, they learn, and together we go out and run these projects, like tree planting, landscaping, helping to refurbish elderly homes, working in other schools, helping at Christmas street fairs or Octoberfest street fairs, or painting children's wings of hospitals, running the bay area's biggest Easter Egg Hunt and Eggstravaganza, helping in the Easter Parade, or Veterans Day Parade, among others.

Gregory Charlop: You're a leading real estate agent, along with being a leading philanthropist, and a lot of the people reading this book are real estate associates. What are some good ways that real estate associates can give back to the community or help out the community or people in need?

J.R. McKee: Joining any community service organization like Kiwanis. Kiwanis happens to be my preferred outlet, but there are many. Rotary International is an amazing organization. Lions International is a great organization. Kiwanis happens to be one of the least expensive organizations to belong to.

We typically do more hands-on projects, whereas clubs like Rotary more often just give money. They do some projects, but it's more of a fundraising organization where they give away lots of money. We give away money too, but not as much. The barrier of entry into the Kiwanis organization is a lot lower, and we tend to do more hands-on projects, interfacing with the community. And our youth organizations are much stronger in general.

Gregory Charlop: How you think real estate agents, individually, could give back or help their communities?

J.R. McKee: By joining a community service organization. Service organizations need support from professionals, as well as regular individuals from every walk of life. As a real estate professional, joining a charitable organization is an amazing opportunity to support the community, to give back, and to get that sense of gratification and sense of balance. It is therapeutic to help by giving back to the community and supporting our children. It balances and offsets the intensity under which we work.

It's also good for marketing. I mean, by default I am so visible through my community giving that it reinforces who I am. It does bring me business, but that's the secondary benefit—not my primary goal. I got involved after an "aha" moment in 2001 or 2002 when I saw a dear sweet 75-year-old member of our club walk into Rosemary Elementary School. Kids just started pouring out of class, ran up and hugged her, and said, "Miss Terri, we love you, so good to see you."

This lady and member of our club would for years go every day into this school in an area that was economically challenged. She would hug these dear sweet children, give them toothbrushes, granola bars and offer touching words of encouragement that these children needed but did not hear frequently enough. When I saw how impactful her service through Kiwanis was, I was moved and said, "Wow, that's something I want to be part of." Twenty years later I'm a key stakeholder in the Kiwanis Club of Campbell and couldn't be prouder to support our little corner of the world.

Gregory Charlop: Real estate agents, as you know, are often pillars of their community. They know a lot of people. They know the pulse of the neighborhood. It seems like they would be a natural fit to join these community service organizations. And, as you said, it seems like it would also be a great way for people to find out about them, and, potentially, even get new business.

J.R. McKee: I agree. Although the business aspect should be secondary and should just be a very pleasurable benefit. I'm resolute in the belief that nobody should ever join an organization purely for business purposes. They should join out of a genuine desire to help and make a difference, by default allowing their generosity and dedication to set a shining example of how we as individuals and professionals make a difference.

Gregory Charlop: Do you find that the larger real estate groups and associations have philanthropic components? What are your thoughts?

J.R. McKee: Well, geographically, from state to state and city to city, there are the National Associations of Realtors, the California Association of Realtors, the Santa Clara County Association of Realtors, and local MLSs. Nearly every organization has some sort of philanthropic involvement. And to the degree that you are more or less engaged, really depends on the stakeholders at each one of those organizations and how aggressive they are or are not. Some are better than others. Some are very involved. Some are doing nothing. And, of course, it's everything in between. Many are serious, and some say they support causes but it's just window dressing for PR.

But most associations do have a division that supports giving programs, particularly here in the Santa Clara area. Many companies, like Coldwell Banker, Keller Williams, Alain Pinel, and the Sereno Group are involved. Each one of these companies has something like Coldwell Banker cares, or Keller Williams cares, or Sereno cares, or Alain Pinel cares. Each one has some sort of division that identifies and supports a cause. The better organizations set goals, create team building opportunities, and truly reach out to support some annual effort using their agents to power a community service event.

Gregory Charlop: A lot of the people reading this book are either brokers or executives with these larger real estate firms. If they came to you for advice about how they could give back to the community or set up a program to give back to the community, what would you recommend?

J.R. McKee: That's a great question because some executives or organizations do it just because they want to create a name for themselves, and they want to be perceived in the community as caring. But they're not fully vested and "all in" on a truly on-going, full-time basis. Don't get me wrong, there are many, many great companies that truly do care, and they're involved at a grassroots level. They jump in and really make a difference in their local community. Some of it's just lip service, and some of it's sincere. I've seen this over the years, but the larger nationwide chains encourage each branch manager to actively participate in the community. And I do see the Coldwells, the Centuries, the ReMax's... they occasionally tackle projects. They go out and work at a street festival, or they go out and support seniors maintain their yards, or they paint a house. Or they do things for the community such as a Christmas toy drive or maybe a winter coat drive. But these are seasonal and not perpetual by their very nature.

In general, I think the big corporations charge their people at a branch level to find local causes and then support them. They do that for visibility, and they also do it for team building and work rapport among their agents. Every branch is only as effective as the leader in that branch and their ability to rally the troops, find a cause, and really jump in and support it.

Gregory Charlop: You're a leading real estate agent. You left the larger companies, and you're working on your own. Do you get the sense that a lot of other top agents will be doing the same thing? In other words, will a lot of them be leaving these larger companies and starting their own business or joining a discount internet brokerage?

J.R. McKee: A lot of the big brokerages offer extremely attractive packages to top producers in an attempt to retain them. I think agents work for large brokerages for a host of reasons, including—but not limited to—recognition, rewards, systems, branding, being viewed as icons within their organization, and more. Many top franchises offer the top two or three performers a very high split that is not known by the masses of the agents ... and not known by very many agents ... to retain them—the top producers—because the 95 percent of the agents who work for the company are on lower splits. The top five percent are on much higher splits because of their volume. But the brokerages need those top agents as icons to continue to attract newer agents because they need to show them, "Look, this is what you could achieve."

So, a lot of agents will stay in that model. But some of them don't like the politics, don't want to be that iconic agent, they don't want to be pestered by other agents looking up at them saying, "Well, how'd you get there? What are you doing? What's making sense? Where are you succeeding? Where are you failing?" And that happens when you are on top of the heap. Everyone wants to know what you're doing to get there. So, there are some who get tired of that bureaucracy, office environment, and dog and pony show by the broker pointing out how they achieved that status. And they're going to want to strike out on their own. They're going to seek out or start their own boutiques or seek virtual office opportunities.

Gregory Charlop: What do you think is the best way to train newer agents? If there are a lot of agents who are largely working on their own, how do you feel the newer agents, or the underperforming agents, could get better or learn the tricks of the trade?

J.R. McKee: Well, first of all, they need to pass their statutorily-required educational requirements that are set up by local and state jurisdictions. Secondly, they need some serious training from either their broker, company, or outside training agency—and not just to succeed, but also for the safety and protection of the consumers they serve. Once they get through that, or do that concurrently with a mentorship program, there should still be a mentorship requirement until each agent reaches a level of competency and production. In my humble opinion, NO AGENT should ever be turned loose without any significant education and training. We have the broker/salesperson relationship where a salesperson cannot work except under the dutiful eye and supervision of a broker. But, that's kind of loose and fast in some organizations that should have a mentorship program where a new agent is assigned a mentor, and at least three, four, five, six transactions are run parallel with a seasoned veteran. That way, the new agent doesn't create a liability for the consumer and/or for the company.

So, statutory educational requirements for state and local guidelines, and then some sort of hands-on, real world training—either from an outside vendor or from the company's in-house vendor and their staff—and then they should have some sort of mentorship program to guide those first transactions so that they don't go too far from where they should be.

CHAPTER 7: THE PATH FORWARD

Real Estate at a Crossroads

Technology is transforming real estate but remember the human touch

You're at a cocktail party. Guests are sipping wine by the crackling fireplace and laughing by the pool. After enjoying some appetizers and chatting with an old friend, you decide to network. You are a real estate agent, after all. You know that connections mean business. But you also don't want to waste your time. It's cold and the party is winding down.

Who should you talk to? Who is most likely to need your help buying or selling a home?

Is there a way you can predict someone's probability of moving?

Yes!

You now have the ability to consider a sea of strangers and immediately know which one will soon be looking for a real estate agent.[68] You walk over, introduce yourself, and secure your next commission.

Is it magic? No, it's artificial intelligence. There is now an algorithm that can determine someone's likelihood to sell their home based on their demographics and internet activity—even before they start searching for a real estate agent. No kidding!

After you secure your new client, your phone buzzes. It's your chatbot calling. The bot has some big news! Someone just visited your website and wants a new home. They're moving to town next month, require a 3/2, and they need help fast. You put down your drink and call the new prospects right away—before they reach another agent.

As you drive home from another successful evening, you get a call from another bot. This time, it's an actual robot! It turns out that your autonomous robot just signed up a family for a condo you're renting downtown. Your robotic friend showed the family around, answered all their questions, and pre-qualified them.

Boom! Three deals in one evening.

You wake up the next morning and enjoy a fresh cup of coffee. Before you finish breakfast, you ask your virtual assistant to order a CMA for your two new listings, contact an appraiser, make arrangements for an inspection, and send a thank you bottle of wine to your last client. You smile to yourself as you finish your croissant, knowing that your VA will make sure that each task is a job well-done.

After a morning jog, you jump on your computer to look for new leads. Your Facebook marketing campaign nets you two new prospects. And, your lead generation service just found you a new client in town looking to sell in the next few months.

Your daughter comes up and asks if real estate was always like this. "No, honey," you say while reflecting on the past. Your mind travels back to the old days.

"We used to make cold calls."

"What's a cold call?" asks your daughter.

"A cold call is when you call random people and ask them if they want to sell their home or buy one. You may not know these people at all and you would try to get them to hire you. Most people you call would either decline or hang up before you finish speaking. It was rough!"

"We'd also wander around public events handing out business cards and hope to run into someone at the grocery store who is looking to buy or sell a home.

Your daughter puts away her cellphone and stares at you with disbelief. "Wow, mommy, that sounds terrible!"

"It was. And when we weren't making cold calls, we would drive around town with flyers and distribute notepads or pens on doorsteps. We'd look for bus stops to place advertisements. And sometimes we'd wait at our expensive real estate offices all day and answer phones, hoping that we'd find a new client during 'floor time.' It was agonizing."

"Once we finally found a client, we'd take them around to 20, 30, even 40 homes before we hopefully found one that they liked. Before virtual tours, our clients had almost no idea what to expect in a house other than what they saw in a few small pictures. We wasted so much time!"

"And don't even get me started on FAX machines!"

"What's a FAX-" your daughter starts to ask.

"Shhhh, honey, it's okay. FAX machines are gone now, they're gone."

After you drive your daughter to school (or, perhaps the car is self-driving, since this is the future!), you get a call from an on-line brokerage. They don't have any physical offices, are high-tech, and take only a small cut from your commissions. They want you to jump ship from your traditional brokerage and join them. A year ago, you would have hung up without considering the offer. After all, you used to feel everyone needed an office and a big-name brokerage behind them.

Now, you're not so sure.

You're a top agent and you're comfortable with technology. You don't need the conference room, copy machine, or all the red tape. And, you'd sure like to keep your commission checks for yourself. Maybe it is time to consider the offer…

Don't just hope for the best

The whole process of transacting residential real estate is nothing like it used to be. However, we still have too many agents, brokers, executives, and systems that are relics of the past.

There are still real estate agents who spend most of their time making cold calls, papering a neighborhood with flyers or business cards, and placing ads on bus stops and shopping carts. They're FAXing out disclosures. They haven't updated their website. They miss most of their inbound leads. And they keep track of old clients on outdated Excel spreadsheets.

These agents use "hope for the best" marketing. They hope that a home seller will see their ad at the grocery store, they hope that the next cold call will create a hot lead, and they hope that all their hard work will pay off.

How can these "hope for the best" agents possibly compete against a salesperson steeped in technology who can target a prospect like a missile? They can't.

There are still brokers who believe they can charge successful agents high commission splits. They spend too much money on offices. And they waste too much time cultivating weak and underperforming salespeople rather than focusing like a laser on their top performers who bring in most of the business.

I have some bad news for these old-school brokers. Your best agents will leave, your underperforming salespeople will almost certainly not become rock stars, and you will never be able to charge enough for your photocopy machine to maintain your fancy office.

What's more, too many real estate brokerage executives aren't investing in technology. They're not developing the tools and aren't willing to purchase novel products from tech startups. They move too slowly when they finally embrace new technology. They maintain large portfolios of lavish offices and conference rooms even though clients would rather meet in their homes. They still cling to the belief that prospects choose an agent by their brokerage rather than the agent's track record or advertising prowess. And they rely too much on their brand name and, therefore, don't take seriously the threat posed by virtual or internet brokerages.

Brokers and execs will find that an increasing share of sales will be made by fewer and fewer top performers. Those elite agents will leave for greener pastures and smaller overhead at the online firms. These traditional brokers will be stuck with empty offices, high fixed costs, and a brand name that adds almost no value. If they don't make some major changes, they may find themselves in the unemployment line next to executives from Blockbuster and Nokia.

Whether you're an agent, broker, or senior executive: failure to adapt to modern technology will drive you into the ground.

Sometimes, when we are involved in a complex task day in and day out, we see things only from the inside. We assume things will stay the same, and we miss the change. After all, change appears gradual and peripheral.

It's like looking at your kids. You don't see any difference from one day to the next. But when your cousin Mary comes to town, she can't believe her eyes. The kids have changed so much since her last visit! But you can't see it. You were still focused on getting them to school and yelling at them to clean their rooms that you missed the bigger picture. You were too caught up in the day to day, and your kids grew up without you noticing.

Real estate has grown up too

The tools of the past like cold calls, untargeted advertising, spreadsheets, and ostentatious offices are worse than useless. They're a waste, a drain. They suck your precious time and energy down a rabbit hole while you miss all the successful new tools and technology.

The game is changing and you're missing it.

For years, we've had too many real estate agents. The trouble is, this is only going to get worse. As we discussed earlier, you'll start to see the top agents vacuum up more and more of the deals. The power will increasingly focus at the top. In addition, as agents start adopting a more virtual presence, fewer and fewer agents will be needed to conduct the same number of transactions. They can, after all, be in more than one place at a time. Finally, a larger segment of homebuyers and sellers will start transacting using novel techniques which will bypass real estate agents entirely.

When you combine the preexisting excess of salespeople, the increased concentration of sales in the top echelon, and the decreased need for agents in the future, you're going to have a lot of salespeople out of work and searching for a different job. The new reality will also squeeze brokers and brokerage firms as they squander valuable time and resources on folks who simply won't make it.

The best-run traditional brokerages that invest in innovation and the top virtual brokerages will (likely) be safe. Internet brokerages have a marginal cost per associate of near $0. If an agent signs up with an internet brokerage and later leaves to become an artist or an accountant, the brokerage has lost little. However, when this same agent drops out of a traditional brokerage, the brokerage itself suffers from all the wasted effort cultivating this novice salesperson.

Taken together, the changes wrought by the combination of new technology, the consolidation of sales by the top agents, and the exodus of buyers and sellers from the traditional transaction process will be profound. Here's what will happen:

- **Agents**: Salespeople will leave the real estate industry in droves. Although the barrier to entry in real estate is small, fewer and fewer people will be able to make a living as a sales associate. Those who do stay will find it increasingly difficult to work part-time. If they survive, they will likely be forced to become a top agent, take on a special niche, or find some technological trick to remain competitive.

- **Top agents**: You are the big winners. Your unmatched track record for closing deals and your sterling reviews are plastered all over the internet. Any homebuyer or seller who invests even 5 minutes researching their agent will stumble on you and insist on hiring the best. You'll clean up the market as fewer and fewer prospects take a chance on an inexperienced salesperson and turn to you for security. Your mastery of technology and the automated office will enable you to handle more and more sales in less and less time. And, finally, your bargaining power with brokers and real estate firms will only improve. You'll capture more of the market and retain a larger portion of your commissions. You will always be in demand, even in the world of iBuyers. Life is good for you.

- **Prospective real estate agents:** As the excess capacity of real estate agents becomes increasingly apparent, it's likely that fewer and fewer folks will choose real estate as a career. Far too many new agents fail. For those who are still interested in real estate (and I hope that some of you will stay interested - since we need you!), perhaps you should consider a different approach and join or create a real estate tech startup, promote blockchain, or focus on a niche.

- **Brokers:** As the internet and virtual brokerages allow one broker to assist more and more agents, we also will likely need fewer and fewer brokers in the future. Brokers will also find it increasingly difficult to attract salespeople, since brokers will no longer be able to rely on their location, size of their offices, or their corporate brand name to attract teammates. It may easily become a race to the bottom for commission splits, and a race to the top for technology.

- **Real estate brokerages:** You're no safer than the brokers. You cannot rely on your company's famous name and respected reputation. Your prospects don't care. Your large portfolio of offices will do you little good as most clients prefer to meet in their home or at a coffee shop, although I highly recommend you read Tony Vitale's contrasting opinion. The trend away from offices will accelerate as Millennials gobble up more and more of the real estate marketplace. Consequently, your ability to squeeze high franchise fees from your brokers will evaporate. Unless you cut costs, embrace philanthropy, target a niche, and develop/deploy novel technology, you will face stiff headwinds competing against internet brokerages and the more tech-savvy upstarts.

- **Homebuyers and sellers:** Along with the top agents, homebuyers and sellers are the biggest winners. You can now research homes and neighborhoods from the comfort of your living room. You can easily identify and hire the top salespeople in their area based on past performance and online reviews. Rather than going to every single possible home, you will be able to tour properties virtually and reserve in-person visits only for the top prospects. And, most importantly, you will likely pay less and less to your real estate agent as real estate transactions continue to streamline.

Perhaps the most striking change of all will be the *rate* of change. Millennials love technology, they expect convenience and immediate results. They're comfortable doing most of their business online and rarely feel a need to go out to stores or offices. They'll expect virtual reality home tours, respond to social media advertising, and have no problem conversing with chatbots instead of real people. As Millennials represent a growing share of both the home transacting public and the real estate community, they will drive accelerated adoption of real estate technology and new business models.

As Millennials become real estate agents, they will naturally gravitate toward technology. Facebook, Snapchat, and Instagram ads will come natively to them. Using their phone to conduct business will be second nature. And, they won't care about the old ways of doing things.

Millennial homebuyers and sellers will be equally irreverent to the old ways. They'll expect everything on their phone (except actual phone calls!), won't want to waste time on endless house tours, and they sure won't pay a premium if their real estate agent hails from a famous traditional brokerage firm.

The path forward

To survive in the real estate business, we must adapt to these profound transformations or go extinct. Fortunately, the path forward is clear—even if it is not easy. Regardless of whether you're an agent, broker, or senior executive, you must undertake three fundamental changes in order to survive in the new world of real estate. You need to embrace technology, expect lower commissions, and focus on winners/niches.

First, you have no choice but to embrace technology. It is well past the point when you can bury your head in the sand and expect everything to blow over. It ain't going away. Now, you must learn to use the new tools. Social media marketing, chatbots, virtual and augmented reality, artificial intelligence, a real estate CRM, and lead-nurturing technology should become part of your arsenal. If you're an agent or broker, I recommend that you start going to classes, read books, listen to The Real Estate Flash on your Alexa, meet with sales reps, sign up for blogs, and just try out various technological tools to see what works for you.

If you're an executive from a large brokerage firm, the process of adopting technology is a bit more complex. I recommend that you attempt to create new technological platforms in-house, but also partner with tech companies and startups to explore emerging new technology. While you need an internal department that understands tech and works to integrate your tech tools, you also need the fresh blood and willingness to experiment that you'll find with outside tech partners.

Your next challenge comes when you try to distribute this new technology throughout your enterprise. Do you force your different branches to use the new tools or make it optional? Do you purchase the new technology centrally or leave it up to the franchises? How do you review technological tools fast enough to get them in the hands of your front-line staff before they become obsolete? These are difficult problems and will require a high level of engagement from senior leadership. Consider working with innovative technological consultants like T3 Sixty for advice about how to spread technology throughout your organization.

Finally, we must all make peace with decreased commissions. The typical real estate salesperson's commission of 5-6 percent originated back in the day when the transacting public was completely dependent on real estate agents. The average homebuyer or seller had no idea what their home was worth, had little to no idea about neighborhood comps, had no easy way of finding new homes, and buyers knew little neighborhood information such as school quality and crime rates. The public couldn't access the MLS and could barely do any research. The public was nearly helpless.

Not anymore.

Now, the general public knows almost everything. They can do their own home value estimates. Heck, they can even ask their Alexa how much their home is worth![69] They know all the listed properties for sale in their target city. If a prospective homebuyer wants to see all the 3 bed / 2 bath condos over 1,500 sq. feet and under $800,000 in Long Island, they can do that in a flash. They know mortgage rates, crime rates, and all about that new shopping complex across town. In short, buyers and sellers can do almost everything themselves.

As a result, the transacting public will be increasingly wary of cutting their real estate agent into 5-6 percent of their deal. They simply don't need to pay that much. And as the Millennials start controlling more of the purse strings, they will be open to new and creative ways to eliminate an expense they view as excessive. They simply won't pay 6 percent commission on a routine transaction.

Therefore, real estate agents should expect that commissions per transaction will drop. This shift in commission rates won't hurt top agents much, but it will profoundly impact everyone else. Agents lower down on the food chain will need to plan accordingly by either leaving real estate, lowering costs, or closing more deals. Under-performing agents will drop out of real estate as their income falls even further. The remaining agents will attempt to extract concessions from their brokers and brokerage firms.

Then, brokers will make less money per transaction, so they also will need to cut costs or increase sales. Brokers can accomplish both of those objectives by transforming into a 'virtual broker' with a mostly online presence. That way, they can manage more agents. Alternatively, brokers can convert their offices into a destination, as Tony Vitale suggests.

As for brokerage firms, their franchise fees will plummet. Brokers will no longer see the value in sending a bunch of their money to a franchise company. Brokers will realize they get little in return from the franchisor's name, and they'll insist on corresponding reductions in charges.

THE NEW REAL ESTATE MARKETPLACE: WINNERS & LOSERS

WINNERS: TECHNOLOGY, VIRTUAL AGENCIES, TOP AGENTS

LOSERS: TRADITIONAL AGENCY MODELS, HIGH COMMISSIONS

As the dominos fall, most brokerage firms can expect a drastic drop in revenue per transaction. As a result, they, too, will need to cut costs or increase sales. This will likely be achieved by shedding physical real estate, reducing employees, and investing in technological tools that will retain the best brokers. In fact, useful technology might be one of the few remaining carrots that most real estate companies will be able to offer their brokers.

All of these changes will ultimately accelerate the drive for more and more technology. The agents need tech to reach more and more clients since their revenue per client will drop; the brokers need tech to attract and manage more top agents and to cut costs; and the real estate companies need more tech to attract more brokers. In short, real estate technology will be weaponized.

Finally, professionals throughout the real estate food chain will need to focus on winners and niches. As discussed in the Agents chapter, the bottom 80 percent of salespeople won't be able to tackle the top folks head-on. Instead, they should opt for a niche or angle—survival through specialization. Target a very narrow property type, buyer, geographic region, or area of technology. Own a small segment of the market and you'll be okay.

For brokers and real estate companies, the story is the same. You, too, will need to specialize and target certain niches. Your company's brand name may be meaningless in general, but you just might be able to build a reputation for highrise condos in San Francisco or senior housing. Brokers, also, will need to focus on winners and specialists. The probability of bringing a chronically underperforming generalist salesperson up to snuff is vanishingly small. You should focus on attracting and retaining top talent or steering your associates into specialties rather than wasting time on those who aren't cutting it.

This focus on top talent might have long term implications for the real estate business as a whole as fewer and fewer new folks learn the ropes. But, as an individual broker, you're in a battle for survival. You need to secure the best people.

In conclusion

This book explores the rapid technological and business evolution of the residential real estate marketplace. As a result, companies and circumstances change in a flash. By the time you read this, some of the individual companies mentioned here may no longer exist. Unfortunately, that is one of the challenges of predictive books.

Having said that, I encourage you to view the rapid change in the real estate landscape as further support of the book's basic premise—the market is changing, and methods of the past won't cut it. Time marches on and waits for nobody. Technology is killing off older companies across all industries. The average lifespan of an S&P 500 company dropped from 60 to

20 years.[70] Startups are on shakier ground. Businesses come and go, victims of the creative destruction of the market. To stay on top, you must keep up with the latest innovations, whatever they may be.

Although this book focuses on technology and business innovation, don't forget the human side of real estate. One reason we all went into this business is to help people find new homes and upgrade their lives. We should use technology to improve efficiency, reach more prospects, and make better deals. But, sitting at our computer, it's easy to lose sight of the bigger picture. Remember, behind your mouse clicks and lead generation tools are real people who need your help. Ultimately, that's why we're all here.

I'd love to hear your ideas. Contact me on LinkedIn or Facebook and let's start a discussion!

Best of luck to you,
Gregory Charlop

[1] https://en.wikipedia.org/wiki/Pareto_principle

[2] https://www.nahb.org/en/news-and-publications/press-releases/2018/04/millennials-leading-the-growth-of-new-home-buyers.aspx

[3] https://www.redfin.com/blog/2018/02/sight-unseen-in-2017.html

[4] https://theamericangenius.com/housing/real-estate-marketing/much-real-estate-professionals-spend-marketing-stats/

[5] https://realestate.nextdoor.com/

[6] http://www.pewinternet.org/fact-sheet/social-media/

[7] https://www.nar.realtor/sites/default/files/reports/2017/2017-real-estate-in-a-digital-age-03-10-2017.pdf

[8] http://www.lumentussocial.com/wp-content/uploads/2016/11/Why-Social-Media-Isnt-Working-for-You-and-How-to-Fix-It-whitepaper.pdf

[9] Private communication

[10] The Fall Oaks town name, website, and email address are entirely fictional. They did not exist at the time of this writing and have no connection to any person or town, real or fictional.

[11] Private communication

[12] http://www.pewinternet.org/2017/05/17/technology-use-among-seniors/

[13] https://www.inman.com/2018/10/31/7-senior-housing-options-every-real-estate-agent-needs-to-know/

[14] https://www.nar.realtor/sites/default/files/documents/2017-Profile-of-International-Activity-in-US-Residential-Real-Estate.pdf

[15] https://www.nar.realtor/infographics/infographic-top-reasons-for-choosing-a-career-in-real-estate

[16] https://www.nar.realtor/research-and-statistics/research-reports/highlights-from-the-nar-member-profile

[17] Referrals and the internet are the top two ways folks find real estate agents

[18] https://www.forbes.com/sites/forbesrealestatecouncil/2018/06/27/why-venture-capitalists-are-investing-billions-into-real-estate-technology/

[19] https://techcrunch.com/2019/03/20/opendoor-raises-300m-on-a-3-8b-valuation-for-its-home-marketplace/

[20] https://www.inman.com/2019/01/21/purplebricks-pivots-to-more-traditional-model-in-us/

[21] https://www.nar.realtor/research-and-statistics/research-reports/real-estate-in-a-digital-age

[22] Heraclitus

[23] https://www.forbes.com/sites/donnafuscaldo/2018/09/26/home-buying-goes-high-tech-as-millennials-become-largest-real-estate-buyers/#3816300d7774

[24] https://www.psychologytoday.com/blog/you-illuminated/201204/brain-scans-show-how-meditation-improves-mental-focus

[25] http://journals.sagepub.com/doi/abs/10.1177/0956797612459659?rss=1&;ssource=mfr&

[26] https://www.psychologytoday.com/us/blog/what-mentally-strong-people-dont-do/201504/7-scientifically-proven-benefits-gratitude

[27] https://sleepfoundation.org/excessivesleepiness/content/how-much-sleep-do-we-really-need-0

[28] https://sleepfoundation.org/sleep-topics/sleep-hygiene

[29] https://www.sleepassociation.org/patients-general-public/insomnia/sleep-hygiene-tips/

[30] http://healthysleep.med.harvard.edu/healthy/getting/overcoming/tips

[31] https://www.amazon.com/Protection-Computer-Readers-Glasses-Shatterproof/dp/B00BQ7KBV4/

[32] https://www.nytimes.com/2015/05/12/upshot/more-consensus-on-coffees-benefits-than-you-might-think.html

[33] https://www.scientificamerican.com/article/the-healthy-addiction-coffee-study-finds-more-health-benefits/

[34] http://annals.org/aim/article/2643435/coffee-drinking-mortality-10-european-countries-multinational-cohort-study

[35] https://www.sciencedaily.com/releases/2004/05/040512041022.htm

[36] https://www.sciencealert.com/here-s-when-you-should-be-drinking-your-coffee-according-to-science

[37] https://www.theatlantic.com/health/archive/2014/03/how-athletes-strategically-use-caffeine/283758/

[38] Placester Life as a Real Estate Agent Survey 2013

[39] The Art of Not Working at Work, The Atlantic, Nov 3, 2014

[40] https://www.quora.com/How-many-hours-on-average-do-realtors-spend-per-client

[41] https://www.nar.realtor/education/courses

[42] https://www.car.org/education/calendar

[43] http://www.dce.harvard.edu/

[44] http://www.ucla.edu/academics/continuing-education
[45] https://continuingstudies.stanford.edu/
[46] https://www.amazon.com/The-Agent-Marketer-Flash/dp/B07DCF39NK/
[47] https://www.fastcompany.com/40438926/linkedin-is-testing-a-new-feature-that-matches-you-with-a-mentor
[48] http://www.prnewswire.com/news-releases/realtor-magazine-seeks-entries-for-2017-volunteering-works-mentoring-program-300397408.html
[49] https://www.nar.realtor/sites/default/files/reports/2017/2017-home-buyer-and-seller-generational-trends-03-07-2017.pdf
[50] https://www.realtown.com/blog/Why-Your-Real-Estate-Business-Needs-To-Hire-a-Virtual-Assistant
[51] https://www.acelerartech.com/blog/virtual-assistant-vs-in-house-employee/
[52] https://www.nar.realtor/sites/default/files/reports/2017/2017-home-buyer-and-seller-generational-trends-03-07-2017.pdf
[53] Since chatbots respond immediately, they'll engage prospects faster than any human can - including you!
[54] https://www.rocketmortgage.com/purchase/get-started
[55] https://www.lenda.com/
[56] https://www.forbes.com/sites/donnafuscaldo/2018/09/26/home-buying-goes-high-tech-as-millennials-become-largest-real-estate-buyers/#5e9455e17774
[57] https://www.redfin.com/blog/2018/02/sight-unseen-in-2017.html
[58] https://www.huffingtonpost.com/danielle-sabrina/rising-trend-social-respo_b_14578380.html
[59] https://www.nar.realtor/research-and-statistics/research-reports/home-buyer-and-seller-generational-trends
[60] http://www.conecomm.com/news-blog/new-cone-communications-research-confirms-millennials-as-americas-most-ardent-csr-supporters
[61] https://www.forbes.com/sites/larissafaw/2014/05/22/millennials-expect-more-than-good-products-services-to-win-their-loyalty/#673e26875697
[62] https://www.forbes.com/sites/sarahlandrum/2017/03/17/millennials-driving-brands-to-practice-socially-responsible-marketing/#6e7cf0ae4990
[63] https://www.fastcompany.com/3012568/blake-mycoskie-toms
[64] We'll see how this changes with Amazon's acquisition of Whole Foods
[65] https://www.statista.com/statistics/226144/us-existing-home-sales/
[66] We covered other powerful ways to differentiate yourself in the Agents

chapter. But, in my opinion, social responsibility is the best way to achieve meaningful and lasting differentiation.

[67] https://www.ssa.gov/news/press/factsheets/basicfact-alt.pdf

[68] There is a great online tool for real estate agents to predict someone's probability of moving. Although this isn't yet available for in-person use (as in this example), such technology is likely to be available soon.

[69] https://www.voiceterpro.com/ is one great example

[70] https://www.cnbc.com/2017/08/24/technology-killing-off-corporations-average-lifespan-of-company-under-20-years.html

Made in the USA
Monee, IL
29 January 2020